THE FIFTH
OLD HOUSE CATALOGUE

Cover illustration: This beautifully proportioned doorway, with lovely leaded fan window and handsome curving staircase, welcomes visitors to the 1825 Porter Mansion, one of four buildings which comprise the historic Middlebury Inn property in Middlebury, Vermont. Photograph by Erik Borg.

Entry hall of the Ronald-Brennan House (1868), now the Filson Club, Louisville, Kentucky. Photograph by Jack E. Boucher, Historic American Buildings Survey.

THE FIFTH
OLD HOUSE CATALOGUE

Compiled by Lawrence Grow

Hayley Gorenberg and Kirstin Olsen
General Editors

THE MAIN STREET PRESS • PITTSTOWN, NEW JERSEY

Compiler:	Lawrence Grow
General Editors:	Hayley Gorenberg
	Kirstin Olsen
Staff Writers:	Vicki Brooks
	Hayley Gorenberg
	Martin Greif
	Kirstin Olsen
Research Associate:	Mariann Arnitz
Art:	John Fox
	M. Henri Katz
	Frank Mahood

Published by
The Main Street Press, Inc.
William Case House
Pittstown, New Jersey 08867

Published simultaneously in Canada by
Methuen Publications
2330 Midland Avenue
Agincourt, Ontario M1S 1P7

Cover design by Frank Mahood

Printed in the United States of America

Library of Congress Cataloging-in-Publication Data

Grow, Lawrence.
  The fifth old house catalogue.

  Includes index.
  1. Historic buildings—Unites States—Conservation and restoration—Catalogs.
2. Buildings—United States—Conservation and restoration—Catalogs. I. Gorenberg, Hayley. II. Olsen, Kirstin. III. Title. IV. Title: 5th old house catalogue.
TH3411.G74 1986   728.3'7'0288029473   86-23659
ISBN 1-55562-001-9
ISBN 1-55562-000-0 (pbk.)

Contents

Introduction

The assembly of a book of this sort is an extremely complex operation. From hundred of sources, the names of craftsmen, manufacturers, suppliers, distributors, artists, dealers in old materials, and consultants and architects are meticulously gathered. Curators of historic houses and museums make many recommendations; other useful suggestions come from contractors and from people active in preservation societies and associated with various private and public agencies. Still others come from you, the users of this biennial publication.

As important as the search is the evaluation of products and services. Approximately 25 percent of these are selected for write-ups, with another 25 percent listed at the end of each chapter. Fifty percent are rejected completely. In the evaluation process, several considerations are paramount. Someone who renders a service must be available on a regular basis and must possess the credentials required to do a proper job; manufacturers and craftsmen must prove that the objects they can supply are designed and executed in a stylistically proper or documented manner and are made of materials which are both durable and fitting. As best as we can, we also try to determine whether products and supplies are sold and delivered in an efficient and honest manner.

After all materials and information are properly evaluated, the task of compiling the write-ups in a useful format gets underway. Since we want the book to be as fresh and up-to-date as possible, it is necessary to rush to print as quickly as we can. Lists can be assembled almost instantly, but the writing of textual material requires careful and thoughtful consideration. Advice on how and when to use various products or services is interwoven with the individual write-ups. Additional lists of suppliers are included for each category covered in the various chapters.

Each *Old House Catalogue* is an entirely new book—word for word. New sources are included on nearly every page, and products or services from a source previously acknowledged are new as well. At the same time, we are summing up in every chapter—either in the text itself or in the list of additional suppliers at the end of each chapter—many objects or services previously featured. One book thus builds on another in a way that we think is most useful to the ever growing old-house market.

The search for original and reproduction old-house materials is guided by three major considerations—time, money, and effort. The urge is always to "improve" things just as quickly as possible with the least possible effort and cost. The temptation to seize on what is readily available and easily worked into place is very difficult to resist if the price is right. But patience has its rewards. There are too many purveyors of old items and manufacturers of new who are all too happy to gratify one's desire for neatness, order, and accomplishment instantly. The question of whether an item is appropriate in style and form should be answered first, but this is by no means the only matter of importance. How durable is the object? How much maintenance will it require? Is it something integral to the expression of a period style or merely a passing fancy to be consigned to the attic or a garage sale ten years hence? The answers to these questions cannot be fully given in *The Fifth Old House Catalogue*. Each house has its own particular problems and needs. The process of finding, evaluating, and using a wide variety of materials, however, can be made a much less frustrating exercise with the use of this book. The process of restoring a room or a complete house should be an invigorating and satisfying project. We're still learning, sweating, and, yes, even smiling, after ten years of tackling the legacy of the past, its problems and its pleasures.

Once again we must express our thanks to the many people who have assisted in the compilation of this biennial publication. Hayley Gorenberg and Kirstin Olsen have guided the Main Street staff in locating new sources of supply and in evaluating and organizing material. Together they have written thousands of letters and made countless calls to produce an avalanche of information that is thoroughly up-to-date. The assistance of friends and associates in the restoration field who have shared their knowledge so freely is greatly appreciated. Some of these are craftsmen or professionals who have offered their own evaluations of particular products, and, in a number of cases, recommended the work of competitors. The preservation/restoration world is still a friendly one inhabited by individuals who enjoy their work and who labor for more than profit. Long may this spirit prevail.

Lawrence Grow
Pittstown, New Jersey
September, 1986

THE FIFTH
OLD HOUSE
CATALOGUE

1.

Structural Products and Services

The most important chapter in any old house resource book should be devoted to such fundamentals as doors, windows, beams, paneling, columns, stairways, etc. These are the nuts-and-bolts elements which give form to a building, along with a good percentage of its style. If a building is not structurally sound, corrective work must be done before rehabilitation or replacement of the decorative elements. But sound construction, in our book, is more than a skeletal matter: a building should "hang together," its proportions should be right, the structural members should relate well to one another, and they must also be able to bear the weight or stress intended for them without difficulty.

Many old buildings acquire an odd look over a period of time. Ill-conceived "add-ons" are thrown up on one side or another. Rather than restoring the basic framework, a choice is made to cover the frame with another coating, perhaps of asphalt or vinyl siding, thereby obliterating the old lines. Possibly the most common horror perpetrated on the old building is the destruction of windows and doors. Segmented picture windows, for example, are often cut to replace a double-hung sash window without any thought given to the rest of the façade.

The sources given in this chapter can provide some of the basic elements which may need replacement. There are also many craftsmen listed who specialize in making the old as good as new. We would urge the reader to make use of real period building materials as often as aesthetically and economically feasible. If copies have to be made, however, make sure that the artisan you choose is willing to be a bit old-fashioned in his approach. It is tempting to accept the easy "period" solutions offered by many manufacturers; styrofoam-like beams, veneered rather than solid doors, and yes, even plastic shutters. It may take just a little more time to find something better, but it will be a bit more durable, and, in the long run, more satisfying to live with.

A gracefully curving wooden staircase designed and built by Tom Dahlke of Dahlke Studios, Glastonbury, Connecticut.

Architectural Salvage

Architectural antiques used to be known as "junk" or "salvage." And in some communities, thoughtless people still call in the salvage or wrecking team to finish off their decrepit old houses. Salvage dealers, however, know that there is money to be made from old windows, doors, flooring, paneling, etc., and unbeknownst to the seller, make arrangements to place at least the better pieces with a big-city treasure hunter. The competition for even run-of-the-mill decorative pieces is growing more fierce each year. Increasingly, even reproduction objects are being presented as antique. It is important, then, that the buyer of old house materials deal with only the most reputable dealers, such as those presented in the following listings.

The Architectural Antique Warehouse

This company demonstrates the principle of *multum in parvo*. It usually carries some objects retrieved from old homes, although it's better known for its collections of reproduction items—bath and lighting fixtures, wood and metal ornamentation, furniture, fencing, mantels, tin ceilings, and doors. A selection of new beveled glass doors and windows in traditional styles is also available. The Architectural Antique Warehouse even does some consulting for renovation and restoration projects and will prepare blueprints or supervise the implementation of repairs or changes.

Literature available.

*Architectural Antique Warehouse
1583 Bank St.
Ottawa, Ontario, Canada K1H 7Z3
(613) 526-1818*

Architectural Antiques

How better to inspire a design for an authentic interior than by walking through authentic antique rooms? Architectural Antiques has preserved several such complete interiors in its 18,000-foot showroom. Standard offerings of mantels, hardware, lighting fixtures, columns, and woodwork are joined by entire staircases, a roomful of plumbing fixtures, entryways, and a prize pair of leaded-glass doors, topped by a matching fan transom. Architectural Antiques will send photographs upon individual requests and provides a locator service if existing stock doesn't satisfy your needs.

*Architectural Antiques
121 E. Sheridan Ave.
Oklahoma City, OK 73104-2419
(405) 232-0759*

Architectural Antiques Exchange

Some stores feature a little bit of everything; Architectural Antiques Exchange features a lot of everything, or at least it seems as if it does. The 30,000-square-foot warehouse is stuffed with fascinating antiques from the 1700s to the 1940s, although the emphasis is on Victorian artifacts. Pine, oak, cherry, walnut, chestnut, and mahogany doors and mantels abound; lustrous oak, mahogany, and walnut paneling is waiting to be used again. If you can't find an original piece that meets your criteria, you can purchase a reproduction door or ask the in-house woodworking shop to make something special. It's easy to spend hours looking at the other antique items in the store, which usually include stained glass, front and back bars, mirrors, lighting fixtures,

balustrades, newel posts, columns, pedestal sinks, ironwork, ornate frames, marble carvings, and fretwork. Architectural Antiques Exchange will be happy to pack its merchandise and to ship it anywhere.

Literature available.

Architectural Antiques Exchange
709-15 N. 2nd St.
Philadelphia, PA 19123
(215) 922-3669

Architectural Salvage Co.

Warmth isn't just a temperature with an antique mantel from Architectural Salvage. Reclaimed mantels enrich a vintage interior with historic woodwork. Cherry pieces, carved with vines or flowers, are among the more ornate selections. Designs in oak may include shelves, beaded columns, or even a repeating ornament of wooden owls. Other services from Architectural Salvage include carpentry and building with architectural antiques, as well as restoration of antiques (with special expertise in stained glass).

Brochure available.

Architectural Salvage Co.
103 W. Michigan Ave.
Box 401
Grass Lake, MI 49240
(517) 522-8516

Architectural Salvage Cooperative

Non-profit Neighborhood Housing Service aids, advises, and makes loans to individuals who take on house renovations in its target neighborhoods. In the course of performing their services, members of the firm saw building materials making trips to the trash heaps and decided to do something about such a criminal waste. Neighborhood Housing Service's Architectural Salvage Cooperative now offers for sale bath and lighting fixtures, windows, tile, columns, hardware, and mantels, among many other reclaimed items.

Architectural Salvage Cooperative
909 W. 3rd St.
Davenport, IA 52803
(319) 324-1556

Canal Company

Because this company deals in antiques rather than reproductions, its stock fluctuates; an item may be easy to find one month and difficult the next. This is not to say that Canal's merchandise is limited in variety. On the contrary, the diversity of the architectural antiques typically on hand is staggering. On an average day at the company, you'd be likely to encounter claw-foot bathtubs, wood doors, French doors, desks, mirrors, wall sinks, faucet handles, mantels, moldings, quilts, curtains, shutters, tiles, tables, and several types of glass. If you're looking for a particular item, give Canal a call. The staff will search its inventory to see if the object is in stock.

Literature available.

The Canal Co.
1612 14th St. N.W.
Washington, DC 20009
(202) 234-6637

Great American Salvage

From a cramped garage to showrooms in Vermont, New York, Florida, and Connecticut, Great American Salvage has spent its half dozen years growing, building, adding, finding. French doors, beveled glass, lighting fixtures, stonework, mantels, and bars only begin the catalogue of Great American Salvage's inventory. Request the in-house newspaper for quarterly updates on Great American Salvage's unusual discoveries during reclamation and salvage jobs.

Literature available quarterly.

Great American Salvage Co.
34 Cooper Sq.
New York, NY 10003
(212) 505-0070

Whit Hanks

A newly expanded, 15,000-foot showroom makes Whit Hanks one of the largest retailers of architectural antiques in Texas. Specializing in massive, oversized pieces like a terrific street clock

14

from London and this oversized entryway of beveled glass and Belgian pine, Whit Hanks also offers 1000 unique mantels, iron gates, and general antiques. After working with architectural antiques for many years, Whit Hanks now restores antiques as well as selling them. The firm will respond to all inquiries with photographs and information on one-of-a-kind pieces.

Whit Hanks
1009 W. 6th St.
Austin, TX 78703
(512) 478-2101

Nottingham Gallery

For those who love antique glass but not high prices, Barbara Arrindell's Nottingham Gallery offers a selection of affordable doors and windows. The company's stock consists entirely of antique English stained and etched glass, most from the turn of the century. The pieces are made primarily of clear textured glass with interesting use of line and strong, basic colors used sparingly. Nottingham Gallery often visits antique shows around the country and has a mailing list to which you may add your name; since the stock shifts constantly, the company offers no brochure or catalogue.

Nottingham Gallery
339 Bellvale Rd.
Warwick, NY 10990
(914) 986-1487

Ohmega Salvage

Poke around in the yard at Ohmega Salvage and you'll turn up an eclectic selection of rebuilt kitchen fixtures, marble mantels, Peerless, Hajoca, and John Douglas toilets, among other treasures. Ohmega takes special pride in its antique and contemporary stained and beveled glass doors, which the firm repairs, restores, or reproduces to order.

Ohmega Salvage
Box 2125
2407 San Pablo Ave.
Berkeley, CA 94702
(415) 843-7368

Pelnik Wrecking

A doomed building may seem an unlikely candy shop, but for sixty years Pelnik Wrecking has been salvaging "all the goodies" from buildings slated for demolition. Pelnik's has amassed a phenomenal collection of mantels, sinks, corbels, railings, heart pine timbers, and more. Especially choice are windows—beveled, etched, and stained glass. This slender window of zipper-cut beveled glass is a valuable prize of architectural salvage. Lodge a specific request for photographs and see what Pelnik's offers you from its trove.

Pelnik Wrecking Co., Inc.
1749 Erie Blvd. E.
Syracuse, NY 13210
(315) 472-1031

PHOTOGRAPHY BY JULES

Urban Archaeology

Some say the Parisian department store Au Bon Marché was the apogee of Art Deco. Decide for yourself by visiting the complete circa 1920 interior, preserved at Urban Archaeology. The grand staircase, bronze balconies, leaded-glass skylights, plaster moldings, and copper railings are typical of the items available from this firm. The unusual showroom and four warehouses contain Art Deco, Art Nouveau, and Victorian relics, as well as antique slot machines, barber shops, and ice cream parlors. Urban Archaeology can replicate some items if your demands exceed what is available. The firm employs an excellent mold maker and carver for just this purpose. Make your request, or visit New York City and Urban Archaeology directly.

Urban Archaeology
137 Spring St.
New York, NY 10012
(212) 431-6969

Wooden Nickel Antiques

Scouring the Midwest for all that's old and intriguing, Tim Miller and Mike Williams acquire objects for Wooden Nickel Antiques. The company sells mantels, doors, lighting fixtures, beveled glass, stained glass, back bars, and hardware made between 1880 and 1920. Reproduction corbels are also available. No brochure is distributed, but you can phone or write to see whether a particular item is in stock. If you live in the area, feel free to take a look at Wooden Nickel's stock in person.

Wooden Nickel Antiques
1408 Central Pkwy.
Box 991531
Cincinnati, OH 45202
(513) 241-2985

Reproduction Building Materials

It is amazing just how sophisticated the market for reproduction building materials has become. For years there has been a plentiful supply of period fabrics, papers, and lighting fixtures. Now, one can also purchase new old-style brick, whole tin ceilings, doors and windows, lumber for flooring or wainscoting, roofing materials, and stair systems suitable for various types of old houses. This happy circumstance is due largely to a renaissance in traditional craftsmanship. More and more people have learned how to use old methods to produce materials such as mortise-and-tenon paneled white pine doors

and 12-over-12 windows. Of course, the demand for old style products has grown proportionally. Sometimes you have to wait in line to get what you want from a particular craftsman, but your investment of time and money will be amply rewarded.

Since the quantity and quality of reproduction building materials have grown almost geometrically in the past few years, the listings that follow are organized by subject, viz., Brick and Stone, Ceilings, Doors and Windows, Lumber, Roofing Materials, and Stairs.

suitable for traditional homes. What's special about Glen-Gery, however, is that it doesn't simply make fine standard bricks. It also makes handmade bricks formed in wooden molds, each unlike any other. Measuring 2¾" high by 4" wide by 8½" long or 2¼" high by 3⅝" wide by 7⅝" long, and thus larger than standard bricks, they are available in a rainbow of reds, burgundies, tans, browns, whites, buffs, and pinks.

Glen-Gery also offers a design and technical assistance service which enables you to consult with an engineer. Finally, for solving design problems, adding interest to a surface, or re-creating traditional detailing, the company offers a large selection of molded and extruded brick shapes. Wall caps, coping, bullnoses, watertable, sills, corners, step treads, and arches are among the standard shapes, and the company will execute custom designs on request.

Literature available.

Glen-Gery has branches in several mid-Atlantic, northeastern, and midwestern states. For further information or to locate the branch nearest you, contact:

Glen-Gery Corp.
6th and Court Sts.
Box 1542
Reading, PA 19603
(215) 374-4011

Brick and Stone

Locating supplies of the type of masonry material originally used in an older building is a task requiring considerable patience. Whether your aim is to patch up a small area, restore a whole expanse of wall, or add a complementary addition, you will have to seek out the specialty dealer or producer. Architectural antiques suppliers sometimes carry an

inventory of old brick; salvage yards are another good source. Manufacturers of old-style brick may be able to help you if you forward a sample to them. Stone is somewhat easier to come by, as most varieties popular in the past, such as brownstone, slate, fieldstone, marble, and granite, are still quarried today.

Aged Woods

It's almost impossible to find fieldstone today, except in the foundations of old farm buildings, so that's where Aged Woods goes to get it. Dismantling structures that cannot be used safely, the company salvages all the building materials that it can—including multicolored fieldstones which can be used for facing surfaces, fireplaces, interior walls, and some floors. Aged Woods also sells blue-gray Peach Bottom slate for roofs or walls.

Brochure available.

Aged Woods
Division of First Capital Wood
* Products*
147 W. Philadelphia St.
York, PA 17401
(800) 233-9307

Glen-Gery

If it's made of brick, Glen-Gery is likely to have it; if the company doesn't have it, it will probably make it. For nearly 100 years, Glen-Gery has been making bricks, so it's not surprising that it manufactures the basics very well. Its machine-made, sand-molded bricks are among the finest available and come in a multitude of sizes, colors, and textures

New York Marble Works

The veins of impurities that render marble so delicate are, ironically, the source of striking colors that recommend its use in protected indoor spaces. Hues of red, black, green, and gold, polished to a high sheen, are rare luxuries for tabletops, pedestals, and floors. New York Marble Works offers marble and granite in over 400 colors, in tile sizes ranging from 6" by 6" to 20" by 20". Custom designs, restoration (often using color-matched epoxies), and replacement for everything from fireplaces and furniture to handsome marble floors issue unrivaled from the inventory of this firm.

Brochure available.

New York Marble Works, Inc.
1399 Park Ave.
New York, NY 10029
(212) 534-2242

Superior Clay

For superior structural protection, top walls with coping formed from vitrified clay. Unfazed by harsh weather, the tough clay surface pieces from Superior Clay sport special features such as grooved tail inserts that guarantee tight bonds between pieces. Reinforcing drop sides also cleave to mortar in waterproof joints. Single slant, double slant, streamline, and camelback styles provide the variety to suit any architectural style.

Brochure available.

Superior Clay Corp.
Box 352
Uhrichsville, OH 44683
(800) 848-6166

Terra Cotta Productions

The decades around the turn of the century were the heyday of terra-cotta construction. Authentic and economical restoration of historic structures from that era is now possible with help from Terra Cotta Productions. Experts in ceramic design, backed by thorough historic research and mass production capabilities,

Terra Cotta Productions manufactures strong, solid terra cotta with buff clay from its own clay mine. The plant capacity of Superior Clay Corporation, representing half a century's experience, allows production of custom terra cotta, matched to originals by size, color, and design, as well as stock architectural tile. Terra cotta cleans easily, and proper maintenance renders it proof against fire, natural elements, and pollution

for centuries. Terra Cotta Productions assesses what each job will require by using photographs, sketches, measurements of pieces needed, and a sample of the original terra cotta for analysis.

For further information, contact:

Terra Cotta Productions, Inc.
Box 99781
Pittsburgh, PA 15233
(412) 321-2109

Ceilings

Ceilings in most period rooms are fairly simple. They may contain a center medallion or rosette but little else. Nineteenth-century Americans often attempted to spice up overhead space with special printed papers. This was an inexpensive way to make up for the lack of plasterwork or carved ornament. Another way of decorating the ceiling was to use composition or plaster borders and corners along with a center medallion.

Dovetail, Inc., has reproduced just such a design. In the late 1800s metal ceilings became quite popular for commercial spaces. They were decorative and inexpensive. Fortunately, they have been rediscovered; unfortunately, they have been overused in theme-park-like restaurants. Metal ceiling might be used in the kitchen of a private home today, but the historical precedent for such residential use is difficult to document.

Other ceilings include the Adams, which shows flowery details in 1" relief, while the Barton's balanced design includes leafy accents (1½" relief). Install these ceilings yourself with a saw, drill, tape measure, putty knife, sand paper, chalkline, and caulking gun. Professional help is required only for the plaster skim-coating of the remainder of the ceiling. Call on Dovetail with any questions that arise.

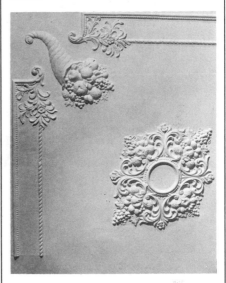

Brochure available.

Dovetail, Inc.
Box 1569
Lowell, MA 01853-2769
(617) 454-2944

AA-Abbingdon Affiliates

Compared with the fanciful metal ceilings of the late 19th century, today's ceilings seem unbearably dull. AA-Abbingdon's Prestplate metal ceilings were designed to reproduce the interesting lighting effects of those older surfaces. Over twenty styles, all sold in 2' by 8' sheets, feature pineapples, bold sharp lines, delicate beading, classical motifs, geometric designs, and intricate floral patterns. It's easy to find something you like. Ten cornice patterns increase the variety of this company's stock. The ceilings can be finished with any oil-base paint, clear lacquer, or polyurethane.

Brochure available.

AA-Abbingdon Affiliates Inc.
2149-51 Utica Ave.
Brooklyn, NY 11234
(718) 258-8333

In Canada, AA-Abbingdon's products can be obtained from:

The Architectural Antique Warehouse
1583 Bank St.
Ottawa, Ontario, Canada K1H 7Z3
(613) 526-1818

Ceilings, Walls & More

The slogan "decorative ceiling panels for gracious interiors" well describes some of the wares of Ceilings, Walls & More. Authentic metal patterns are faithfully copied in a sturdy, lightweight, non-porous polymer or vinyl.

Custom designs are also available. Choose from many traditional patterns, including Rosette, the egg and dart molding of Empire, the floral Victoriana, fleur-de-lis Excelsior, the rococo Covington, or the decoratively gridded Jeffersonian. Filler panels are available in simple Chain, Sunburst, or Star/Lattice. Installation is easy—panels can be scored and cleanly snapped to fit any space. A generous coating of adhesive allows application to sheetrock, plaster, or existing panels. Use oil-based spray paint on the panels, or leave a natural finish.

Brochure available.

Ceilings, Walls & More, Inc.
124 Walnut St.
Box 494
Jefferson, TX 75657
(214) 665-2221

Dovetail

For the renovator who covets the carved and molded opulence of a decorative ceiling, Dovetail offers the same beauty in an economical option. Single elements have been cast into substantial panels, simplifying installation and reducing cost. Specialized corner pieces, border friezes, moldings, and central medallions compose three different 15' by 18' ceilings. Cornucopian, double-framed by beaded and roped borders, sports a centerpiece of fruit and a woven horn, in 2" relief, at each corner.

W.F. Norman

Fin-de-siècle decorative interiors often featured pressed metal ceilings that were light, permanent, and pretty. From turn-of-the-century dies, Norman offers steel, brass, or copper ceilings in time-honored styles: Victorian, Romanesque, Rococo, Oriental, Greek, Gothic, Empire, Colonial, and Art Deco. An army of cornices, moldings, and beam covers provide flattering details for your designs, and most of the panels themselves can double as decorative coverings for bars, cabinets, or walls. Other practical advantages include the metal ceiling's fireproof quality and the fact that the metal effectively hides water damage and cracks. Easily installed, in panels of up to 2' by 4', the ceilings take a variety of paints and platings.

Brochure available.

W.F. Norman Corp.
Box 323
214-32 N. Cedar St.
Nevada, MO 64772-0323
(800) 641-4038

Missouri customers, call collect:
(417) 667-5552

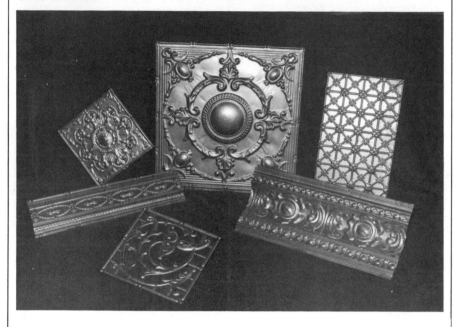

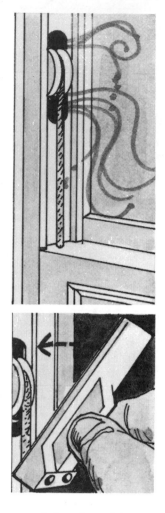

Doors and Windows

Finding a good door can be as difficult as finding a good man to hang it properly. There are aluminum exterior doors with a baked finish that look all right but pull right away from their frames in a year or two; there are hollow interior wood doors which are light as a feather to handle but won't stay shut for very long. We've tried lots of doors, inside and out, and we're ready to settle for a good, solid wood door—as thick as possible. The same goes for screen and storm doors. Since they are particularly exposed to the elements, it is important that they be well made. Aluminum or vinyl may be easy to put up and take down but until these materials are proven to take more than a few years wear and

tear, we'll stick with wood, thank you.

Windows are like doors. They are never easy to handle. In hot weather they stick and in cold they leak. Windows that are properly framed, that have sash with panes that are well puttied, and that are provided with suitable hardware shouldn't stick and won't leak. But they still do both. We don't know any solution to the problem. We do know that we'd just as soon have handsome, solidly built windows that add character to the house. Most old houses don't look right with modern sash. There are lots of suppliers who will help you to maintain the old image in good shape.

home, and there's nothing you can do about it. Anderson Pulley Seal, however, has invented an inexpensive way to save quite a bit of money. The company's little white or brown seals fit quickly and easily over the pulleys in old windows, covering the slots and reducing heat loss by as much as thirty-five percent. When properly caulked, weatherstripped, and sealed with Anderson's products, your old windows will be as energy-efficient as good-quality new windows.

Brochure available.

Anderson Pulley Seal
Box 19101
Minneapolis, MN 55419
(612) 827-1117

Architectural Antiques West

The most difficult question you'll have to answer abut this company's superb French doors is which you like best. Several stan-

Anderson Pulley Seal

It's frustrating to know that heat is seeping from your house. You

know that you're paying more than you should to warm your

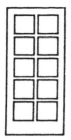

dard styles, including model 10/5, shown here, are kept in stock. This door comes in five widths from 2′ to 3′ and stands 6′8″ high. Most sizes are available in both Douglas fir and red oak, and if you're willing to wait a little longer, the company can make them in walnut, mahogany or any other wood that you prefer.

Custom sizes can be ordered, and several types of beveled, etched, and glue chip glass can be selected. Architectural Antiques West also makes what it calls its "custom" collection of French doors, which consists of styles not regularly kept in stock. Three examples are shown here; they can be fitted with clear glass or with beveled glass in four colors: clear, bronze, smoke gray, or peach. If you prefer to emphasize wood rather than glass, the company can provide you with a choice of carved and paneled doors in American red oak and Honduras mahogany. Special features of some of these doors include carving on both sides, beveled glass inserts, arched tops, and matching sidelights.

Architectural Antiques West has distributors throughout the United States. To locate the one nearest to your home, contact:

Architectural Antiques West
3117 S. La Cienega Blvd.
Los Angeles, CA 90016
(213) 559-3019

Architectural Components

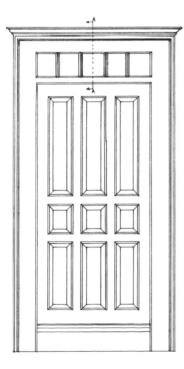

Workmanship of the 18th and 19th centuries may be inimitable, but it's not necessarily any less painstaking than museum-quality contemporary work by Architectural Components. Using construction techniques based on research into Georgian, Federal,

and Revival styles, the firm produces sturdy doors which come in double thicknesses or insulated designs. Cut from eastern white pine, pieces are milled and dried, mortise and tenon joined, and held with square pegs. In addition to its doors, Architecural

Components stocks plank window frames, small pane window sash, and moldings styled after Connecticut Valley originals. Custom work includes French doors, paneled items, sash, and cameo, casement, or fanlight windows. Contact Architectural Com-

ponents with your specific requests.

Brochure, $3.

Architectural Components
Box 249
Leverett, MA 01054
(413) 367-9441

Beech River Mill

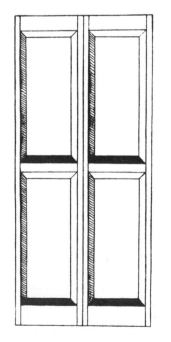

Founded in 1856, the Beech River Mill still uses genuine water-powered, Victorian mortisers, planers, and an antique rabbeting and beading machine. Custom sized, the wooden doors that Beech River Mill turns out are of unquestionably high quality. A

folding door shows an upper section of narrow panels over a single raised panel at the bottom. The door may be 1⅛" or 1⅜" thick, and the cross rail may be positioned at the height you specify. This four-panel louver door is also available with raised

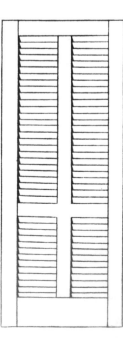

solid panels across the bottom. Clear, dry pine is the standard material, but Beech River Mill can use ash, cherry, cypress, mahogany, and oak as well.

Catalogue, $3.

Beech River Mill Co.
Old Route 16
Centre Ossipee, NH 03814
(603) 539-2636

Combination Door Co.

For all their Old-World appeal, vintage homes are usually none too energy efficient. Windows and doors will guarantee drafty chill in winter and steep bills for summer air conditioning, unless you turn to such firms as the Combination Door Company for help. Sound doors of solid ponderosa or sugar pine (wood doesn't conduct the chill) feature aluminum screen and tempered glass inserts in order to function as screen or storm doors. Each door is fitted with an adjustable vinyl and aluminum sweep that nestles at the sill to keep heated or air-conditioned air from escaping. The Combination Door Company cuts every door from 1¹⁄₁₆″ thicknesses of clear, kiln-dried wood treated with preservative and water-repelling compounds. Use paint, or keep a natural finish as you wish. The circle-top door, shown with both sets of seasonal hardware, demonstrates the "Easy Change" system at work. Another door is shown with four panels of airy screen. Also shown are variations on a charismatic octagonal window, both equipped with ⅛″ thick tempered glass.

Brochure available.

Combination Door Co.
Box 1076
Dept. OH
Fond du Lac, WI 54935
(414) 922-2050

Creative Openings

"Screeeek . . . . . slam!" According to Creative Openings, that (and not the dry rattle of cheap aluminum) is the inimitable sound of an authentic hardwood screen door. From kiln-dried walnut, teak, mahogany, old growth Douglas fir, and ash, Creative Openings assembles and finishes each door by hand.

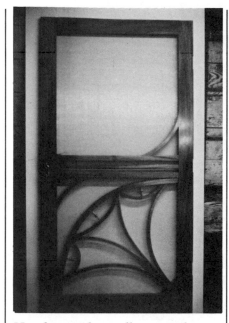

Hand-turned spindles, a tradition from the 1880s, accent the doors with spokes of ebony, maple, cherry, purpleheart, and other woods. Hardware is brass, bronze, or chrome. Easily replaceable bronze insect screens accompany all doors and can accept protective coatings to resist rust. Styles include Victorian, Colonial, Mission, and many other period designs. Storm window inserts can equip the doors for foul weather, and Creative Openings can often match screen doors with solid doors, some with hand-beveled or stained glass.

Brochure available.

Creative Openings
Box 4204
Bellingham, WA 98227
(206) 671-6420

Dovetail Woodworking

Few things are more irritating than knowing what you want and being unable to find it. All too frequently, old house lovers encounter this sort of frustration when looking for doors and windows. The craftsmen who built houses 200, 100, or even 50 years ago brought individuality to their work; today, standardization has left sashless, doorless gaps in fine old structures. Dovetail Woodworking attempts to solve the problem by specializing in hard-to-find, irregular shapes and

sizes. The company can reproduce almost any design, and it makes its sashes, storm windows, and doors from solid wood for efficient insulation and natural beauty.

Brochure available.

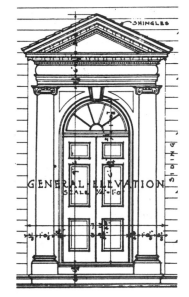

Dovetail Woodworking
550 Elizabeth St.
Waukesha, WI 53186
(414) 544-5859

Fypon

Fypon's "entrance systems" showcase the company's exceptional Molded Millwork, a dense polymer that you can work with drills, nails, or field carpenter tools. Don't worry about warping or rotting—and insects can't harm Molded Millwork, either. Different crossheads, or Peaked, Ram's Head, Acorn, or Sunburst pediments crown openings that vary by several feet within dif-

ferent styles of entrances. Pilasters trim to the desired height, and the entire system is easily installed. A creamy barrier coating takes oil-base primer and top coats, and the completed system requires very little upkeep. Other Molded Millwork items include custom bay and bow window roofs, window heads, door trim, moldings, and brackets.

Catalogues and sample sections available.

Fypon, Inc.
22 W. Pennsylvania Ave.
Stewartstown, PA 17363
(717) 993-2593

Glass Arts

Best known for its wide selection of elaborate beveled-glass panels, Glass Arts also makes nine styles of handsome doors from solid Appalachian red oak. All measure 6'8" high by 3' wide by 1¾" thick and are designed to accommodate single beveled panels or triple-glazed tempered glass. Mortise and tenon construction and oak pegging make the doors strong enough to be treasured by future generations. If red oak doesn't suit your needs, or if you'd like to match the design of another door in your house, Glass Arts will build a door to your specifications or execute its standard styles in oak, mahogany, walnut, or soft maple. Particle core veneer doors are also available for those who'd prefer to avoid the high cost of solid wood.

Catalogue available.

Glass Arts
30 Penniman Rd.
Boston (Allston), MA 02134
(617) 782-7760

Historic Windows

Beauty, styling in the spirit of the 18th century, and the natural effectiveness of wood as an insulator make interior paneled shutters a wise choice. Historic Windows makes several designs to your size specifications, including the three-paneled Annapolis. The company recommends that it be used only on windows at least 48" high to maintain the shutter's classic proportions. Half and Dutch shutters are also available. Four half shutters are usually required for each window; eight Dutch sections are needed—four for the bottom and four for the top. Windows narrower than 26" may need only two or three half shutters or four to six Dutch shutters. All of Historic Windows' products are available in white oak, rustic knotty oak, red oak, rustic knotty walnut, rustic knotty cherry, knotty pine, white oak, white maple, white birch, natural birch, pecan, and hickory. Wormy chestnut, clear walnut, and clear cherry are sometimes available. All shutters are ¾" thick. If you'd like to see a sample of a particular wood, a single raised panel measuring 8" by 12" is available for inspection. The price of the sample is refundable if it is returned within sixty days of the shipping date.

Brochure available.

Historic Windows
Box 1172
Harrisonburg, VA 22801
(703) 434-5855

Ideal

Obviously, the house that comes to stand behind the handsome door illustrated here has lots to live up to. One of Ideal's new Hartford Entrances, this imposing structure, made of white Ponderosa pine, comes in three styles. Opt for antique leaded glass, or choose clear leaded lights or divided lights with wood mulls. The distinctive panes of "water" glass, the cut gems achieved through beveling, and clear "ice crystal" glass unite in the full leaded lights that grace these transoms. Ideal equips these doors inside and out, with interior trim for elliptical caps, brick molding, cap piece, and fluted pilasters and mull casings.

Brochures available.

Ideal Co., Inc.
Box 2540
Waco, TX 76702-2540
(817) 752-2494

The Joinery Company

Authenticity is paramount in the manufacture of The Joinery Company's six-panel heart pine doors. Like the antique originals, these doors are hand pegged, raised on one side and flat on the other, and equipped with panels which are all made from the same plank. The panels are floating to help prevent splitting or fracturing due to the gain or loss of moisture. They are positioned in such a way as to reveal symmetrical, aligned graining. A choice of hand-planed or sanded surfaces is available. The Joinery Company also makes fine board-and-batten heart pine doors.

Kenmore Industries

Kenmore owes its excellent reputation to superb doorways like the ones described here. Model 510 has cast leaded paterae

at the joints, an elliptical leaded fanlight, carved capitals and pilasters, and a closed triangular pediment. Model 610 is an Adam-style entrance using a carved, draped frame with a choice of four half rounds and leaded sidelights surrounded by columns

24

with carved capitals. Kenmore is in the process of adding several new designs to its line, including a doorway with a pineapple motif and carved bolection molding and two broken-pediment doorways with horizontal leaded glass in a choice of sunburst or gothic styles.

Brochure, $3.

Kenmore Industries
Box 34, One Thompson Sq.
Boston, MA 02129
(617) 242-1711

Mad River Woodworks

Delicate white stencilwork or ornamental gingerbread woodwork turns Mad River's screen doors into decorative treasures. The company has reproduced four designs that were popular in the 1860s and manufactures them using double-doweled corner joints and knives ground especially for the cutting of the framework parts. All doors are built to your specifications, and a charcoal-gray aluminum screen is included. Plexiglass can be easily installed to make an all-weather storm door. To enable you to match the door to your exterior color scheme, it is left unfinished, ready for the paint or stain of your choice.

Catalogue, $2.

Mad River Woodworks
Box 163
Arcata, CA 95521
(707) 826-0629

Maurer and Shepherd Joyners

An entranceway can enhance or destroy a home's period look. It naturally draws the eye, and it must withstand more scrutiny than most other parts of a house's exterior. Maurer and Shepherd's entranceways prove more than a match for close examination. The one illustrated here is a splendid example of the company's work. All surfaces are hand-planed; all joints are mortise and tenon, held together by wooden pegs. Maurer and Shepherd also makes man-

tels, wainscoting, flooring, shutters, window sashes, window frames, and $^{15}\!/_{16}$"-thick interior doors in any panel configuration desired. All work is custom-made and done by hand.

Brochure available.

Maurer and Shepherd Joyners, Inc.
122 Naubuc Ave.
Glastonbury, CT 06033
(203) 633-2383

Midwest Wood Products

Midwest Wood's restoration projects include rebuilding paneled doors, porch windows, and screens. Attention to historic detail is a prime goal, and, with that priority in mind, Midwest Wood qualifies as a superb source for authentic window sash, an important element in recreating a period façade.

Send SASE for brochure.

Midwest Wood Products
1051 S. Rolff St.
Davenport, IA 52802
(319) 323-4757

Old Wagon Factory

Shunning veneers and composite boards, the Old Wagon Factory uses for its doors solid spruce and Douglas fir, fitted with brass or cast iron. Hand built, with mortise and tenon joints and plexiglass panels with aluminum screen, its Victorian doors have proved highly popular. Choose these decorated storm and screen doors to protect you from the weather or to invite a breeze inside. Doors from the Old Wagon Factory are available in custom sizes, or in the usual 32" by 81" or 36" by 81".

Catalogue, $2.

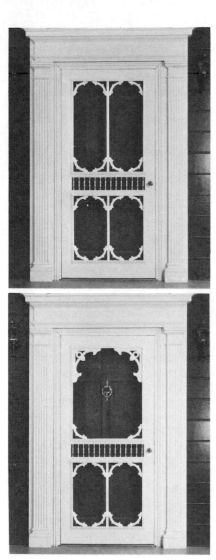

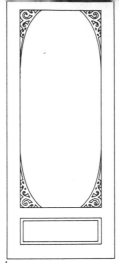

The Old Wagon Factory
103 Russell St.
Box 1427, Dept. OC86
Clarksville, VA 23927
(804) 374-5787

Remodelers' & Renovators' Supply

"No aluminum is allowed in our neighborhood," vows Remodelers' & Renovators' Supply, referring to an attractive selection of wooden screen doors manufactured by the company. Choose the Warm Springs, with pierced patterns in each corner, opt for the scrolled curves of the Oval, or draw your own style and let Remodelers' & Renovators' build it for you. Every door is custom cut from 1⅛" thicknesses of mixed grain fir. Solid glueing and doweling ensure lasting use. Stain and seal your door, which arrives presanded, and choose a solid brass

doorknob and lever set from Remodelers' & Renovators', if you like. Hardware comes in antique or polished brass. The firm can construct any of these doors as storm doors at your request. Remodelers' & Renovators' will ship to any corner of the United States.

Catalogue, $2.

Remodelers' & Renovators' Supply
512 W. Idaho
Boise, ID 83702
(208) 344-8612

Sheppard Millwork

If it's variety that you seek, don't fail to look at Sheppard Millwork's selection. Thirty-six door styles with various raised and flat panel and light combinations, three attractive louvered doors, eleven types of folding paneled or louvered doors, and seven sidelight designs are available. All are made of high-quality solid kiln-dried lumber and can be bored for knobs and locks if you choose. They are shipped sanded, unfinished, and without hardware, but they can be pre-hung in the jamb style of your choice and hinged. Doors with lights are sold without the glass. If you don't

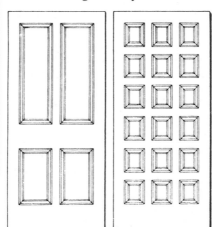

find anything you like in Sheppard's extensive collection, suggest a design to fill your needs. Custom work is frequently executed by the company; all custom doors are built with stile and rail construction and hardwood dowels.

Catalogue available.

Sheppard Millwork, Inc.
21020 70th Ave. W.
Edmonds, WA 98020
(206) 771-4645 or
(206) 283-7549

Somerset Door & Column

Although wood columns are this company's specialty, doors and windows are always in stock. Solid-wood doors are available with panels, louvers, and various light arrangements. Six standard windows, including a trapezoid, quarter, and half rounds, and the round and octagonal models shown here, are all of use for

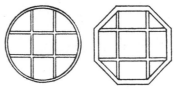

historical restoration. Custom millwork is also undertaken, so if you don't find exactly what you need in Somerset's brochure, don't despair; call and describe what your project demands.

Brochure available.

Somerset Door & Column Co.
Box 328
Somerset, PA 15501
(800) 242-7916
(800) 242-7915 (PA)

Lumber

If you are searching for boards or beams or even a small heavy strip of wood to replace a lintel or door saddle, you probably won't find what you want at the local lumberyard or home center. The usual response to a question concerning the availability of something other than the softest pine is that the better grade woods are simply not available any longer. That is not true. The truth is that the average building materials supplier makes his money from plywood, various types of composition board, sheetrock, and pine durable enough to frame a house. Consequently, other specialty lumber dealers have established themselves throughout North America. All stock quantities of newly cut domestic and foreign timber such as quality white pine and oak, and many also keep a supply of recycled Southern heart pine. These dealers usually maintain an inventory of the more elegant woods used for interior work. If you need to have boards milled and finished in a particular manner, the specialty supplier probably can help.

Aged Woods

Few things are more appropriate to an old house than the time-enhanced beauty of old wood. Used for exposed beams, furniture, cabinets, doors, flooring, or paneling, old wood has a comfortable and solid look that's hard to match. Aged Woods offers several species salvaged from old buildings, inspected, treated for insects if necessary, and cleaned with water or steel brushing. Planks or beams are usually available in pine, oak, walnut, and rare American chestnut. Twenty-five-year-old cypress is also sold for use in damp areas. You can purchase samples of various woods if you like; the price will be refunded if you place an order.

Brochures available.

Aged Woods
Division of First Capital Wood
Products
147 W. Philadelphia St.
York, PA 17401
(800) 233-9307

Carlisle Restoration Lumber

Carlisle is a source of wide-board lumber that you might have trouble locating near your home. Expertly milled square-edged pine ranges from 14″ to 21″ in width. It can be obtained with shiplapped edges in widths between 8″ and 12″ as well. Oak planks are milled in 5″ to 10″ widths. All three types of lumber range from 8′ to 16′ in length. Carlisle also sells pine feather-edge clapboards.

Literature available.

Carlisle Restoration Lumber
Rte. 123
Stoddard, NH 03464
(603) 446-3937

Cedar Valley

When it comes to shingle siding, the combination of easy installation and superb weather protection is hard to beat, and Cedar Valley's products excel in both categories. Two-course or three-course panels, attached to $\frac{5}{16}$″-thick plywood with special staples, make mounting the shingles simple and precise. The problem of uneven nailing is eliminated, and stress is better distributed. The placement of a 30/30/30 Kraft paper barrier between the shingles and the plywood eliminates the need for a separate sheet of building paper.

Cedar Valley's shingles are attractive as well as functional. They are made of western cedar, which weathers to a rustic gray; the staples are invisible, and there's little need for obtrusive face nailing. A patented system hides joints between panels, and you can choose the exposure length of the shingles. Standard lengths are 6″, 7″, 8″, 12″, and 14″; custom lengths may be specified.

Literature available.

Cedar Valley Shingle Systems
985 S. 6th St.
San Jose, CA 95112
(408) 998-8550

Granville Manufacturing

The last machine for manufacturing quartersawn clapboards was built in 1910. Only three mills still operate to produce these boards today. Granville, Vermont's mill has turned out clapboards since 1857, and many of them, even unpainted, still cover and protect New England homes. Quarter-sawn boards, each a tapered section reaching from the log's center to its surface (minus bark), result in straight grain for each board, while the easier "resawing" methods of manufacturing clapboards yield a warp-prone curved grain. Straight grain, furthermore, holds stains and paints better. Select from four widths of white and red spruce and white pine, in 2′ to 6′ lengths. Three grades are available: clear clapboard; boards with no more than one blemish or knot each; or the "cottage" grade, with a rustic look engendered by numerous knots and blemishes (guaranteed not to impair use).

Catalogue, $1.

Granville Manufacturing Co., Inc.
Rte. 100
Granville, VT 05747
(802) 767-4747

Mad River Woodworks

Mad River Woodworks has fallen in love with Victorian millwork—its ornate and fanciful style and its special grace. Work from these craftspeople will have you charmed, too. Of particular interest is Mad River's many styles of decorative siding. Majestic redwoods yield a naturally enduring wood. Clear kiln-dried sections of this material, cut in various decorative patterns for distinctive and practical siding, take stain and paint or show to advantage in a natural finish.

Catalogue, $2.

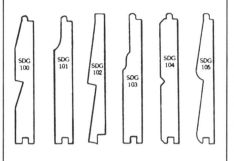

Mad River Woodworks
Box 163
Arcata, CA 95521
(707) 826-0629

Mountain Lumber

Longleaf heart pine is Mountain Lumber's specialty. Retrieved from structures built before 1900, this fine wood can be used for floors, paneling, beams, doors, moldings, cabinets, and mantels. Rough-sawn boards and rough-sawn or hand-hewn beams are available, as well as stair treads and risers. Paneling comes in several types: ⁷⁄₁₆″-thick panels with flush shiplap joints and random lengths of 4″ to 8″; ¾″-thick panels with tongue and groove flush joints and random lengths of 4″ to 10″ in what Mountain Lumber calls its "naily grade," and ¾″-thick panels in random lengths of either 4″ to 8″ or 4″ to 10″. The latter two sizes have tongue and groove construction with a choice of beaded or "V" joints. The company's president, William G. Drake, welcomes visits to the showroom, which is located five minutes from the Charlottesville airport. If you call ahead, someone will be glad to pick you up at the airport and drive you back afterward.

Brochure available.

Mountain Lumber Co.
Rte. 2, Box 43-1
Ruckersville, VA 22968
(804) 985-3646 or
(804) 295-1922

The Woodworkers' Store

Sometimes it's simply impossible to find good hardwood lumber near your home. Retailers don't carry what you need, or else what they have is unacceptable. Don't give up the search; it's possible to order what you need by mail. The Woodworkers' Store, based in Minnesota, sells birch, hard maple, walnut, cherry, white oak, and Honduras mahogany by the inch. You can buy precisely as much as you want, although each piece must be at least 6″ and no more than 60″ in length. The lumber comes in five board widths—1¾″, 2¾″, 3¾″, 4¾″, and 5¾″—and three thicknesses—½″, ¾″, and 1¾″. Thinner boards are available. All boards are surfaced on both top and bottom and have straight parallel edges. They are guaranteed to have at least one side free of defects. The Woodworkers' Store also has retail outlets in San Diego, Minneapolis, Seattle, Denver, Boston, and Columbus, Ohio.

Catalogue, $1.

The Woodworkers' Store
21801 Industrial Blvd.
Rogers, MN 55374
(612) 428-4101

Roofing Materials

A good roofing material is indispensable for any old house, and its application must be carefully done. A leaking roof can cause no end of structural problems which may be extremely expensive to correct. When one considers just how many square feet of a building's exterior may be covered with roofing material, its importance is better understood. Although much of it is often out of sight, it cannot be out of mind. This is especially true in the majority of North American regions where a roof is traditionally inclined to ward off the elements. Only in arid regions, such as the Southwest, where rainfall is slight and snow rare, are roofs traditionally flat. Many modern builders have learned to their regret that flat roofs collect rather than shed the elements. Why they couldn't figure this out in advance is puzzling. But, then, who ever said that modern builders have it over the old?

Blue Ridge Shingle

Blue Ridge Shingle explains that unfinished shingles, known as "shakes", will soon deteriorate. Choose hard, durable white oak shingles that weather to a silvery gray. Blue Ridge issues three grades of these recommended shingles, differing in texture and percentage of heartwood in their composition but each an investment in the weatherproofing of your old house.

Brochure available.

Blue Ridge Shingle Co.
Montebello, VA 24464
(703) 377-6635 or
(919) 395-5333

C & H Roofing

With its unusual rolled eaves and gables, C & H's "Country Cottage Roof" has a cedar shingle pattern that sets it apart from others. C & H's new catalogue and installation guide instruct ambitious homeowners in the simple steps of assembling their own Country Cottage Roofs. Pre-cut framing elements allow builders to adapt standard roof frames to accommodate a roof from C & H. Special roof features include the upward curve of "eyebrow" dormers, rolling roof vents (complete with wooden louvers), and various cleverly bent shingles. The flowing nature of these roofs begs your imaginative input, and C & H's design specialists will ad-

vise you on your very own interpretation of the Country Cottage Roof.

Catalogue available.

C & H Roofing, Inc.
1713 S. Cliff Ave.
Sioux Falls, SD 57105
(605) 332-5060

Cedar Valley

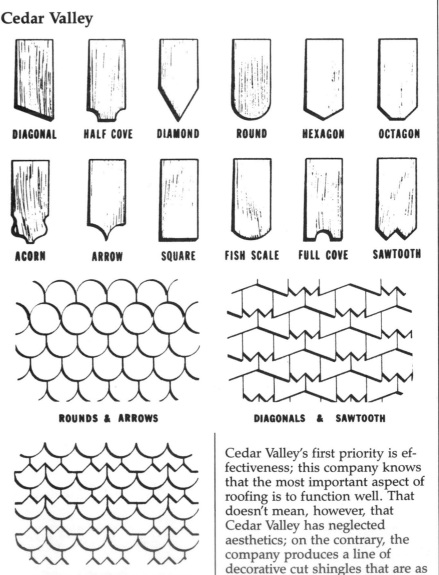

DIAGONAL HALF COVE DIAMOND ROUND HEXAGON OCTAGON

ACORN ARROW SQUARE FISH SCALE FULL COVE SAWTOOTH

ROUNDS & ARROWS

DIAGONALS & SAWTOOTH

ROUNDS, SAWTOOTH & OCTAGONS

Cedar Valley's first priority is effectiveness; this company knows that the most important aspect of roofing is to function well. That doesn't mean, however, that Cedar Valley has neglected aesthetics; on the contrary, the company produces a line of decorative cut shingles that are as attractive as any wood shingles you'll find. Made of western red cedar, they can be coated with a clear stain, painted with oil-base or acrylic paints, or left to weather to a natural gray. They are sold in boxes of about 100 pieces, but they are also available in two-course panels with a maximum exposure of 7½". Cedar Valley suggests combining different shingle types to create unusual designs; a few examples are shown here.

Literature available.

Cedar Valley Shingle Systems
985 S. 6th St.
San Jose, CA 95112
(408) 998-8550

Mad River Woodworks

Why think of your house's roof as merely a device for keeping out the rain? Properly covered, it can be a festive decoration as well as a durable shelter. Mad River's attractive redwood shingles can help your roof contribute to your home's appearance of authenticity; such shingles have been protecting homes in California for over 100 years. A number of shingles, measuring either 5" or 6" in length, are available in several styles, including hexagons,

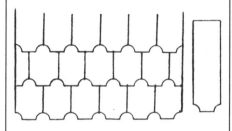

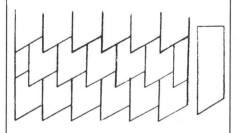

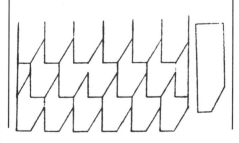

diamonds, and octagons. The indented Halfcove, sharp Diamond, and unusual Sawtooth versions are shown here.

Catalogue, $2.

Mad River Woodworks
Box 163
Arcata, CA 95521
(707) 826-0629

Mister Slate

Customers from Maine to California have purchased Mister Slate's roofing products, and they had some good reasons to do so. The company's new and salvaged roofing slate is easily installed and long-lasting; of the latter virtue, owner Chuck Smid notes that slate has been around for over 100 million years. Various sizes are available, and the tiles can be trimmed in diamond, scallop, or octagonal shapes for an especially decorative appearance. If the size or shape you'd like is not sold, Smid will custom-cut it. He'll also do his best to match your slate color for repairs. Black, greens, grays, purples, and even rare reds are usually in stock.

Literature available.

Mister Slate
Smid Inc.
Sudbury, VT 05733
(802) 247-8809

W. F. Norman

Galvanized steel or solid copper, Norman's shingles and tiles are back in production. This company began manufacturing roofs in 1908. Many of the very first roofs still exist, attesting to the supreme durability of Norman's functional, elegant product. Resilient and practical, these roofs withstand hail and fire, winter and broiling

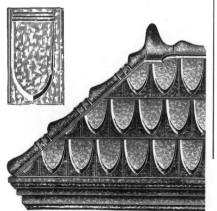

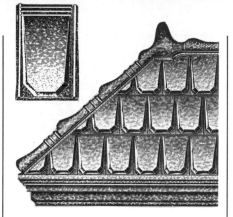

summer weather. Spanish and Mission tiles maintain their popularity, and Victorian and slate-like Normandie shingles enjoy a healthy following as well.

Brochure available.

W. F. Norman Corp.
Box 323
214-32 N. Cedar St.
Nevada, MO 64772-0323
(800) 641-4038

Missouri customers, call collect:
(417) 667-5552

Rising and Nelson

For more than a century, Rising and Nelson has been producing colored slate from its Vermont quarries. The slate's density, fire and water resistance, low maintenance cost, and ability to be installed over other roofing materials make it effective and practical. Its various colors, including black, gray, sea green, dark emerald, dark reddish purple, and red, make it a wise choice from an aesthetic standpoint as well. Some of the colors soften or acquire a brown or buff patina with age, and others remain unchanged by exposure to the elements. Lengths run from 10" to 24" in 2" increments; widths are random. Two textures are available. The smooth slate ranges from ³⁄₁₆" to ¼" in thickness, and the rough slate from ³⁄₁₆" to 1". If you wish, Rising and Nelson will make use of its capable design service to help you plan your roof.

Literature available.

Rising and Nelson Slate Co., Inc.
West Pawlet, VT 05775
(802) 645-0150

Stairways

A stairway can be the most dramatic element in a house: how many Hollywood movies feature a stairway scene, with the heroine descending into the arms of romance or danger? While a stairway must be sturdy, it should also have some flair—if not grandeur. Old house builders understood this and were not satisfied with constructing a straight up-and-down path. Nearly every old stairway curves gracefully at some point—top, bottom or middle. All of the suppliers (of complete staircases and of parts) in the following listings understand something of the charm of the well-wrought bridge between floors.

Curvoflite

Combine various molded or champhered handrails with standard, champhered, or turned balusters and posts for a unique spiral staircase that you design for the desired degree of period ambience. From beautiful woods like red oak, poplar, mahogany, birch, and walnut, Curvoflite's treads and risers form various graceful right- or left-hand helixes in a range of diameters.

Curvoflite also builds bars,

cabinets, raised paneling, hand-turned balusters, doors, and mantels.

Brochure available.

Dahlke Studios

Tom Dahlke's art demands he play the hybrid of sculptor-engineer. A custom designer and builder of curving wooden staircases, Dahlke came to stair design through Oakland's California College of Arts and Crafts, experience in sailboat maintenance that taught him laminating techniques for delicately curved wood, and a penchant for getting the best of tough design problems.

Curvoflite
205 Spencer Ave.
Chelsea, MA 02150
(617) 889-0007

Dahlke delves deep with his research, and when he uncovers the suitable historical motifs, he uses them imaginatively in his work to produce pieces that cleave to the period without plagiarizing designs. Using laminations of wood slivered to thicknesses of $3/32$", Dahlke bends and glues dozens of layers, with a resulting curved piece that looks like a twist of solid wood. The staircase shown here bespeaks Tom Dahlke's talent and delivers a breathtaking effect in the house it graces.

Brochure, $2.

Dahlke Studios
Box 1128
Glastonbury, CT 06033
(203) 659-1887

The Iron Shop

Perfect for tight spaces and simple in design, spiral staircases can often solve difficult problems. If you like the look of metal, take a look at The Iron Shop's easily assembled kit for a steel staircase with a vinyl handrail. All fasteners are included, and all parts are primed flat black. The Iron Shop even includes a spray can of the primer in case the finish is scratched during shipping. Available options include oak or embossed treads, an oak handrail, fancy spindles, and assorted parts that give your staircase a custom look.

If you prefer the warmth of wood, however, the company's oak staircase kit may be to your liking. Made of beautifully grained, kiln-dried solid oak from Kentucky, Indiana, and Tennessee, it has 1¼"-thick treads supported by dovetailed gussets, a hollow cen-

tral hub that measures 5" in diameter, and a 2½"-high by 1⅜" wide curved railing.

The metal staircase kit comes in eight sizes, ranging from 3' 6" to 7' in diameter; the oak staircase is available only in 4' and 5' sizes. Both kits are custom-built to meet your floor-to-floor height specifications.

Brochure, $1.

The Iron Shop
Dept. OHCF
Box 128, 400 Reed Rd.
Broomall, PA 19008
(215) 544-7100

The Joinery Company

The beauty of a solidly built wooden staircase can make an entrance hall a majestic sight, and for most 17th- and 18th-century homes, its authenticity is undeniable. The Joinery Company manufactures heart pine stair parts that will enable you to achieve a look that only fine materials and painstaking craftsmanship can bestow. At the Joinery Company, everything is

manufactured by hand, and you'll find everything you need. Stair treads are made of 1¼"-thick by 12" deep boards milled to 1" by 11" with nosing profiles, and they can be hand-planed or sanded, depending on your preference. Treads with vertical grain are also available. Risers, which may also have vertical graining, are made of 1" by 8" boards milled to ¾" by 7¾" with square-edged profiles.

The company also sells scotia molding for use between treads and risers, Georgian-style hand rails, turned or 1" square by 36"-high pickets, and newel posts. Two standard posts are made—Georgian, with a square post, raised panel cap, and ogee molding; and Deerfield, with a square base and hand-carved top. Turned newel posts are made on request. The Joinery Company invites visits to its showroom.

Brochure, $5.

The Joinery Co.
Box 518
Tarboro, NC 27886
(919) 823-3306

Schwartz's Forge

If the staircase you want seems impossible to find, have a talk with Joel A. Schwartz. Schwartz uses his extensive training, research, and experience to create ironwork that is durable, attractive, and rich in detail; his work has been exhibited at the Museum of Contemporary Crafts in New York City and at the Renwick Gallery of the Smithsonian Institution. His commissions for New York residences have included an imposing two-story spiral staircase, an undulating stair railing with a wild vine motif, and a five-story stairway that features a smoothly curving top rail and gently bending posts ending in spirals at their tops and bottoms.

Literature available.

Schwartz's Forge & Metalworks
Forge Hollow Rd.
Box 205
Deansboro, NY 13328
(315) 841-4477

Somerset Door & Column

Best known for its wood columns, Somerset also makes an attractive circular stairway. Built of solid hardwood, the stairway has a gentle curve that lends elegance to a room or to an entrance hallway. Its simplicity and grace make it appropriate for most

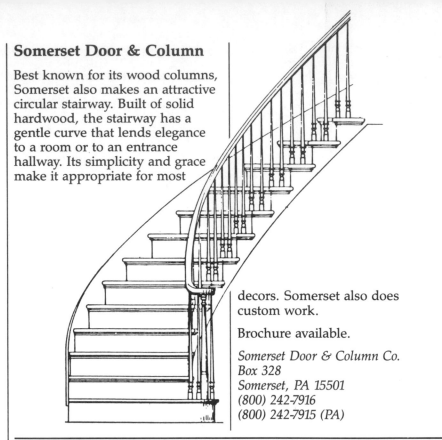

decors. Somerset also does custom work.

Brochure available.

Somerset Door & Column Co.
Box 328
Somerset, PA 15501
(800) 242-7916
(800) 242-7915 (PA)

Steptoe & Wife

Victorian-style cast-iron staircases are Steptoe & Wife's specialty. In addition to two spiral staircases, the 5'-diameter Barclay and the 4'3"-diameter Albany, the company makes an elegant straight model, the Kensington. Perfect for front entrances, patio exits, porch steps, and interior applications, cast-iron staircases are a welcome alternative to unsightly concrete. Measuring 36" wide, each elaborate open fretwork riser is composed of four castings bolted together. Order as many risers as you need; if you're using more than three, steel channels will provide extra support. If you like, you can add brass and steel railings or decorative cast-iron balusters.

Catalogue available.

Steptoe & Wife Antiques Ltd.
322 Geary Ave.
Toronto, Ontario, Canada M6H 2C7
(416) 530-4200

33

Sunshine Architectural Woodworks

There's no need to interrupt beautiful wainscoting between floors. Available in a variety of hardwood species, Sunshine's angular wainscoting allows you to apply the beauty of wood to the angular elevations of staircases as well as horizontally. Simply supply a few measurements and Sunshine will custom-manufacture the paneling; the company's catalogue provides instructions for taking the measurements. If you have any questions or problems, call Sunshine; they'll be glad to help you.

Catalogue, $4.

Sunshine Architectural Woodworks
Rte. 2, Box 434
Fayetteville, AR 72701
(501) 521-4329

Vintage Lumber

Only centuries of slow, steady growth could produce the tight-grained heartwood of the longleaf pine. Naturally immune to insects and decay, the wood was coveted, cut for homes, bridges . . . even the keel of the *U.S.S. Constitution*. Retrieved wood from these structures seems to be quite a prize, since lumbermen have felled the great pine forests, destroying the needed conditions for them ever to grow again.

Vintage Lumber offers stair parts from this reclaimed heart pine. Treads, risers, landing and return nosing, etc.—all have been resawn from antique timbers.

Vintage Lumber & Construction Co., Inc.
9507 Woodsboro Rd.
Frederick, MD 21701
(301) 898-7859

Consultants and Architects

Almost everyone needs advice in putting an old house back together or in renovating some part of it. Consultants and architects can help tremendously with such preliminary steps as inspecting a building before it is purchased, digging out the building's history, and drawing up a recommended list of restoration or renovation steps to be taken. Once the direction is clear and the plans have been drawn up, a contractor is usually called in to perform most of the work. The architect or consultant need not step out of the picture entirely at this point; he is usually willing to supervise the contractual work.

Architectural Resources Group

The San Pablo Bay, California town that produced more TNT than any other during World War II eventually took the name of the black powder its plant produced: Hercules. After the plant shut down and even the sheep that had grazed the area (to cut the chance of disastrous grass fires) were gone, a score of Colonial Revival and Queen Anne homes still stood. A baker's dozen of these buildings, relocated in a nationally listed historic district, still display their classic architecture, thanks to the work of the Architectural Resources Group. Original wood shingles and millwork were restored. Necessary replacements were matched to antiques. Interior work, such as the ornate decoration of Colonial Revival entrance halls, was faithfully preserved. Modern additions, sometimes entailing complete plumbing systems, were executed to leave the village basically undisturbed.

Architectural and design services from Architectural Resources Group make projects like this one feasible. Contact the firm for further information.

Architectural Resources Group
Pier 9
The Embarcadero
San Francisco, CA 94111
(415) 421-1680

Carson, Dunlop

The house captures your heart, but how do you squelch doubts about antique constructions, nuances of maintenance over the years that may harbor impending costly repairs? Let Carson, Dunlop & Associates ease your mind with the information to make an expertly informed decision. Partial or full inspections, conducted six days a week, yield honest evaluations; an on-site verbal report precedes the prompt written summary. Carson, Dunlop is the first Canadian firm in the American Society of Home Inspectors and holds certification from the Association of Professional Engineers of Ontario.

Brochure available.

Carson, Dunlop & Associates
597 Parliament St.
Suite 85
Toronto, Ontario, Canada M4X 1W3
(416) 964-9415

Clio Group

Named after the Greek muse of history, the Clio Group began with a pair of architectural historians and a restoration architect commissioned to plan exhibits honoring the American bicentennial. Today, the Clio Group's projects dot the United States. The National Register of Historic Places lists over 100 buildings and a score of historic districts that have been included because of the research and certification surveys of the Clio Group.

Government services to meet the standards of local, state, and federal agencies are available from the Clio Group. Historic Structure Reports, Historic Sites Surveys, and National Register nominations are deftly handled. Restoration services may include entire building plans or minute materials analysis for an individual room. The Clio Group has accrued much experience working with developers in such areas as Chicago's South Loop Printing House District and Philadelphia's Powelton Village Historic District. Superb academic training qualifies members of the Clio Group to present a host of lectures and seminars. The firm's excellent architectural photography often facilitates drafting, as well as marketing and publicity projects.

CLIOX, the Clio Group's innovative computer program, was originally developed for projects in historic areas of Philadelphia but can be adapted to serve other areas for informative studies. The program makes a wealth of valuable data readily accessible, with listings of specific buildings, architects, owners, construction dates, materials, sizes and locations.

Brochure available.

Clio Group, Inc.
3961 Baltimore Ave.
Philadelphia, PA 19104
(215) 386-6276

maintaining historic areas. Additional technical services include one of the United States' few private laboratories for analyzing plaster, paint, and mortar, either for duplication or for documentation. Community Services Collaborative also provides landscape architectural services, cultural resources surveys, adaptive reuse studies, and redesigning for energy efficiency.

Community Services Collaborative will respond by letter to any inquiry.

Community Services Collaborative
1315 Broadway
Boulder, CO 80302
(303) 442-3601

Jamie Gibbs and Associates

Nine years of experience, seven of them as the head of his own private practice, have taken Jamie Gibbs across three continents. His specialty is the creation of traditional interiors, and his work in this field has encompassed a wide range of architectural styles. Gibbs has also written several books and frequently gives lectures and conducts study tours through famous houses, many of which are not usually open to the public.

Jamie Gibbs and Associates
Landscape Architects and Interior
* Designers*
340 E. 93rd St., Suite 14C
New York, NY 10128
(212) 722-7508

The Color People

Specializing in Victorian structures, James R. Martin's consulting firm chooses colors that make buildings look their best. Tasteful color schemes tailored to your needs are developed on the basis of your personal preferences and painting budget, the building's architectural history, the location, the interior colors, and the colors of brick or roof tiles. Much of the company's business takes place by mail; you send Martin requested photographs and information, and he sends you an easily understandable packet of instructions to give to your painter.

Brochure available.

The Color People
1672 Madison St.
Denver, CO 80206
(303) 388-8686

Brian G. Hart

You need not compromise historic integrity when use requires an addition to original architecture. Brian Hart's architectural and planning services include designing compatible infill structures for historic districts and adding another wing or story to an existing building. Evaluative services cover conservation, restoration, adaptation, and rehabilitation. Various research and inspection services, as well as inventories

Community Services Collaborative

The charm of a historic building doesn't always translate to peace in the community around it. Defusing of tensions between neighborhood merchants and residents in a historic district provides an example of the effective techniques in public relations that are just one aspect of Community Services Collaborative.

Let this consulting firm guide you through the necessary statements, maps, and photographs to place a building on the National Register. The firm can draw up guidelines for modifying period structures and can back up those guidelines with sound preservation ordinances, free of the vague or arbitrary clauses that are pitfalls in

WEST ELEVATION

and feasibility studies are additional specialties offered. Hart's work has focused mainly on the West Coast.

Brian G. Hart
4375 W. River Rd.
Delta, British Columbia, Canada
V4K 1R9
(604) 946-8302

clients, is headed by registered architect Carol Hickey and Elvin Hess, a designer and construction consultant whose experience includes running a restoration contracting company. The firm's work for individuals and businesses has included the preservation, restoration, and renovation of historic buildings dating from the late 1700s.

Two such projects were the renovations of a Lancaster, Pennsylvania carriage house for use as a guest house and of Washington Hall in York, Pennsylvania, an 1850 warehouse which was converted into an apartment building. The exterior and lobby of Washington Hall are shown here.

Whether the company is restoring a structure to its original appearance or adapting it for a new use, its staff tries to retain as much of the original building as possible. Hickey/Hess also provides consulting services, historical research services, and assistance in completing U.S. Department of Interior forms.

Hickey/Hess Architecture and Design
230 Harrisburg Ave.
Lancaster, PA 17603
(717) 394-6053

Hickey/Hess

Old house lovers in Maryland and central and western Pennsylvania can get architectural assistance from Hickey/Hess. The small firm, which takes pride in its personal approach to its projects and

Mackall & Dickinson Architects

Formerly called Louis Mackall and Partner, Mackall & Dickinson Architects is expert at projects in-

Is your old house picture perfect? Then let Jack Nixon preserve it in an exquisite architectural rendering. With a full house of design, building, calligraphy, and illustration awards, Nixon has directed his talents to soft pencil illustrations of at least 20" by 16". Homes, businesses, or religious structures receive his careful attention, beginning with sharp photographs, scheduled during the time of year that sees the most flattering lighting pattern cast against the building. This 1843 hotel in Brooklyn, Michigan, entered in the National Register of Historic Places, will last as long and as beautifully on top-quality drawing paper as it will in durable brick.

Brochure available.

Nixon Design Studio
835 15th St.
Wilmette, IL 60091
(312) 256-3531

Preservation Associates

Let Preservation Associates guide you through the maze of planning, revitalizing, and registering necessary for protecting historic structures. Providing a substantial fund of information and records of restoration and preservation materials and methods, as well as the expertise to ascertain what must be preserved in a vintage building, Preservation Associates is obviously prepared to help fanciers of old homes. The firm is expert in readying applications for certification with the National Register of Historic Places.

Preservation Associates
207 S. Potomac St.
Hagerstown, MD 21740
(301) 791-7880

The Preservation Partnership

Founded in 1977, this firm is New England's oldest private historic preservation consulting practice. The staff of eight, which includes architects, architectural historians, and architectural conservators, has an impressive collective

volving historic buildings, such as the addition designed for an 1870 Italianate farmhouse in Hartford, Connecticut, illustrated here. The addition consists of a master bedroom and straddles an enclosed porch added forty years ago. Mackall & Dickinson also operates Breakfast Woodworks, a restoration contracting company.

Mackall & Dickinson Architects
50 Maple St.
Branford, CT 06405-3590
(203) 488-8364

Nixon Design Studio

Restorations Unlimited can begin helping before you even move into your house by performing inspections of structures. You'll know about problems that might arise and what it might cost to fix them. The firm also offers historical color consultation, preparation of floor plans and elevations, assistance with paperwork, and assistance for do-it-yourselfers. If you don't want a general contractor but need information about the best tools, materials, and approach for a certain aspect of your project, give this company a call. Of course, if you are in the market for a general contractor, Restorations Unlimited will be able to provide everything you need, from millwork and flooring to stenciling and paper hanging. Available services include electrical work, plumbing, glasswork, plastering, tiling, roofing, and masonry.

Brochure available.

Restorations Unlimited, Inc.
124 W. Main St.
Elizabethville, PA 17023
(717) 362-3477

Contractors

Builders with the skills necessary to execute restoration or renovation work successfully can be difficult to find. Nearly every area of North America, however, has at least a few of these talented individuals. In addition to basic construction techniques, the old-house contractor must be very familiar with various period styles, old-fashioned building methods, and the types of materials which can be appropriately used. How to locate such a history-sensitive contractor? The listings that follow will be helpful, and, if one individual cannot help you, he may be able to lead you to another who can assist. The best recommendation, however, is still a house that has been successfully restored or renovated. If possible, visit a few of these homes, and find out by whom the work was done.

educational and professional background. Among the projects which the firm has tackled are the restoration of historic Ferrin Hall at Barrington College in Barrington, Rhode Island, including supervision of the first phase of the roof repairs, and the restoration of a historic row in Bedford Square, Boston, illustrated here. The Preservation Partnership offers a number of valuable services to the consumer. Half-day property inspections will help you decide whether you really want a particular house. You'll find out the structure's historical value and physical condition, what repairs are needed, and even how much they'll cost. If you decide that you still want the house, the firm will oversee the repairs for you, if you like.

For the serious restorer, The Preservation Partnership offers help with grant applications and other paperwork. To ensure the most accurate restoration possible, a Historic Structure Report can be compiled. This may take days, weeks, or even months as the staff painstakingly researches the house's background, prepares drawings and specifications, removes and dates nails, and un-

covers and matches layers of paint.

Brochure available.

The Preservation Partnership
345 Union St.
New Bedford, MA 02740
(617) 996-3383

Preservation Services

Preservation Services offers expert analysis and design advice for both conservation and adaptive reuse. The firm will document every aspect of a historic structure and offers help with grant applications and nominations to the National Register. Direct specific inquiries for projects of any size to:

Preservations Services, Inc.
1445 Hampshire
Quincy, IL 62301
(217) 224-2300

Restorations Unlimited

Working on houses, museums, churches, and offices, this company provides a number of valuable services for anyone interested in restoring, remodeling, or adding to an old building.

Anderson Building Restoration

The expert craftsmen at Anderson Building Restoration return aged structures to their original glory, cleaning and restoring antique masonry with state-of-the-art techniques. These photographs show details of a Newport, Kentucky metamorphosis. The James Wiedemann House, a building on the National Register of Historic Places, showed massive injury to red sandstone decoration, demanding artistic and scientific skill to repair. Using patch material from Edison Chemical Systems, Anderson transformed cracked details, often rebuilding missing segments of the original, until no sign of damage remained. The artistic talent is obvious; the technological back-up was crucial.

Anderson has found Diedrich Chemicals' cleaning products ideal for most jobs. Surfaces cleaned with Diedrich products skirt the pitting, erosion, dulling, and general deterioration wreaked through sandblasting by using water-soluble, biodegradable substances that preserve finely carved detail and even protect the masonry skin that repels water and dirt. By using only the safest products of restoration technology, Anderson respects history and devotes itself to preserving architectural legacies for the future.

For further information, contact:

Anderson Building Restoration
923 Marion Ave.
Cincinnati, OH 45229
(513) 281-5258

For further information on Edison products, contact:

Edison Chemical Systems, Inc.
25 Grant St.
Waterbury, CT 06704
(203) 597-9727

For information on Diedrich, contact:

Diedrich Chemicals Restoration
* Technologies, Inc.*
300A E. Oak St.
Milwaukee, WI 53154
(800) 323-3565

Architectural Reclamation

Whether taking apart and restoring a historic trolley car (stripping woodwork, lifting off paint to reveal a stenciled canvas ceiling, custom milling wood to replace rotting or nonexistent work, and final painting and refinishing) or renovating a brick mansion down to the custom-made shutters, Architectural Reclamation's thorough contracting work commands respect.

While Architectural Reclamation focuses on assisting homeowners with restoration work, the firm's skills occasionally transform more unusual projects. Shown here is part of the restoration of Georgetown, Ohio's, Brown County Courthouse. Fire damage demanded re-constructing the bell and clock tower to withstand both natural forces and strict building codes.

Nothing will stop this firm from achieving a period effect. Architectural Reclamation often employs authentic parts salvaged from demolished buildings. When

necessary, new parts are crafted to match originals, and Architectural Reclamation's artists won't hesitate to learn a particular process or even to find the period tools to produce a particular effect.

Experience statement available.

Architectural Reclamation
312 S. River St.
Franklin, OH 45005
(513) 746-8964

Koeppel/Freedman Studios

Formerly Ornamental Plaster Restoration, Koeppel/Freedman is a small specialized company dedicated to the art of preservation, custom architectural restoration, and design. The firm's services include moldmaking from existing elements, hand remodeling by skilled artists, re-creation of lost detail from photographs, drawings, or blueprints, and the creation of new ornaments for appropriate application within the context of existing architecture. Interior work is hand-modeled or cast in plaster and reinforced for structural durability. Plaster/fiberglass composites are available where lighter weight is advised. Most exterior casts are done in epoxy-fiberglass, cement, or a combination of both elements. Marble repair, as well as terra-cotta repair, is also available. Koeppel/Freedman can serve as consultants in any of these areas, both to the individual home-owner, and to other professionals within the restoration and design fields.

In addition to these three-dimensional services, the firm also provides painting services, which include color matching and re-creation of original processes, as well as decorative painting of restored plasterwork. Koeppel/Freedman also specializes in trompe l'oeil painting of wall murals, floors, screens, and furniture.

Since all work is customized, the firm offers no literature, but mail and telephone inquiries are welcome.

Koeppel/Freedman Studios
386 Congress St.
Boston, MA 02210
(617) 426-8887

Steven P. Mack Associates

From the authentic whitewash he mixes himself to barnraising par-ties (bluegrass band included), Steven P. Mack's restorations of antique houses and barns are rife with authenticity. Ever since he fell in love with a windowless shambles that seemed more an oversized bird roost than a house—entailing a restoration of its rotting floor that was "like replacing the soles in your shoes while standing in them" — Mack's been hooked on historic preserva-tion. Mack's services include design, architectural work, the supply of building materials, and preservation. He specializes in rescuing old structures facing demolition, dismantling them (with photographic documenta-tion), and storing them to be erected again.

Steven P. Mack Associates
Chase Hill Farm
Ashaway, RI 02804
(401) 377-8041

M.J. May

M.J. May's contractors specialize in restorations of period buildings—from the floor up. After stripping and refinishing, May can install ceramic or wood floors. Repairs for drywalls and plaster walls, innovative carpentry work that doubles for the original, fretwork, windows, and wall-paper—M.J. May completes them all. A bonus: May will even locate just the architectural antiques that have eluded you in your own treasure hunts.

Brochure available.

M.J. May Antique Building
Restoration
505 Storle Ave.
Burlington, WI 53105
(414) 763-8822

Tom Moore's Steeple People

High or hard-to-reach places are just like home to the Steeple Peo-ple. Cupolas, rooftops, steeples, ceilings, and bell towers receive the benefit of this company's restoration know-how. Some tasks frequently performed are restor-ing gold leaf, repairing metal ceil-ings, making and installing cop-per gutters and downspouts, and fixing roofs made of slate, metal, or Spanish tile. Although most of the company's work is done in New England, where it will issue written estimates free of charge, commissions are accepted from anywhere in the country.

Tom Moore's Steeple People
21 Janine St.
Chicopee, MA 01013
(413) 533-9515

Old World Restorations

When an heirloom piece of porcelain is chipped or an antique stained-glass window broken, it can be heart-wrenching. For-tunately, there's a company that specializes in restoring such ob-jects to their former beauty. Old World Restorations restores and conserves oil paintings, frames, porcelain, glass, china, ivory, stone, wood, pottery, gilding, sculpture, stained glass, metal, marble, and other materials. In

most cases the repairs are invisi-ble to the naked eye. Just send the object to Old World; a brochure available from the company gives good packaging and shipping in-structions. An examination of the object will take place and a writ-ten estimate will be prepared before any work is begun.

Literature available.

Old World Restorations, Inc.
Columbia/Stanley Bldg.
347 Stanley Ave.
Cincinnati, OH 45226
(513) 321-1911

River City Restorations

Like a doctor with a fragile pa-tient, River City Restorations stabilizes the ailing structure of a historic building. The firm then attends to details that are not critical to stability, but are crucial for authenticity. Millwork, masonry, and delicate finishes and decorative artistry all benefit from scrupulous attention. From floorplan changes to papering, graining, and stenciling, the River City motto, "If we can't do it, it can't be done," stands strong.

Brochure available.

River City Restorations
623 Collier
Box 1065
Hannibal, MO 63401
(314) 248-0733

Riverbend Timber Framing

Riverbend Timber Framing reinstates the historic timber fram-ing of the first North American colonial houses as a dramatic ex-posed element in homes today. The great strength of this framing allows huge open spaces and breathtaking high-ceilinged rooms. The exacting craftsman-ship and durable materials in timber-framed colonial American homes have sustained these buildings for 350 years—a dura-tion dwarfed by a thousand-year-old Japanese temple and by Euro-pean buildings over twice the age of their American relatives. An added merit—timber framing makes efficient use of wood resources, requiring less raw

naments cast in Portland cement, epoxies, fiberglass-reinforced plastic, and other synthetic materials.

Russell Restoration of Suffolk
5550 Bergen Ave.
Mattituck, NY 11952
(516) 765-2481

Reproduction Period Homes

The rediscovery since World War II of the clean, honest lines of early American architecture has been marked by the diffusion of thousands of ready-made house designs or plans. The majority of such designs leave much to be desired. Regional differences were great in the 17th and 18th centuries, and it is often difficult to determine whether a particular modern plan derives from Massachusetts (Sturbridge), the Middle Atlantic states, or Virginia (Williamsburg). Late Georgian high-style elements are often applied to a simple clapboard house with casement windows dating from the 1600s. Brick laid with an inappropriate mortar is often juxtaposed with cedar shakes and both are combined with fake stone facing to form what can only be described as an abortive mess. Most of the modern designs are drawn with the use of assembly-line synthetic materials in mind. Unfortunately, use of such substitutes is a waste if the appearance of an authentic period house is the only aim.

If you wish to start from scratch and to build a new home that meets minimal historical standards, it would be best to consult a knowledgeable custom builder. Some restoration specialists, such as Preservation Associates, can help you in this respect. The skills of the housewright and joiner have not been completely lost. Old skills have been relearned in workshops across North America; new materials can be handled and used in a way that is honest and convincing. And there are ready-made plans which can be adapted to your particular needs.

lumber than stud framing or log construction, and generating much less sawdust waste than results from sawing two-by-fours.

Riverbend's custom sheathing panels, with laminated foam cores, strengthen and insulate the timber-frame homes that contain them. The use of stress-skin panels converts the work of laying exterior sheathing, insulation, and drywall into one economical step.

To accommodate growing interest in timber framing methods, Riverbend presents lectures and provides several informative books and periodicals on timber framing for the owner-builder. Riverbend's design services will guide you in adapting timber framing to suit your particular needs.

Brochure available.

Riverbend Timber Framing, Inc.
Box 26
Blissfield, MI 49228
(517) 486-4566

Russell Restoration of Suffolk

When a craftsman has mastered his medium, it's made obvious by his versatility, the quality of his work, and his willingness to accept challenging projects. It's apparent that Dean M. Russell has achieved this level of skill in plaster construction. From restoring a ceiling to making his own jigs for drawn moldings, he seems able to handle almost any aspect of the craft. Working for local museums and historical societies as well as for individuals, Russell makes flexible molds, niches, curved moldings, domes, arches, various ornaments, and even complete interiors with nothing but bare walls as a starting point. His company also produces or-

Historical Replications

The first step toward the building of a beautiful reproduction house is designing it. Historical Replications simplifies this crucial phase of the project by providing four portfolios of reproduction house plans. Each portfolio contains twenty to thirty line drawings and floor plans of different house styles, listing overall dimensions, ceiling heights for each floor, and square footage for each structure. Working drawings of any house can be ordered from the company. If you and your builder want to alter the design slightly, go ahead, but for major changes Historical Replications suggests that you send a sketch and describe what you'd like to adapt. The company will adjust the plans for you and make sure that your design will be safe. Custom plans can also be developed; send a sketch and information to the company, and you'll get an estimate of the time and cost of creating a suitable design.

The house shown here is a 2,522-square-foot Victorian structure with a dramatic foyer open

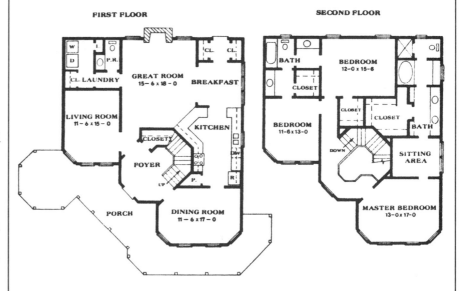

all the way to the tower ceiling. It's from the company's original portfolio, which contains diverse houses, from an Acadian cottage to a reproduction of the Holly Springs, Mississippi, home of 19th-century senator General Cary Marshall. Other designs were inspired by a multi-gabled home in Norcross, Georgia and an 1842 parsonage in Madison, Georgia.

The Louisiana Collection contains homes with a Southern flavor that

measure between 1,448 and 6,264 square feet. There is a heavy emphasis on French Colonial and Greek Revival designs. The Classic Cottage portfolio features smaller houses measuring between 853 and 1,997 square feet. A wide range of styles are represented, including Cape Cod, Georgian, Victorian, farmhouse, Greek Revival, English, French, and Acadian. Historical Replications' newest portfolio is called

Colonial Heritage and contains Georgian, Federal, Williamsburg, saltbox, Dutch, and Greek Revival house plans.

For further information, contact:

Historical Replications, Inc.
Box 13529
Jackson, MS 39236
(601) 981-8743

McKie Wing Roth

Straightforward and simple, house designs from McKie Wing Roth have few corners, fewer ornaments. Solid styles, without waste or distraction, characterize this firm's work. Windows are small-paned for character, authenticity, and security. Shutters and dormers appear only when functional. The modern platform style of framing replaces colonial post and beam methods to allow for wiring and insulation, economy, and freedom of design. Roth's folios include thorough studies of foundation, floors, heating and wiring, masonry and chimney, siding, roofing, and trim. The Montsweag House, first built in 1973 in Maine and illustrated here, has the central fireplace Roth deems vital to a house's character, and the standard interior finish of white plastered walls with pine trim, doors, and flooring. It's hard to imagine a more handsome saltbox adaptation.

Catalogue available.

McKie Wing Roth, Jr.
1001 Bridgeway, #234
Sausalito, CA 94965
(800) 232-7684

Second Floor

First Floor

Schools and Study

Courses and workshops in traditional building methods, architectural styles, and the interior design of period buildings are very popular. These educational programs are especially useful to the do-it-yourselfer, but they are also instructive for anyone who is about to become involved in restoration or renovation work. Listed are only major, well-established programs. There are many other seminars and lectures sponsored by preservation groups which are held from time to time throughout North America. The preservation organization in your area is likely to have information on similar programs.

Campbell Center

Melding history and high tech to show the advantages of both, the Campbell Center's workshops span a creditable range of topics. Under the heading of "Museum Collections," you may choose Computerization for Museum Collections or Ceramics and Glass: Technology and Care. Check "Architecture" for Rehabilitation of Wooden Structures and National Register: How to List a Place. "Furniture" offers Hands-on Furniture Conservation and Conservation of Gilt Wood. A seminar faculty of active professionals provides expert instruction. The twenty-one summer workshops range from two to five days in length and are situated in the town of Mt. Carroll, Illinois, itself a registered historic district.

Newsletter available.

Campbell Center
Box 66
Mt. Carroll, IL 61053
(815) 244-1173

Heartwood

It's an unusual proposition: Take two or three weeks off to live in Massachusetts' Berkshire Hills—and learn to build a house. Six months out of the year, Heartwood runs a series of instructive

classroom demonstrations, discussions, slides, and modelings. Students then move to the yard or the shop to put what they've learned into action . . . or into wood, or foundation, or plumbing, or electrical wiring. Resources include hands-on training, an exhaustive library, and access to power tools, as well as introductions to site preparation, building codes, structural principles, and safety measures. In line with Heartwood's goal of beautiful and economical houses, the courses explore methods of passive solar heating and cooling, as well as state-of-the-art insulating tech-

niques. Heartwood uses Sam Clark's *Designing and Building Your Own House* as a text. For prospective students with tight schedules and interest in specific topics,

Heartwood offers week-long workshops in basic carpentry, timber framing, contracting, cabinet-making, and renovation.

Brochure available.

Heartwood School
Johnson Rd.
Washington, MA 01235
(413) 623-6677

Preservation Associates

Preservation Associates has amassed enough knowledge in the field of preservation technology to publish four books and dozens of articles on the subject. Part of putting this knowledge into practice includes conducting four college-level courses in construction methods and architectural history. Preservation Associates offers lectures and seminars and maintains a 12,000-item photographic library, which facilitates lectures, publications, or instruction series geared to many different areas.

Brochure available.

Preservation Associates
207 S. Potomac St.
Hagerstown, MD 21740
(301) 791-7880

Riverbend Timber Framing

Learn to raise a timber frame home—enroll in a seminar from Riverbend Timber Framing. Classes cover design, contracting (financing, material purchases, scheduling, etc.), frame construction, and enclosure using stress-skin panels. Riverbend has chosen and now markets various hand and power tools, from a rawhide mallet to a reversible drill, to facilitate your project. Also available from Riverbend are magazines such as *Fine Homebuilding* and several excellent books, including *Building the Timber Frame House* and *The Framed Houses of Massachusetts Bay 1625-1725*.

Brochure and newsletter available.

Riverbend Timber Framing, Inc.
Box 26
Blissfield, MI 49228
(517) 486-4566

Other Suppliers of Structural Products and Services

Consult List of Suppliers for addresses.

Architectural Salvage

Jerard Paul Jordan
Nostalgia, Inc.
Spiess Antique Building Materials
Sunset Antiques, Inc.

Brick and Stone

Architectural Salvage Co.
Jamie C. Clark
Diamond K. Co.
Great American Salvage Co.
Rising and Nelson Slate Co., Inc.

Ceilings

Architectural Antique Warehouse
Architectural Salvage Co.
The Canal Co.
Chelsea Decorative Metal Co.
Remodelers' & Renovators' Supply
San Francisco Victoriana

Doors and Windows

Accurate Metal Weather Strip Co.
Aged Woods
Architectural Antique Warehouse
Architectural Antiques Exchange
Architectural Salvage Co.
Art Directions
The Canal Co.
Central Kentucky Millwork Inc.
Classic Architectural Specialties
Eagle Plywood & Door Manufacturers,
  Inc.
The Fireplace Mantel Shop
Whit Hanks
Iberia Millwork
Jerard Paul Jordan
M.J. May Antique Building Restoration
Mountain Lumber
Nostalgia, Inc.
Ohmega Salvage
Pelnik Wrecking Co.
Silverton Victorian Mill Works
Spiess Antique Building Materials
Wooden Nickel Antiques

Lumber

Blue Ridge Shingle Co.
Central Kentucky Millwork Inc.
Diamond K. Co.
Vintage Lumber

Roofing Materials

Aged Woods
Vintage Wood Works

Stairs

American Ornamental Metal Co.
Architectural Salvage Co.
Classic Architectural Specialties
The Fireplace Mantel Shop
Mountain Lumber
Sheppard Millwork, Inc.

Consultants and Architects

Angel House Designs
Entourage, Inc.
The Renovation Source

Contractors

William H. Parsons & Associates

Schools and Study

The Clio Group, Inc.
The Preservation Partnership
Restorations Unlimited, Inc.
R. Wayne Reynolds

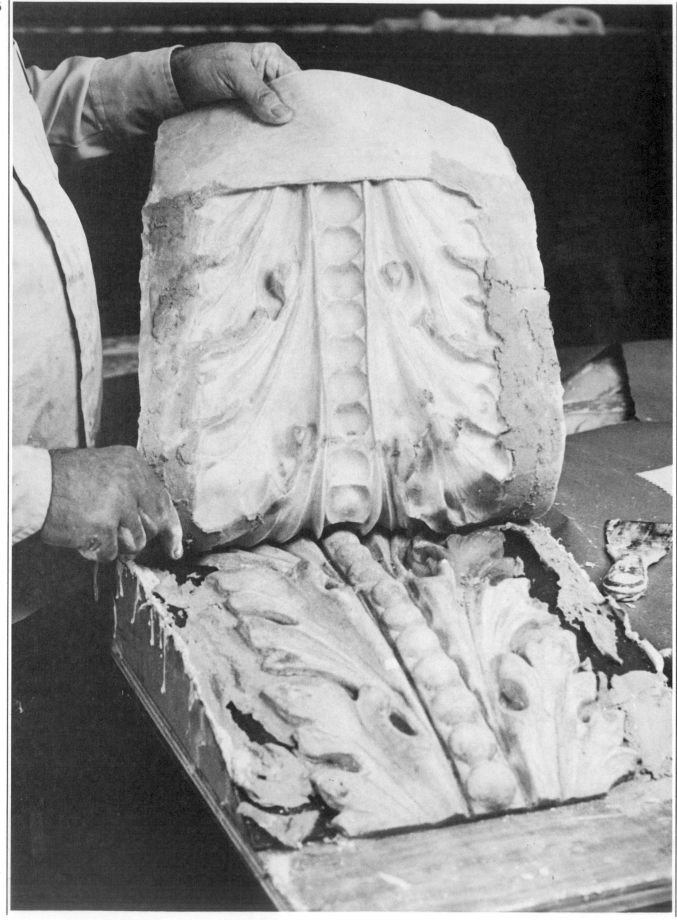

2.

Architectural Decoration

The decorative architectural elements are those which serve no structural purpose but finish off the exterior framework of a building and its interior spaces as well. Of wood, plaster, metal, composition, and modern synthetics, these are the moldings, window and door casings, corbels and brackets, medallions and corner blocks. Properly fashioned, these elements endow a house with character. The line, the basic skeleton, is more fundamental, but we are more apt to notice only the way in which a building or room is dressed—the manner in which it is decorated.

Of all the elements, moldings are the most important. Cornice moldings appear both inside and outside a building. Shoe and base moldings may finish off lower walls. Window and door frames or casings are—in an older building—made up of one or more moldings. Elaborate door assemblies such as appear at the main entrance of a Georgian Colonial or Federal-style building are very complex constructions and moldings are their principal component.

The most beautiful old buildings are generally thought of as those which are the most elaborately turned out. The very term "old" as applied to architecture implies the use of the decorative element rather than the purely functional or "modern." In the 1980s we are being swept into a new wave of romanticism, of the decorative. Some abhor the move back in time to broken pediments and mindless gingerbread and prefer to label the movement escapist. Whatever its psychological dimensions, the new appreciation of the ornamental is to be welcomed if it brings with it a return to the same type of craftsmanship achieved during the late-19th century in the Arts and Crafts period. Unfortunately, much of the newly romantic is as tacky as the sleekly modern. One has to proceed cautiously across the commercial minefield of decorative objects, as the territory is full of "instant gratification." Packaged nostalgia—a bracket weighing as much as a soda cracker or a molding with the profile of a jagged tin can—is too readily available. Instead, turn back to the basics of good design and workmanship as outlined in these pages.

Molded plaster ornaments, faithful to antique originals, by Dovetail, Inc., Lowell, Massachusetts.

Glass

Proper glass can be as important to the appearance of a period house as paint, moldings, or other trimmings. The differences between new plate glass and that used in the past are not readily noticeable by most people, but these can be considerable. Many homes have lost their old windows, transoms, or other glass panels. To replace them with modern plates of glass, however insulated they may be by double or triple glazing, can despoil a façade. This is especially true if the glass being replaced is stained, etched, or engraved.

Old window glass is not easy to obtain. A number of the restoration suppliers and consultants included in this chapter have a supply on hand from time to time. Reproduction panes can be obtained from a number of the glass workshops across the country and from Blenko Glass.

Blenko Glass

All sheets have some bubbles and a texture like early American window glass. Stock sheets are approximately 18" by 23" untrimmed. The glass is priced at $5.99 per square foot.

Blenko Glass Company, Inc.
Milton, WV 25541
(304) 743-9081

Etched, textured, and engraved glass is somewhat easier to obtain. A number of firms in North America kept going in the 20th century with commissions for churches and public institutions. With the resurgence of interest in things "Victorian," these old companies have been joined by many enterprises run by the young in heart and body who find glassmaking an exciting and profitable craft.

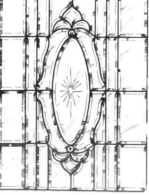

Architectural Antiques West

Careful hand beveling and assembly, rigorous inspection, a chemical wash to finish the metal, and a final cleaning by hand give these glass windows the proper period look. Architectural Antiques West creates a number of transoms, sidelights, and panels in Victorian, Edwardian, and Art Nouveau styles. A dazzling display of diagonal lines forms a breathtaking window, available in two sizes: 36½" high by 21⅝" wide (model B-1) and 36½" high by 27⅝" wide (model B-2). A more sedate design makes the second window shown here a perfect accent for almost any Victorian room. It is sold in the same sizes as model W-1 and W-2.

Architectural Antiques West is a wholesaler only; however, its products are sold by distributors throughout the nation. To find the one nearest to you, contact:

Architectural Antiques West
3117 S. La Cienega Blvd.
Los Angeles, CA 90016
(213) 559-3019

Curran Glass & Mirror

New York City's Tiffany & Co. has shown Patrick Curran's sculpture in laminated architectural glass. His work has been commissioned for Avon Corporation and the North American Division of the Bank of America. Curran's glasswork, whether it be etched panels of peacocks or beveled emerald and sapphire glass in a Victorian door, is nothing less than superb. Examine the leaded scallops and teardrops in the window illustrated to appreciate the skill and grace that show, crystal clear, in fine glasswork. Doors, mirrors, sidelights, signs, tabletops, and windows—Curran makes them all. Curran's custom work includes hand-cut stenciling, etching, leaded stained glass that uses bevels and glass jewels, glass bending, silvering, and electroforming of metals on glass. An expert restorer of antique leaded windows, Curran knows how to care for his art as it's come through the ages.

Brochure, $1.

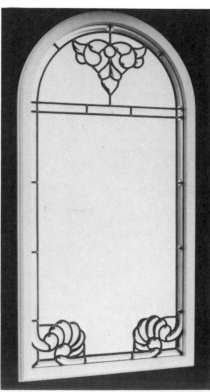

Curran Glass & Mirror Co.
30 N. Maple St.
Florence, MA 01060
(413) 584-5761

Electric Glass

If ordinary windows bore you, but you want more light than stained glass admits, you might consider installing clear beveled glass windows. They retain the interesting shapes and classic, old-fashioned beauty of stained glass while more easily permitting vision and the entrance of sunlight. Electric sells a wide variety of standard designs, two of which are shown here. Overture is a versatile style with elements of both floral and geometric motifs; the panels illustrated measure 63" high by 27½" wide. Nouveau combines curves and points to make a fin-de-siècle pattern. The sidelight is 72" high and 12" wide; the door panels are 66½" high and 27½" wide.

Brochure, $3.

Electric Glass Co.
One E. Mellen St.
Hampton, VA 23663
(804) 722-6200

and ruby-colored glass. The complete window is, quite simply, stunning.

Brochure available.

Ferguson's Cut Glass Works
4292 Pearl Rd.
Cleveland, OH 44109
(216) 459-2929

Glass Arts

Capable of reproducing an almost endless variety of styles and patterns, Glass Arts specializes in taking a customer's rough ideas and measurements and turning them into a dazzling piece of leaded glasswork. For a fee, which is deducted from the cost of the panel, the studio will produce a detailed scale rendering based on your specifications. A brochure of sample designs, including the 30"- square flower panel and the

Ferguson's Cut Glass Works

A master glass cutter and beveler in the brilliant style, Cary Ferguson creates windows, entranceways, room dividers, and decorative mirrors that pierce the eye with their colors and clarity. This window, called "Perfection," is typical of his style. The four

petals and center are elaborately cut, but the deft use of color wrestles with the intricate cutting for command of the viewer's attention. The interlocking bands are a deep, bright blue, interrupted at points by triangular or diamond-shaped slivers of clear

40″-high by 30″-wide stylized iris shown here, is available to give you some starting ideas.

The company also etches glass by means of the precise abrasive technique. Mirrors, signs, tabletops, room dividers, windows, and entryway lights in a number of glass types and colors can be inscribed with Victorian or Art Nouveau designs. The real specialty at Glass Arts, however, is hand-beveled glass. One hundred and thirty-five different panels, designed to fit standard door and window frames, are available.

Catalogue of beveled panels available.

Glass Arts
30 Penniman Rd.
Boston (Allston), MA 02134
(617) 782-7760

Golden Age Glassworks

From the restoration of a 3½′-high by 4½′-wide window with a classical theme to the creation of a vivid yellow lampshade bordered with scarlet flowers and foliage in several shades of green, Barbara Arrindell displays skill and ingenuity. Working with verbal hints, photographs, drawings, and her own artistry, she creates eye-pleasing panels like her "Victorian Cut Flowers," a detail of which is shown here. Measuring 24″ high by 54″ long, it features a bowl of deep-blue irises and gracefully intertwined yellow roses. Although she excels at re-creating many styles, Arrindell is at her best when tackling natural subjects—vines, trees, flowers, or entire pastoral scenes. She also manages Nottingham Gallery, which specializes in the sale of antique English windows.

Sets of slides or photographs, $2 each.

Golden Age Glassworks
339 Bellvale Rd.
Warwick, NY 10990
(914) 986-1487

Great Panes Glassworks

If you like the look of antique etched glass, you can custom order it for an exact fit to doors, windows, tabletops, signs, or mirrors, and enjoy your own favorite art design, skillfully reproduced. Photo-stenciled sandblasting techniques practiced by Great Panes Glassworks yield perfect copies of the pattern you submit. Stock artwork is also available, with representative period designs including flowers in a six-pointed star, an oblong with more abstract floral details, and highly embellished Victorian panels. The economical photo-stenciling process provides lasting results on whatever glass you specify. Choose any thickness of colored glass; tempered, laminated safety or plate glass; mirror; or request slate, marble, or jade. Camera and art services, as well as a panel of design consultants, are available to you at Great Panes.

Brochure available.

Great Panes Glassworks, Inc.
2861 Walnut St.
Denver, CO 80205
(303) 294-0927

Kraatz Russell

Transoms and sidelights of Kraatz Russell's custom glass are perfect for early American houses. Blown, cooled, heated and spun, the firm's glass has that "wavy" quality of 18th-century glass that is totally absent in the modern product. Founded during the American bicentennial, Kraatz Russell has continually expanded its projects in bull's eye, decorative, and leaded glass. Newly available is the hand-blown sheet glass known as "Restoration Glass." Imported and custom cut, this glass suits windows in 18th-century buildings perfectly.

Brochure available.

Kraatz Russell Glass
Grist Mill Hill
RFD 1
Box 320C
Canaan, NH 03741
(603) 523-4289

Pocahontas

Impeccably executed etching is characteristic of the beautiful, antique glass designs at Pocahontas. An ornate grid of spades and

diamonds, flowering into tiny circles and curves at every junction, or elaborate floral patterning, with opulent beads and chains, are just two of Pocahontas's rich designs. Entire nature scenes, cherubs, patterns of flowers and leaves—each choice sparkles in crystalline clarity against its milky background. Your precise measurements, which include paper or cardboard patterns for ovals and arches, guarantee a custom fit for every piece of work from Pocahontas. Choose double-strength glass (⅛" thick) for cabinet doors, windows, transoms, and ornamental work, ¼" plate glass to suit transoms and picture window lights, or ¼" safety laminate glass for entrance doors and sidelights or hazardous areas. Solar bronze tinting, light

in ⅛" thicknesses, deep brown in ¼" thicknesses, is an option for any style.

Brochure available.

Pocahontas Hardware & Glass
Box 127
Pocahontas, IL 62275
(618) 669-2880

J. Ring Glass Studio

Exquisite beveling and an elegant design distinguish these glass windows, created by J. Ring. The studio is skilled in the manufacture of such pieces, with the capacity to make bevels up to 1½" wide. Another specialty is the reproduction of bent glass panels for lamps and windows; J. Ring is expert at restoring Handel and Tiffany lamps. The firm also resilvers mirrors, etches glass by both the abrasive and acid methods, constructs and restores stained and leaded glass windows, and glue-chips glass in featherlike patterns. No catalogue is available, as J. Ring does custom work almost exclusively.

J. Ring Glass Studio
2724 University Ave. S.E.
Minneapolis, MN 55414
(612) 379-0920

Sunflower Glass Studio

Karen and Geoff Caldwell's work speaks for itself. Their one-of-a-kind windows and panels testify to the couple's skill and artistry. Intricate beveling done in the studio, brilliant jewels, textured clear glass, and subtle use of colors give Sunflower's creations a dazzling elegance. The Caldwells also create lighting fixtures and will repair glass. Call for an appointment to visit the studio for a

look at some unusually beautiful original pieces.

Sunflower Glass Studio
Box 99, Rte. 523
Sergeantsville, NJ 08557
(609) 397-1535

Venturella Studios

Tom Venturella's glasswork may be quite familiar to lecture audiences, readers of the *New York Times,* and visitors to many of New York's private galleries. Beveled, etched, and stained glass—mixing lead, copper foil, and glass as media—demonstrate the talent that has sparked museums to call in Tom Venturella as a consultant. Nearly two decades of work with stained glass stand behind Venturella Studios. Commissioned for both restoration and for original artwork, Venturella exercises techniques he acquired from various American schools and from work and study in Italy and France. Pieces in period styles include the modernistic windows shown here, which demonstrate the harmony of free-thinking design and the demands of sound structure—

ELLEN KARDELL

guarantors of permanence—in which Tom Venturella takes pride.

Brochure available.

*Venturella Studios
32 Union Sq. E. Rm. 1110
New York, NY 10003
(212) 228-4252*

Victorian Glassworks

K. Ellen Kardell, owner of Victorian Glassworks, makes her home in a 1903 Logan Circle-area townhouse that is in the midst of a decade-long historical renovation. Hundreds of clients country-wide, including churches, restaurants, residences, and the Smithsonian Institution, have commissioned period-inspired windows from the studio in her turn-of-the-century house. The two designs shown here, one 45" by 54", the other a narrow 17" by 40", showcase the leaded grids, swirls, and jewels that characterize Kardell's array of custom designs. Kardell is often engaged in consultation for leaded glass restoration projects and has conducted exhaustive research in 18th- and 19th-century designs by combing historical society libraries, the Library of Congress, and the National Archives. This research fueled her skill in the age-old methods of leaded glass design and glass painting.

Victorian Glassworks forms every piece from superior-grade, hand-

ELLEN KARDELL

made American and European sheet glass. Styles span Aesthetic, Art Nouveau, Classical Revival, Contemporary, Figurative, Landscape, and Renaissance Revival. Victorian Glassworks' newest feature is a selection of intricate sidelights and transoms, adorned with jewels, hand-blown glass, and bevels.

Brochure and photographs, $3.50 (refundable with order).

Victorian Glassworks
904 Westminster St. N.W.
Washington, DC 20001
(202) 462-4433

Williams Art Glass Studios

Intricate custom beveling and sandblasted designs in plate or flashed glass or mirrors make this firm's work distinctive. The studio and showroom are crowded with brilliantly colored doors and windows. Bits of beveled colored plate glass gleam like gemstones; textured glass plays with the light. Those who feel compelled to bypass Williams' exquisite designs in favor of original pieces should still pay a visit to the showroom. It always contains restored Victorian, Art Nouveau, and Art Deco doors and windows; note, too, that Williams shares its space with Sunset Antiques, a dealer in antique windows.

Brochure available free of charge.

Williams Art Glass Studios, Inc.
22 N. Washington (M-24)
Oxford, MI 48051
(313) 628-1111

Ornamental Metalwork

Architectural iron is one of the most appealing products of the 19th century. This was the great age of cast iron. Today fountains, fences, gates, lawn sculptures of animals, window grilles for frieze windows, and roof cresting and finials are still objects of admiration. Antique cast iron can be found in some salvage yards and antique shops but it is growing more scarce each year. There are foundries that will reproduce old patterns or custom produce replacement parts. Don't forget, however, that a blacksmith may be able to help you out. His forge is a mini-foundry, although the smithy is likely to prefer wrought iron objects to those which are cast. Among the sources of fine reproduction period metalwork are the firms that follow.

Architectural Iron

Praising the fine quality of cast-iron designs over the "corrupted" mass production used to make wrought iron today, Architectural Iron reproduces superb traditional designs from precision molds and molten metal. Several examples of the firm's period designs are illustrated here.

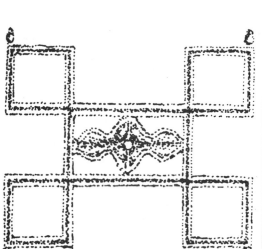

Truly high ornament, this cresting panel is suitable for a Victorian rooftop, all elegance pointed skyward. In 24⅛" horizontal sections weighing 10½ lbs, this ⅜"-thick ironwork reaches 20¼" from feet to highest graceful point.

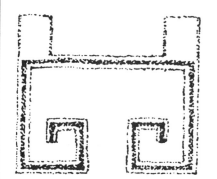

From historic sections of New York City, Architectural Iron has gleaned cast-iron designs for period stair rails. A network of squares around a central ornament, 7¾" high by 6¾" wide, ⅝" thick, provides handsome cast-iron decoration along a railing. Various filler keys, ranging in weight from ¾ to 1½ lbs, slant or stand erect for traditionally accurate cast-iron accent.

Catalogue available.

Architectural Iron Co.
Box 126
Rte. 6W
Milford, PA 18337
(717) 296-7722

Custom Ironwork

Custom Ironwork, formerly called Custom Fabricating, has made its reputation from its superb iron fencing. However, the word "custom" isn't in the company's name for mere show; its skilled craftsmen can match almost any design to produce elegant ornamental iron like this lacy entranceway. Just send a drawing or a photograph, and an estimate will be prepared. The company's standard fencing designs can also be used for decorative purposes,

56

as they were in front of this double house.

Catalogue, $1.

Custom Ironwork
Box 99
Union, KY 41091
(606) 384-4486

W.F. Norman

W.F. Norman has acquired the metal stamping branch of Wilton, Connecticut's, Kenneth Lynch & Sons, continuing nearly a century of sheet metal stamping and hammering. Some unusual and demanding projects executed by the firm have included an armor exhibit and the monumental Pegasus atop the Readers Digest Building. An exhaustive selection of ornaments includes panels of shields, crests, masks, eagles, cherubs, and gargoyles. Ornamental conductor heads and bands for downspouts, available in plain or lead-coated copper, show the high detail that can be skillfully worked into copper, zinc, and other metals. The firm boasts that anything from antique sundials to aircraft wings will be carefully executed to your specifications.

Catalogue, $2.50.

W.F. Norman Corp.
Box 323
214-32 N. Cedar St.
Nevada, MO 64772-0323
(800) 641-4038
Missouri customers, call collect:
(417) 667-5552

Nostalgia

Savannah, Georgia's historic district provides a rich host of models for decorative designs. Among the fine features of the imposing Davenport House (built circa 1815) is a set of dolphin downspouts, a traditional metal spout with a gaping snout to let water run off from rooftops. In Nostalgia's successful attempt to copy this rare design, even the pitting caused by rust is shown. The 8"-deep spout is 5" wide and 59" tall and is typical of Nostalgia's fine metalwork.

Catalogue, $2.50.

Nostalgia, Inc.
307 Stiles Ave.
Savannah, GA 31401
(912) 232-2324

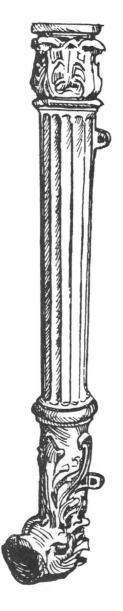

Plaster, Composition, and Polymer Ornamentation

Most old-house interiors are incomplete without a display of complementary moldings, ceiling ornaments, brackets, and other decorative elements. Happily, there are an increasing number of craftsmen extremely skilled in restoring and fabricating new plaster ornamentation. Many of the same imaginative craftsmen also work with compo, as the fibrous alternative to plaster of Paris is termed. Because of the high cost of such specialty work, new lightweight synthetic materials are also being used in place of plaster or composition materials. These are polymer-based products, and they are relatively easy to apply and to finish. Their use has spread even to the bastions of conservative old-house restorers.

American Architectural Art

Call on American Architectural Art to fabricate simulated wood, stone, metal, masonry, or terra-cotta ornamentation. Using special compounds or either gypsum-reinforced, polymerized fiberglass (for interior use) or fiberglass-reinforced polyester (for exterior work), expert artists will execute any style or type of piece. In reproducing period work, American Architectural artists take a cast

from an existing ornamental piece if at all possible. Sculptures, urns, reliefs, cornices, ceilings, and capitals come from the hands of American Architectural Art's craftsmen. Sanding or spackling gives each piece an impeccable surface. The embellishments may be mounted with mortar, mechanical fasteners, or construction adhesives.

Brochure available.

American Architectural Art Co.
Dept. OHC
1910 N. Marshall St.
Philadelphia, PA 19122
(215) 236-6492

American Wood Column

With the finely chiseled look of wood carving, but the strength of a well-formulated modern compound, molded ornaments from American Wood Column are recommended for use in any period building. Chair rails, door trim and facing, dado panels, and crown moldings—all take form from this material which may be glazed, stained, or painted according to your needs. Of particular interest are beautiful ceiling plaques, ¼"-thick composition medallions that reach diameters of 48" to enhance any period lighting fixture. In addition to the usual medallion shape, the ceiling plaques are available in diamond, square, and oblong shapes.

Brochure available.

American Wood Column
913 Grand St.
Brooklyn, NY 11211
(718) 782-3163

Classic Architectural Specialties

Wreaths, flowers, and ribbons; seahorses, cherubs, and shells—the most intricate details of any design may be molded into composition materials for lasting decoration from Classic Architectural Specialties. Exquisite beading and flourishes around handsome medallions add appropriate decorative touches to your period home. On a larger scale, choose brackets and corbels fashioned from high-density polymer, a material that will not rot or warp and is impervious to insects. Decorative ornaments from Classic Architectural Specialties can be nailed, drilled, or sawed with field carpenter tools for easy application. Patching or repairs can be made with wood filler material or exterior glues. In addition to the firm's exceptionally varied array of stock ornaments, it undertakes custom work on request.

Catalogue, $2.

Classic Architectural Specialties
5302 Junius
Dallas, TX 75214
(214) 827-5111

Dovetail

Ever faithful to antique designs, craftsmen at Dovetail have collected many architectural decorations from renovated homes, peeling off layers of paint to repair and sometimes to recarve elements that have been damaged or destroyed over time. The Flowing Leaf ceiling medallion shown here

is the result of just such careful reclamation, mounting, sealing, polyurethane molding, and casting. Strong and light, the Dovetail medallions may be attached with panel adhesive to set off a lighting fixture or fan.

Among Dovetail's ornamental elements to frame a room are cornices like the Federal Acanthus shown here, a classic pattern of flowers and leaves with a 4½" pro-

jection, 7½" drop, and 3⅞" pattern repeat.

The interior shown is rich in brackets and other cast ornaments. Of particular note is the Singing Gallery piece above the mantel. Sculpted by 15th-century artist Luca Della Robbia, the piece had been broken and was repaired and recarved by Dovetail to allow reproductions of the 44¼" by 19" (6" relief) artwork. Other ornaments include various gypsum-based columns (reinforced with fiberglass), capitals, frets, and finials.

Brochure available.

Dovetail, Inc.
Box 1569
Lowell, MA 01853-2769
(617) 454-2944

Fypon

Fypon is a prime supplier of specialty polymer millwork that is custom fit to your needs. The firm offers a wide array of ceiling medallions in a myriad of styles and sizes, carefully formed inside and outside corner blocks, a complete line of molding and many other architectural ornaments. On a larger scale, Fypon creates columns, complete with decorative bases and Corinthian capitals.

Catalogue available.

Fypon, Inc.
22 W. Pennsylvania Ave.
Box 365
Stewartson, PA 17363
(717) 993-2593

San Francisco Victoriana

304-06

304-15

304-13

You can expect high quality and a large variety of designs from San Francisco Victoriana. The company's fiber-reinforced hand-cast plasterwork, like its excellent millwork, is among the best we've seen. Detailed brackets recapture a 19th-century aura of luxury. The Italianate model, 304-06, is 13½" high by 8" wide by 5½" deep. An acanthus and shell motif makes the Classic bracket (304-13) worthy of its name. It measures 8½" high by 5½" wide by 10½" deep. The Hamilton Square (304-15) is 13½" high and deep and 5" wide. Other models incorporate flowers or mythological figures.

The plaster ceiling medallion, a common Victorian decoration, is to be found in all its splendor and variety at San Francisco Victoriana. Roses, ribbons, fruit, faces, and stylized leaves are lavishly spread over the eye-catching surfaces. Not only does the company carry fine versions, like the 28" Liberty Street (301-15), of the ubiquitous circular center-pieces, but it also creates medallions in hard-to-find shapes. San Francisco Victoriana also makes egg-and-dart decorations,

301-15

leaf or drapery festoons, capitals, and cornices in a number of traditional designs. The catalogue provides simple, helpful instructions for installing these plaster ornaments.

Catalogue, $3.

San Francisco Victoriana
2245 Palou Ave.
San Francisco, CA 94124
(415) 648-0313

Turncraft

Turncraft produces composition capitals equipped with weight-bearing wooden plugs that can be crafted to fit columns of any size or style. A transparent weather-proofing compound adds durability to the various designs, which include Scamozzi, modern and Roman Ionic, Greek Erechtheum, Roman Corinthian, and Temple of the Winds, all of which are handsome variations on classical architectural elements. A double coating of oil paint and non-rusting, countersunk screws (sealed against water) ready the ornamental capitals for installation.

Brochure available.

*Turncraft
Box 2429
White City, OR 97503
(503) 826-2911*

Victorian Collectibles

If you suddenly found yourself the owner of almost fourteen hundred Victorian wallpaper patterns, what would you do? Florence Schroeder found herself in that position, and she went into business reproducing them. The two styles of molding shown here are taken from the designs of 9" border patterns found among Schroeder's Brillion Collection. Their delicate floral motifs make them an appropriate decoration for almost any Victorian room. Victorian Collectibles makes several other styles of moldings; all are made of plaster or foam and then hand-painted.

Brochure, $2.

*Victorian Collectibles Ltd.
845 E. Glenbrook Rd.
Milwaukee, WI 53217
(414) 352-6910*

J.P. Weaver

The J.P. Weaver Company specializes in the design and manufacture of custom staff moldings and fine carving reproductions. From its collection of over 8,000 carvings, it can replicate any period in architectural history through Art Deco. Using a composition formula that has been a family secret since the 19th century, the company produces ornaments that are so sharp in reproduction that the most minute detail of the original is in clear relief. Every ornament is handmade. Designs are usually a combination of pieces to make a larger composite design. The average thickness of the ornaments varies from ¼" to ½" with some relief of 1". The sizes varies from ½" diameter to pieces that are 12" by 12". Weaver ornaments are pliable and self-bonding. When lightly steamed, they can be molded to curves and radiused arcs. The ornaments can be self-bonded to wood, drywall, mirror and metal, or any tight, dry, smooth surface. They can also be pre-painted, steamed, and installed on another color surface. Once installed, the oils evaporate and the ornaments take on a rock-like hardness and have a life span of 150 years. Having produced composition ornaments for countless movie palaces of the 1920s and '30s, and for Hearst's inimitable San Simeon castle, J.P. Weaver knows all there is to know about composition ornamentation and its place in architectural history.

Brochure available.

J.P. Weaver
2301 W. Victory Blvd.
Burbank, CA 91506
(818) 841-5700

are made from clear kiln-dried eastern white pine. Architectural Components also makes excellent shutters, doors, windows, and paneling.

Brochure, $3.

Architectural Components
Box 249
Leverett, MA 01054
(413) 367-9441

Applied Wood Ornamentation

Such ornamental items as moldings, brackets, finials, columns, spindles, newel posts, and railings lie very much at the heart of period interior and exterior decoration. Depending on the style of your old house, at least several of these elements will come into play. Door and window casings, of course, are standard items in every old building; it is only in recent times that these openings have been left as unadorned holes in the wall. Such casings in old houses are usually comprised of a series of handsome

moldings and panels. Moldings similarly make up and define paneled doors and may delineate ceilings from walls, and walls from floors. There are thousands of types of moldings and decorative ornaments that can be used in a period room or outside the house on a porch or to embellish entryways, windows, gables, and roof lines. Producers of period millwork are found everywhere in North America, and what they cannot supply from stock they will custom manufacture.

American Wood Column

An excellent source of fluted or plain wood columns, American Wood Column furnishes interior and exterior pieces appropriate as colonnades, room dividers, or window treatments. Simple Doric-capital-columns are stock items, in base diameters of 6", 8", or 10" and heights of 8' or 9'. Custom order more elaborately decorated columns, which American Wood Column will cut to half, two-thirds, or quarter round.

The artisans at American Wood Column specialize in producing turned spindles, balusters, table legs and bases, lamp bases, and newel posts. Describe the designs and woods you prefer. The firm's stock is very large; its capacity for custom work, even larger.

Brochure available.

American Wood Column
913 Grand St.
Brooklyn, NY 11211
(718) 782-3163

Architectural Components

Authenticity is paramount in the manufacture of Architectural Component's moldings. Each item in the collection of wood trims is an exact reproduction of an 18th-century original. Ranging in complexity from the simple, versatile ⅝" by 1¼" ogee band molding to a beautifully crafted chair rail, all

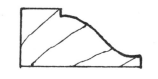

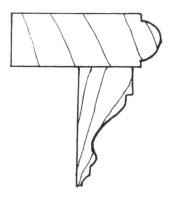

Art Directions

Grand front and back bars command attention in any room. The imposing wooden structures from Art Directions can be built to scale, suitable for a private home or a restaurant. Among the canopy bars, take note of the Grey Eagle bar, every piece, including ionic columns, hand cut from oak and carefully rubbed to a rich sheen. Accents of brass and stained glass complete the design. The Star Times bar exemplifies imagination within a traditional framework, from glossy brass rail to stained glass canopy insets in a pattern created for Art Directions alone. Free-standing front bars include the Aspen, with panels and other details in relief.

To outfit an entire area, Art Directions will design booths, façades, paneling, and table tops. The firm can incorporate decorative glass, mirrors, and lighting into its pieces, and your choice of stains finishes the entire project in tones ranging from golden oak to dark walnut.

Catalogues available.

Art Directions
6120 Delmar Blvd.
St. Louis, MO 63112
(314) 863-1895

Artistry in Veneers

Wood veneer enhances dull surfaces with naturally rich accents. Short, decorative lengths of veneers are commonly available, but long veneers, in strips 5" to 12" wide, are quite scarce. Turn to Artistry in Veneers for 7' lengths that suit exceptional paneling projects. The firm cuts sheets of veneer in sequence from flitches, guaranteeing like texture, figure, and color. Exotic woods are another specialty of the firm, with seldom-seen species including pearwood, teak, anigre, Golden Afrique, acacia, wormy chestnut, French olive ash, four different types of rosewood, and dozens of others.

Catalogue, $1.

Artistry in Veneers, Inc.
450 Oak Tree Ave.
South Plainfield, NJ 07080
(201) 668-1430

Bay Waveland

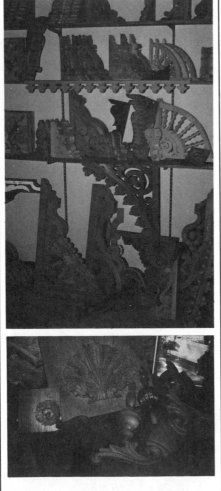

Select red cypres yields the extensive selection of Victorian gingerbread trims available at Bay Waveland. Brackets in a wide variety of styles and sizes are a specialty, as are hand-carved items, especially finials. The company sells wholesale and retail and will ship anywhere; you might also like to examine its mantels, porch swings, and

benches. Owners P.C. Leech and Steve Barron invite visits to their showroom.

Brochure available.

Showroom address:

Bay Waveland Woodworks
1330 Hwy. 90 W.
Waveland, MS 39576
(601) 467-2628.

Inquiries should be sent to:

Bay Waveland Woodworks
Rte. 4, Box 548
Bay St. Louis, MS 39520

Beech River Mill

If you believe that "the success of an architectural design depends on attention to finishing touches," then you and Beech River Mill agree. Offering shutters for any architectural style, Beech River's design services extend to faithful duplication of antique designs. From drawings, photographs, or an original sample, Beech River re-creates history, often working from over 100 antique patterns. The company that once built blinds and shutters for original Pullman Co. trains now fabricates shutters for interior and exterior use today. Louvered shutters; plain, raised panel shutters; or panel-top shutters with cutouts of trees, ships, bells, candles, and other designs are available for outdoor use. Interior designs include louvered and movable louvered styles or a solid, raised-panel design that couples insulation with eye appeal. Clear wood, completely dried, goes into the mortise-and-tenon joinery (the firm eschews dowels and staples) that ensures long use. High quality has characterized Beech River Mill for 130 years, and the tradition is not about to change.

Catalogue, $3.

Beech River Mill Co.
Old Rte. 16
Centre Ossipee, NH 03814
(603) 539-2636

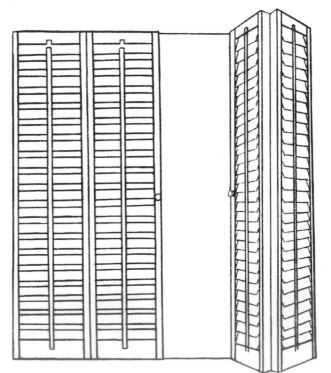

Bendix Mouldings

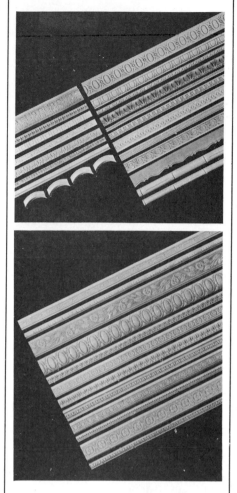

Both variety and quality make Bendix an outstanding supplier of wood ornamentation and moldings. The company makes and sells almost fifty types of ornaments and rosettes, over fifty styles of carved wood moldings, six dentil moldings, three scalloped untextured moldings, eight overlays made of flexible birch plywood and backed with glue, and thirty-nine embossed moldings, plus various beaded, rope, bolection, and crown moldings. They are sold in random lengths of 3' to 15', with most pieces ranging from 6' to 10' in length. The beaded styles are sold only in lengths of 2½' and 3'. Samples of the moldings and carvings are available.

Catalogue, $2.

Bendix Mouldings, Inc.
235 Pegasus Ave.
Northvale, NJ 07647
(800) 526-0240
(201) 767-8888 (NJ)

Classic Architectural Specialties

What is a Victorian house without a proper gable? Classic Architectural Specialties supplies a suitable array of gable finishes in various pitches. This hemlock, white pine, and masonite piece (approximately 59" tall) is handsomely carved to finish your home in style. And as long as you're on top, pick a turned roof finial, easily modified to suit a turret, if desired. Other decorative wooden items stocked by the firm include a bevy of posts, spindles, and post tops. Ask about what you don't see in the catalogue but would enjoy having. The inventory at Classic Architectural Specialties extends well beyond the pieces mentioned here and in the firm's literature.

Catalogue, $2.

Classic Architectural Specialties
5302 Junius
Dallas, TX 75214
(214) 827-5111

Cumberland Woodcraft

Cumberland offers a full line of Victorian-style woodwork designed to put the finishing touches on your house. Although the company also makes exterior ornaments, it is their line of interior items that merits special notice. It includes bead board paneling, carved column capitals, bar rail moldings, ceiling treat-

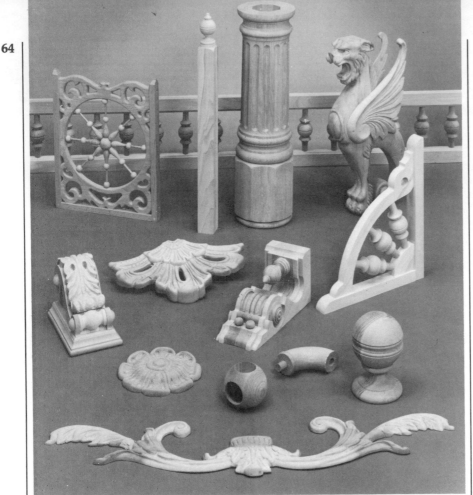

HAYMAN STUDIO OF COMMERCIAL PHOTOGRAPHY

The Fireplace Mantel Shop

From the dignified simplicity of the Supreme Court Double Bead and Cove (model FMS 287) to the massive elegance of the Colonial casing (model FMS 218), The Fireplace Mantel Shop's clear white pine moldings bring an aura of old-house authenticity to your home. If you prefer hardwood to white pine, choose from custom woods that include poplar, red oak, mahogany, birch, cherry, and walnut. For a neoclassical look, choose fluted or reeded moldings. Model FMS 303, featuring wide fluting, is ¾" thick and 5½" wide. Narrower fluting is available on model FMS 304, which is 1¼" thick and 5½" wide. The columnar appearance of FMS 308 is enhanced by its slight outward curve. It measures ¾" thick and 4½" wide. The Fireplace Mantel Shop's moldings have a maximum length of 16'; custom designs can almost always be executed.

Catalogue, $2.75.

The Fireplace Mantel Shop, Inc.
4217 Howard Ave.
Kensington, MD 20895
(301) 564-1550

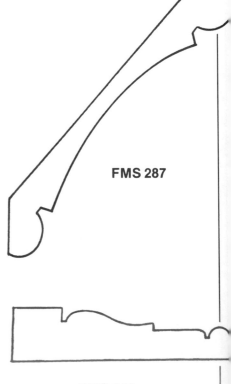

FMS 287

FMS 218

ments, screens, and partitions. The photographs show a few of Cumberland's many solid-oak and poplar interior brackets, corbels, carvings, elaborate moldings, and fretwork grilles. All of the company's wood ornaments are made from high-quality hardwoods.

Catalogue, $3.75.

Cumberland Woodcraft Co., Inc.
Drawer 609
Carlisle, PA 17013
(717) 243-0063

Gazebo & Porchworks

Gazebo & Porchworks offers several types of wood trims in addition to its line of outdoor swings and structures. The selection includes a variety of shoes, fillets, and oak or hemlock rails. The rails are sold in increments of 2′ with a maximum length of 16′. Two styles of gable trims are available; one has spindles and fanciful curves, and the other features a stylized sunburst design. Sturdy corbels ranging in thickness from 3″ to 5″ are also sold; an example measuring 23½″ high by 5″ wide by 9″ deep is shown.

Catalogue, $2.

Gazebo & Porchworks
728 9th Ave. S.W.
Puyallup, WA 98371-6744
(206) 848-0502

Marjory & Peter Holly

Marjory and Peter Holly's distinctive Victorian embellishments bring out the full character of your old house. Custom-cut latticework is both rare and unparalleled for delicacy and true Victorian flavor, and, like railings, spindles, and porchposts, can be customized by the couple for your home. Scroll-cutting is available, and the Hollys also cut various woods, suited for either interior or exterior use, to make beautiful moldings and brackets.

Shown here is the Hollys' work at the beginning of a project to restore the J.B. Hudson House in

Minneapolis, Minnesota. The Hollys glory in this type of custom work and invite you to contact them for further information.

Brochure available.

Marjory & Peter Holly
3111 2nd Ave. S.
Minneapolis, MN 55408
(612) 824-2333

Iberia Millwork

Practical, versatile, and expressive of many moods, shutters have wide and justified appeal. From standard components, fabricated to custom sizes, Iberia Millwork's shutters grace numerous restoration projects. Solid wood rails and warp-resistant laminated stiles of first growth heart redwood form Iberia's exterior shutters. Interior shutters come in stain-grade white cypress and Ponderosa pine or paint-grade yellow poplar. Custom rolling slat shutters are Iberia's specialty, but the firm can furnish fixed louver, panel bottom, and round- or angle-topped shutters, as well. Iberia recommends using its $^{15}/_{16}$″-thick shutters when possible; $1^{1}/_{16}$″ and unusually thick shutters are also available. Other items from Iberia include cabinets, French doors, and various types of custom millwork.

Brochure available.

Iberia Millwork
500 Jane St.
New Iberia, LA 70560
(318) 365-5644

Mark A. Knudsen

Mark A. Knudsen works for exacting customers "who know what they *won't* settle for." A quarter of a century's experience with hand tools and machinery renders Knudsen expert in hand-turning spindles or posts with up to 16″ diameters and lengths of 14′. Using a German tracer lathe, the artist can machine-turn 50″ pieces with 12″ diameters. Another lathe produces ornamental or spiraling turnings for vases or lamp bases. If you're still not convinced, write for Knudsen's references!

Brochure available.

Mark A. Knudsen
1100 E. County Line Rd.
Des Moines, IA 50320
(515) 285-6112

Mad River Woodworks

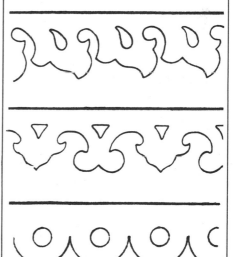

Ornamental woodwork is a specialty at Mad River. The company carries almost everything you'd need, from lacy brackets and corbels to sawn or turned balusters to the gingerbread running trims shown, which measure 5″ high by 96″ long by ¾″ thick. Six graceful styles of spandrels are also available and are hand-assembled. The length of the

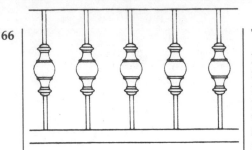

woodwork depends only on your specifications; model SS-100, shown here, is 12" high and 1½" deep.

Another Mad River product is one which we applaud wholeheartedly. Metal gutters can be unsightly, but well-built, attractive wooden gutters can be next to impossible to find. Fortunately, however, Mad River makes a pleasant-looking and useful redwood gutter which comes in random 8' to 20' lengths and measures 3½" high and 3½" deep.

Catalogue, $2.

Mad River Woodworks
Box 163
Arcata, CA 95521
(707) 826-0629

Mountain Lumber

Mountain Lumber is justly famous as the largest supplier of quality heart pine in North America. The same high standards for selection and grading that go into Mountain Lumber's production of flooring and paneling informs the company's millwork. Kiln-dried clear-grade heart pine is custom cut for beautiful moldings, including crown moldings, bed moldings, chair, backband, and Scotia moldings. Then, of course, there is the combination of moldings that is used to create a custom-designed Mountain Lumber mantelpiece. Specialists in custom woodwork, the company invites you to discuss your millwork needs with its skilled craftsmen and designers.

Brochure available.

Mountain Lumber Co.
Rte. 2
Box 43-1
Ruckersville, VA 22968
(804) 984-3646 or
(804) 295-1922

The Old Wagon Factory

If you're looking for a porch railing that's different from most, but not so different that it loses its period flavor, The Old Wagon Factory has one with a delightful fleur-de-lis and tulip design that may suit your needs. Made by hand from solid spruce, it adds a cheerful look to almost any indoor or outdoor setting. The length between posts should not exceed 8'; The Old Wagon Factory suggests that you hang the railing 3" off the ground, making it 28" tall. Posts can also be purchased to match it. Both the posts and the railing are sold primed and ready for paint.

Catalogue, $2.

The Old Wagon Factory
103 Russell St.
Box 1427, Dept. OC86
Clarksville, VA 23927
(804) 374-5787

Pagliacco Turning and Milling

Faithful to old designs and equipped with modern methods, Pagliacco manufactures sturdy wood decorations from dried California redwood. Although other species are used occasionally, the company prefers redwood for its strength and resistance to decay and termite infestation. Pagliacco's porch posts are especially attractive. Reproduced from drawings in catalogues issued between 1870 and the early 20th century, they come in twenty-one styles, 6" and 8" widths, and three standard heights—8', 9', and 10'. Those illustrated here have the proportions of 9' posts. Larger sizes can be made on request. The posts accept rails between 36" and 42" high and coordinate well with Pagliacco's equally fine balusters and newel posts. Shipped sanded and ready for finishing, they should be primed and painted with oil-base products. If your selection will be bearing an unusual amount of weight, the company recommends that it fashion your order from Douglas fir.

The firm also makes redwood columns, available in five shaft styles with turned wood or a choice of eight composition capitals. The two shown here, the Doric capital and Attic base combination and the Greek Doric style, are each manufactured in twelve standard sizes. Diameters at the shaft bottom range from 8" to 30", and height is determined by your specifications. The shaft may be fluted or plain, and four shapes are available: full, half, three-quarter for corners, and two-thirds for placement against walls. Pagliacco takes a good deal of care to ensure that its columns are authentic in proportion and accurate in architectural detail.

Catalogue, $6.

Pagliacco Turning and Milling
Box 225
Woodacre, CA 94973
(415) 488-4333

REM Associates

Inside and outside, your windows should reflect the appreciation of quality evident elsewhere in your old house. REM Associates provides interior and exterior shutters that can create that effect. Made of pine, they are available with fixed or movable louvers or with raised panels. The interior shutters also come in an open frame style to which wallpaper or fabric inserts can be attached. Interior shutters will be painted or stained according to your preference; REM will be happy to match your stain if you send a color sample. Exterior shutters can be painted by the company or left untreated and are provided with solid-brass hardware for mount-

ing. REM can also duplicate old shutters or produce its standard designs in custom sizes.

Literature, $2.

REM Associates
Box 504
Northborough, MA 01532
(617) 393-8424

Remodelers' & Renovators' Supply

Porches and staircases get a little help from Remodelers' & Renovators' Supply. Two hemlock spindles—the Georgetown, with its elaborate center section, and the simpler Colonial — can suit a variety of needs. The Colonial comes in six sizes ranging from 12" high by 2" wide and deep to 36" high by 4" wide and deep. The more slender Georgetown has seven sizes, from 36" high by 2" wide and deep to 96" high by 4" wide and deep.

GEO.-
TOWN

COL.

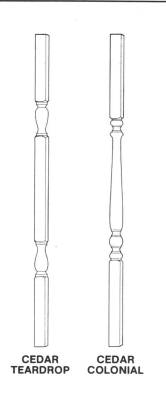

CEDAR TEARDROP   **CEDAR COLONIAL**

Cedar spindles designed specifically for outdoor use are also available. Elegant additions to any porch, they measure 36" high by 2" wide and deep and come in two styles—Teardrop and Colonial.

Porch posts in ponderosa pine are available in six sizes. The smallest is 8' high and 4" square; the largest is 9' and 6" square; You may select the smooth, graceful

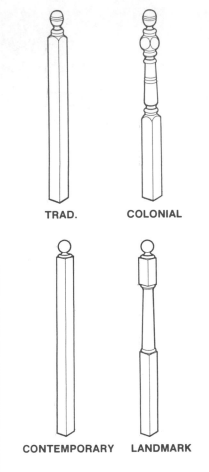

TRAD.   **COLONIAL**

CONTEMPORARY   **LANDMARK**

New Orleans or the sturdy Colonial.

Don't forget to take a look at the company's hemlock newel posts, which can be made in oak on request. The elaborate Colonial and the Traditional, with its simple design and ribbed ball, come in four sizes, ranging from 48″ high and 3⁵⁄₁₆″ wide and deep to 60″ high and 4³⁄₈″ wide and deep. Two newel posts with smooth balls are also sold. A very plain style called Contemporary and a slightly more detailed post called Landmark come in 50″ and 66″ heights and measure 3⁵⁄₁₆″ wide and deep.

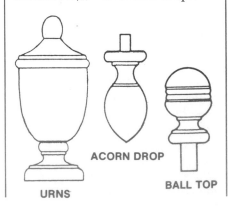

URNS   **ACORN DROP**   **BALL TOP**

Remodelers' & Renovators' Supply has urn, acorn drop, and ball top finials to finish wood-trimmed areas in style. For walls, doors, windows, and ceilings, the company offers a selection of moldings in D-grade pine. Other woods, including oak, fir, and mahogany, can be substituted if you desire. For more information, call or write the company.

Catalogue, $2.

Remodelers' & Renovators' Supply
512 W. Idaho
Boise, ID 83702
(208) 344-8612

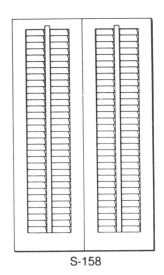

S-158

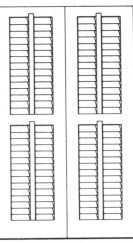

S-159

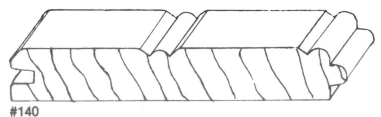

#8263

#140

Sheppard Millwork

Grinding their own knives and executing their turnings by hand, the staff at Sheppard Millwork produces a wide variety of high-quality ornamental woodwork. The company's stock includes two styles of sturdy shutters (models S-158 and S-159); a 1⁹⁄₁₆″-tall, gently-curving picture mold (model 8263); an unusual beaded ceiling mold (model 140); and an ornate cornice mold formed by the combination of three individual moldings. The complete selection of trims incorporates dentil moldings, casings, baseboards, a fireplace mold, stops, plinth blocks, rosettes, handrails, and a bar rail as well. In addition, Sheppard can match existing moldings or create new ones from drawings.

Catalogue available.

Sheppard Millwork, Inc.
21020 70th Ave. W.
Edmonds, WA 98020
(206) 771-4645 or
(206) 283-7549

Shuttercraft

Solid pine shutters trim a colonial or Victorian home in style. Thin, plastic copies don't compare, and they boast no lasting advantage, either. Correctly sealed wooden shutters from Shuttercraft will last as long as your house, and the firm's naturally ventilating wood shutters won't encourage rot in the wooden siding they cover. Galvanized yoke pins are similarly durable. Use hinges for moveable shutters, or install shutters as a fixed decorative accent. Large shutters may also be ordered as door panels with a center rail at doorknob level.

Brochure available.

Shuttercraft
282 Stepstone Hill Rd.
Guilford, CT 06437
(203) 453-1973

Silverton Victorian Mill Works

At Silverton, George Crane replicates turn-of-the-century moldings and millwork. This historical line of over 350 moldings, headblocks, baseblocks, casings, wainscoting, and base-board is available in a standard stock of premium-grade pine and oak. Redwood, mahogany, and other exotic woods are offered on a custom basis. Because of the variety of millwork offered, the old-house devotee can plan the woodwork of his home around a wide array of Victorian styles. A catalogue is available which il-lustrates the various moldings of-fered as well as over forty detailed construction drawings showing the typical uses. Illustrated here is just a sampling of Silverton's stock: repeating ornaments, plate rails, and exterior window trim.

Catalogue, $4.

Silverton Victorian Mill Works
Box 850-OHC
Silverton, CO 81433
(303) 387-5716

Somerset Door & Column

Columns do something for Classical Revival homes that nothing else can. Used inside or outside, they add a touch of period grandeur. Somerset Door & Column specializes in these elegant decorations, offering seven styles and six ornamental capitals. The firm will also manufacture custom columns in any shape and in any size up to 40' high and 40" in diameter. Sturdy tongue-and-groove joints and uniform wood thickness along the entire column length keep the structure strong. A number of wood species are kept in stock, including clear northern white pine, clear heart redwood, Pennsylvania sound knotty white pine, and poplar. All of the wood is fastened with water-resistant glue and primed; columns over 12" in diameter receive the additional protection of black asphalt waterproofing on the inside.

The simple, smooth styling of Somerset's Tuscan column (model 110) makes it appropriate for almost any application. It comes in thirteen standard sizes, ranging from 5" in diameter at the top of the shaft and 6" at the bottom to 25" at the top and 30" at the bottom. Bases measure between 1½" high by 8" wide and deep and

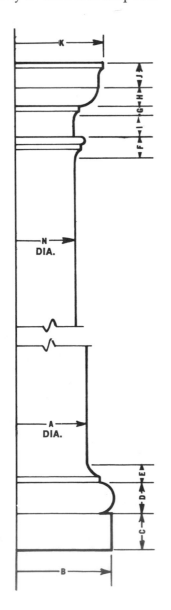

7½" high by 40" wide and deep, and heights of capitals and bases range from 3⅞" and 3½" to 18⅜" and 16⅝".

Brochure available.

Somerset Door & Column Co.
Box 328
Somerset, PA 15501
(800) 242-7916
(800) 242-7915 (PA)

Sunshine Architectural Woodworks

Ridges, notches, and graceful curves combine in Sunshine's collection of fine window and door casings. These trims are usually made of poplar, although they are also available in walnut, cherry, mahogany, or oak. You can paint them if you like, but all are flawless enough to look their best when simply stained. They are shipped in random lengths of 10' to 16'.

Sunshine also manufactures handsome raised-panel shutters.

Made exclusively from solid hardwood, they're perfect for colonial settings and are built to your specifications. Several panel combinations are available.

Catalogue, $4.

Sunshine Architectural Woodworks
Rte. 2, Box 434
Fayetteville, AR 72701
(501) 521-4329

Turncraft

Decorative wood from Turncraft dresses up any home. From grand box or classic columns to delicately turned spindles, these products are excellent additions to authentic decor. The box columns, available in plain or fluted styles and heights of 8' or 10', as well as the round columns, in heights varying from 8' to 20' and diameters ranging from 6" to 20" (according to load capability required), are cut from finger-jointed staves of ponderosa or sugar pine. After edge-gluing, Turncraft readies them for primer and paint by applying water repellent and preservative and sanding the finished column.

Exterior spindles and railings of red cedar contain natural oil that preserves them against harsh weather. In colonial or teardrop styles, the spindles suit patios, landings, garden screens and gates, among other uses. Other spindles come in colonial, Georgetown, Mediterranean, planter, and Williamsburg styles. Use 8" spindles as room dividers. Sturdy newel posts, in lengths of 48" to 60", serve indoors and out, in various traditional styles. Porch posts come in various sizes. With or without corbels, the pine or hemlock posts accept stain or paint to complement any color scheme.

Brochure available.

Turncraft
Box 2429
White City, OR 97503
(503) 826-2911

Vintage Wood Works

Almost every location in a Victorian house can benefit from Vintage's products. Indoors, use ornate shelves in a variety of sizes to hold books, dishes, and whatnots; the company will manufacture almost all of them in any length you desire. An enormous selection of ¾"-thick brackets can be used in many locations. Heavier 1½"-thick brackets are available for exterior use.

Thick corbels decorate the outside of the house, turning ordinary corners into festive spaces. They add a look of permanence and substance where thinner trims would look flimsy. None of Vintage's corbels are less than 3" thick. The roof can be adorned with ¾" running trim. The design at the bottom left of the photograph, called Fleur, stands 3½" high and is shipped in 48"-long sections.

Doorways, foyers, and the spaces between built-in cabinets can be enhanced by the addition of spandrels. Simple ball-and-dowel versions are available, as well as the scrolled designs illustrated and a few with turned spindles instead of balls. Vintage will manufacture them in any length to the nearest ¹⁄₁₆". Wood grilles can serve the same purposes and are sold in two styles: the large, elaborate

Queen Victoria and the smaller, daintier Shell. The Queen Victoria is 19⅛" high and comes in 47⅝"-long and 60"-long sizes; the Shell is 10¼' high by 18¾" long. Both are ¾" thick with 1½"-thick frames.

110. ¾" x 24" x 6½"

For dramatic entranceways, Vintage makes striking arches. The Sun Ray measures 26" high by 62" wide by 1½" thick and consists of two brackets interrupted by a 2" by 2" drop. Headers can enliven doors and windows; model 110 is 6½" high, 24" wide, and ¾" thick.

While you're trimming your house with gingerbread, don't forget gable decorations. Model 42-140, called Old Lace, has 38"-

long sides and is available in any standard roof pitch. For the ambitious, there's a design called the Flying Circle Gable. Measuring 72" long at the bottom and made only for a square roof pitch, it takes some skill to install.

Catalogue, $2.

Vintage Wood Works
Dept. D 691
Box 1157
513 S. Adams
Fredericksburg, TX 78624
(512) 997-9513

Frederick Wilbur

If you can't find what you need at a company that only stocks a few molding designs, if you have a bed finial that needs matching and no one will do it for you, or if you simply appreciate the look of hand-carved wood, you need the services of Frederick Wilbur. His architectural carvings for churches, businesses, municipal buildings, and individuals are done completely by hand. Exquisitely designed and often intricately detailed, his pieces make the most of the extraordinary natural beauty of wood. This mantel corner, decorated with flowers, leaves, and a classical urn overflowing with fruit, is an example of Wilbur's work. If you'd like to employ his services, notify your architect or interior designer.

Literature available.

Frederick Wilbur
Box 425
Lovingston, VA 22949
(804) 263-4827

The Woodworkers' Store

All the classic molding designs are available at The Woodworkers' Store. Specialty moldings include panel and bamboo styles and half-round or full-round poplar rope patterns in five sizes. French Provincial-style trim in oak, birch, or walnut adds an elegant touch to doors, walls, and cabinets. The Woodworkers' Store also carries several types of carved and embossed hardwood moldings, perfect for frames, furniture, paneling, fireplaces, or walls. They apply easily with brads and glue.

You can shop at one of the company's retail stores in San Diego, Minneapolis, Seattle, Denver, Boston, or Columbus, Ohio, or write for more information about ordering products by mail.

Catalogue, $1.

The Woodworkers' Store
21801 Industrial Blvd.
Rogers, MN 55374
(612) 428-4101

26 E. 3rd St.
Bethlehem, PA 18018
(215) 865-2522

The Fireplace Mantel Shop

Finding cabinetry to match your house's style is made easier with The Fireplace Mantel Shop's three cabinet designs. Each can be modified by the addition of reeded or fluted pilasters, an arched top, raised-panel doors on the upper portion, a plaster shell, or, as in this case, Chippendale-style glass doors. The basic unit, D-501, is also shown here. It is open on the top with two raised-panel

Cabinetry

Finding a craftsman who can execute traditional cabinetry such as bookcases, cupboards, chimney breasts and mantels, and room ends is not as difficult as it used to be. Ten or fifteen years ago, one nearly had to kidnap an old-fashioned carpenter from a rest home. Some of these octogenarians, however, passed down their skills to a new generation of woodworkers, and these artisans have inspired yet others. They are found in nearly every North American town and

village, working quietly in their shops on furniture and millwork, and reproducing one-of-a-kind traditional cabinetry pieces. Included here are also suppliers of materials for do-it-yourself projects. For further leads to professionals who can produce cabinetwork for you, consult chapter 9 on furniture, chapter 5 on heating and cooking for suppliers of mantels, and the preceding section of this chapter on applied wood ornamentation.

Marion H. Campbell

Reproductions and restorations of fine antique woodwork are no problem for Marion H. Campbell. Custom work is this craftsman's specialty; this built-in corner cabinet is one of a pair that was designed to match the room's existing paneling and molding. Campbell also makes exceptionally fine furniture.

Brochure, 50¢.

Inquiries may be mailed to Campbell's home address:

Marion H. Campbell
39 Wall St.
Bethlehem, PA 18018
(215) 865-3292

If you wish to visit the workshop or to call during business hours, Campbell can be reached at:

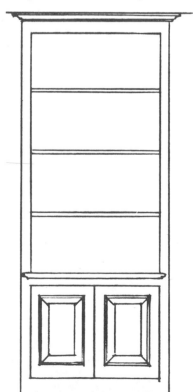

doors at the bottom. These doors may be either ¾" or 1⅛" thick and may be lipped or flush. One stationary shelf of solid kiln-dried sugar pine rests behind the doors. Two heights, 96" and 108", are available; the 96" cabinet is fitted with three sturdy ¾"-thick sugar pine shelves which may be adjustable or stationary. The 108" cabinet comes with four shelves. Both sizes are 36" wide and have an interior depth of 11¼". The sides and backs may be built of plywood or of solid wood; sugar pine is standard, but a host of hardwoods are available as well, including poplar, red oak, cherry, and walnut.

Catalogue, $2.75.

The Fireplace Mantel Shop, Inc.
4217 Howard Ave.
Kensington, MD 20895
(301) 564-1550

The Joinery Company

In addition to its line of superb heart pine flooring, The Joinery Company also offers a complete selection of heart pine millwork: cabinetry, mantels, doors, stair parts, wainscoting, and molding. The firm's cabinetmakers hand build these special products, using authentic colonial methods and details. Their old-world standard of quality results in millwork and furniture that is consistently excellent.

When Colonial Williamsburg selected The Joinery Company to craft its flooring of longleaf heart pine, it chose both extraordinary expertise and materials. This excellence characterizes all other projects at The Joinery, as well. A kitchen full of cabinetry, rich-grained and warm, is elegant, strong, and loyal to Old World traditions. The vertical grain used for all framework, rails, and stiles won't warp. The planks forming the door panels are color- and grain-matched solid wood. Drawer and cabinet bottoms are formica laminate. Ball bearing drawer guides are the strong and silent type. According to The Joinery, "When you have

developed an eye for detail, compromise is unthinkable."

Catalogue, $5.

The Joinery Company
Dept. OHC
Box 518
Tarboro, NC 27886
(919) 823-3306

Paneling

Paneled walls and wainscoting are among the most handsome features of many old houses. Colonial interiors often feature paneled room ends which incorporate a fireplace and closets on each side. Victorian interiors are more likely to make use of wainscoting, generally in that space defined by a baseboard below and a chair rail above, the section of a wall technically termed the dado. Talented home craftsmen can duplicate such paneling using specially milled lumber or veneer, supplies of which are noted in the following listings. Renovators or restorers seeking professional help can turn to a number of specialists for supplies, design assistance, and construction. Many of the craftsmen and suppliers noted in the section on applied wood ornamentation will also assist with paneling projects.

Architectural Components

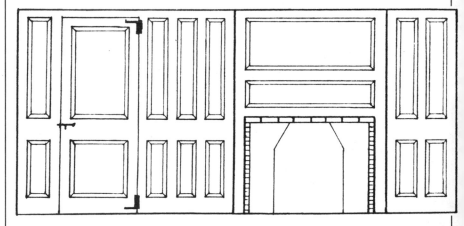

Do you need assistance in bringing a period room to life? Architectural Components will help you to design a raised-panel wall that suits the room and your taste. Then the firm will construct the paneling, typically of ¹⁵⁄₁₆"-thick clear kiln-dried eastern white pine, but sometimes of cherry, poplar, oak, or another type of hardwood. Mortise and tenon joinery is used exclusively, and the surfaces are hand-planed. Featheredge or beaded wainscoting is also available.

Brochure, $3.

Architectural Components
Box 249
Leverett, MA 01054
(413) 367-9441

Marion H. Campbell

This exquisite cherry-paneled library is the work of Marion H. Campbell. The civil engineer-turned-cabinetmaker specializes in custom architectural woodwork, although he makes equally attractive furniture. So thorough and skilled is Campbell that he

vaged from bottoms of sawmill ponds and rivers, into new paneling, achieving boards of antique wood, cut for the first time. Heart-Wood has new wood that's just as exceptional as its antique lumber. Choice cypress paneling is a rarity—call on Heart-Wood to supply it.

Brochure available. Wood sample, $5.

Heart-Wood, Inc.
Rte. 1, Box 97-A
Jasper, FL 32052
(904) 792-1688

The Joinery Company

Using authentic colonial methods of craftsmanship, The Joinery Company manufactures raised-panel wainscoting that looks the way you've always thought fine millwork should. The solid woods used to make the wainscoting include yellow pine, heart pine, cherry, birch, maple, oak, and walnut. Among the standard features of the paneling are hip-raised or featheredge panels, vertical-grained stiles and rails, hand pegging, color and grain matching, and hand-planed or sanded panel faces. All the trim—a chair-rail, an apron, and a two-piece base—is included.

Brochure, $5.

The Joinery Company
Box 518
Tarboro, NC 27886
(919) 823-3306

Maurer & Shepherd Joyners

Few reproduction room elements are more convincing than wood paneling. Its presence adds a richness that nothing else can. Maurer & Shepherd's wood paneling, with its lovingly hand-planed surfaces, is no exception to the rule. Like all of the company's wood products, it is custom-made entirely by hand. Maurer & Shepherd is also known for its fine interior and exterior doors, mantels, flooring, shutters, and windows.

Brochure available.

was selected by a private collector to re-create a case for a clock movement built by David Rittenhouse, an eminent 18th-century clockmaker and an associate of Benjamin Franklin's. However, we need not attest to Campbell's talents; the elegant mantel and walls shown here accomplish this for us.

Brochure, 50¢. Inquiries may be mailed to Campbell's home address:

Marion H. Campbell
39 Wall St.
Bethlehem, PA 18018
(215) 865-3292

If you wish to visit the workshop or to call during business hours, Campbell can be reached at:

26 E. 3rd St.
Bethlehem, PA 18018
(215) 865-2522

Carlisle Restoration Lumber

The materials for pine or oak paneling are available at Carlisle Restoration Lumber, which sells boards that are perfect for the purpose. Square-edged 14″ to 21″ wide pine and 5″ to 10″-wide oak are kept in stock, as is 8″ to 12″-wide ship-lapped pine. Carol and Dale Carlisle provide instructions for installing and caring for their paneling.

Literature available.

Carlisle Restoration Lumber
Rte. 123
Stoddard, NH 03464
(603) 446-3937

Craftsman Lumber

The toughest part of Craftsman Lumber's restoration and reproduction projects is finding the wide boards of white pine, so plentiful when colonists built their homes. Knotty white pine, kiln dried to a moisture content between 6% and 8%—as dry as is feasible, without promoting cracking—can be planed in various ways to yield excellent wood paneling. Edges are generally featheredged, ship-lapped, or tongued and grooved, with molding or beading as options.

Craftsman Lumber
R.R. 1, Box 65
Ashby, MA 01431
(617) 386-7550

Heart-Wood

Heart-Wood specializes in wood from unusual sources. The firm cuts southern yellow pine, sal-

Maurer & Shepherd Joyners Inc.
122 Naubuc Ave.
Glastonbury, CT 06033
(203) 633-2383

Sunshine Architectural Woodworks

If you like the look of fine hardwood, you might consider installing Sunshine's superb wainscoting. Usually made of kiln-dried poplar, it can also be executed in walnut, cherry, mahogany, or oak. If you'd like to see how the wood looks and feels, a sample can be purchased. It consists of a raised panel and frame measuring about 8" by 11" and can be returned to the company for a full refund.

Two grades of wood are sold—paint grade and stain grade; stain grade is the more expensive. The wainscoting has a standard height of 28", although its exact dimensions depend on your specifications. Sunshine's catalogue contains instructions for taking measurements, and the company urges you to call if you have any questions or problems. The paneling is built to allow the wood to expand and contract without being damaged.

Catalogue, $4.

Sunshine Architectural Woodworks
Rte. 2, Box 434
Fayetteville, AK 72701
(501) 521-4329

Vintage Lumber

Antique lumber demands laborious de-nailing, sawing, kiln drying, and milling to recycle timbers for a beautiful addition to an old home. Antique paneling is available from Vintage Lumber in fir, oak, chestnut, cypress, and white or yellow pine. Newly milled paneling comes in poplar, oak, walnut, cherry, and white or yellow pine.

Vintage Lumber
9507 Woodsboro Rd.
Frederick, MD 21701
(301) 898-7859

Tile Ornamentation

Don't despair if you've just made your first trip to a ceramic tile supplier and discovered that everything on display is either speckled or tinted in a sickly pastel. Unless you are a complete defeatist, you will be ready to search further for tile that is truly attractive and fitting for an old-house interior. In chapter 3 some of the leading suppliers of handsome floor tiles are described. Many of these same firms produce decorative tiles which can be used effectively for fireplace surrounds, hearths, kitchen and pantry counters, and as splashboards.

American Olean

If you're looking for easy installation and versatility, look no further than American Olean's 1" hexagonal ceramic mosaics. The tiles are mounted on 2' by 1' sheets for simple and accurate installation, and the small size of the tiles allows you to create an almost unlimited number of patterns. If you like, you can choose from the company's numerous geometric and floral standard pat-

terns, two of which are shown here. American Olean's hexagonal tiles are also perfect for floor use.

Brochure, 25¢.

American Olean Tile Co.
1000 Cannon Ave., Box 271
Lansdale, PA 19446-0271
(215) 855-1111

Laura Ashley

Laura Ashley's Italian-made tiles come in a dozen designs and five matching solids. Large tiles (8″ squares) should be used as wall ornaments or on floors that do not receive heavy traffic, and may require professional advice for installation. Smaller (6″ squares) tiles are handy wall decorations but are not suited for floor use. Striking traditional designs include the ornate, stylized ferns of Conservatory and the heavier clovers and spears of Quatrefoil.

Home furnishings catalogue, $4.

Laura Ashley
Dept. B117, Box 5308
Melville, NY 11747
(800) 367-2000

Designs in Tile

Designs in Tile is an art tile studio specializing in ceramic tile consultation, design development, material and installation specification, and creation of historic reproductions, traditional patterns, and contemporary designs

using mosaics and hand-decorated ceramic tiles. Inspired by the philosophy and art of the Aesthetic Movement, the firm prides itself on its collaboration with clients, architects, designers, and contractors. The firm operates much in the manner of early art tile studios. While custom work is its specialty, it offers many stock designs which are filled on a custom order basis, thus allowing the greatest flexibility in final color and design.

Current stock designs include Victorian transfer tiles in the Anglo-Japanese style; William DeMorgan-style tiles, a hand-painted historic reproduction series of coordinating tile patterns and mini-murals; folk tiles hand-painted in traditional Pennsylvania German and Northern European styles; Persian Revival

tiles, reproductions of tiles from the Arts and Crafts period; and spring flower tiles executed in the naturalistic style reminiscent of Art Nouveau pen and ink with watercolor washes. Shown here is a Victorian transfer tile and two William DeMorgan tiles.

Designs in Tile's work is on display countrywide. The firm routinely works over long distances and will design tile art to suit any plan you provide.

Catalogue, $3.

Designs in Tile
Box 4983
Foster City, CA 94404
(415) 571-7122

Moravian Pottery & Tile Works

Determined to do more than merely regret the loss of Pennsylvania-German pottery methods, Henry Chapman Mercer (1856-1930) first apprenticed himself to a potter and then built the Moravian Pottery & Tile Works in about 1900. Mercer focused on tiles and mosaics, inventing some designs and culling others from the British Museum and from European castles and abbeys.

Decorative tiles like this 4" by 4" horse can highlight hearths, tabletops, and counters. Others can be used on stands, trivets, and hangers. Multi-tile mosaics, originally for floors, can set off tables and walls equally well. Mercer designed most of these mosaics, centering on themes of history, nature, and the arts and crafts tradition. Colors for these handsome tiles include buff blue, gold rust, beard brown, and cream on red, among many others. Finishes include smoked red, gray, and black; brick red, ranging from dark to light; half-glazed, with a brick red surface and recessed coloring; and several others.

Catalogue, $4.

Moravian Pottery & Tile Works
Swamp Rd.
Doylestown, PA 18901
(215) 345-6722

Saxe Patterson

Saxe Patterson's enthusiasm for the science and inherent beauty of ceramic tile is contagious: one glance at the lovely samples and slides that were sent to us and it is easy to see why. For the past twelve years this business high in the mountains of northern New Mexico has been producing ceramic floor and wall tile. Clay bodies combine purchased raw materials with locally available ingredients; the resulting glazed stoneware is produced in a high-fire process. Tiles are available in a wide range of colors, shapes, and sizes; all are suitable for indoor or outdoor use. The line also includes architectural fixtures such as sinks and faucet parts. Although production is limited, word-of-mouth recommendations have kept the firm busy, and a new catalogue is in the works. Various sets of sample tiles are available: tile and basin colors on 4" x 4" square ($25); tile and basin colors on 2" x 2" square ($25); light colors on 2" x 2" square ($7.50). Fees are refundable with an order of $400 or more.

Catalogue available.

Taos Clay Products
Box 15, Salazar Rd.
Taos, NM 87571
(505) 758-9513

Victorian Collectibles

Emblematic of the era in which their designs were created, the decorative tiles sold by Victorian Collectibles feature graceful floral patterns. The designs are taken from samples of wallpaper from the late 19th century and match the company's reproduction papers. A fine pair of tiles was developed from coordinated papers called Mary Daily Crook. From the ceiling paper came an intricate rose pattern in mauve, gold, Victorian blue, and green on a white background. From the sidewall paper came a fragile garland of mauve and green roses draped across a background of white or Victorian blue. The delicate beauty of these tiles should not be underestimated.

Brochure, $2.

Victorian Collectibles Ltd.
845 E. Glenbrook Rd.
Milwaukee, WI 53217
(414) 352-6910

Helen Williams

Nowhere in this country can you find a larger collection of antique Dutch wall tiles than at Helen William's shop. The 5"-square Delft tiles date from 1600 to 1850, and genuine examples display their authenticity at a glance since they show the tin-glazed finish known as "faience." Early tiles are multicolored, but Delft shows shades of blue and brown. The tile pictured here, portraying Mary, Joseph, and Jesus traveling to Jerusalem, represents innumerable Bible tiles that taught Bible stories to children as they gazed at colorful walls and fireplaces.

Other designs available from Helen Williams include sea animals, flower vases, soldiers, shepherds, mythological animals, ships, and windmills. Williams also offers more recent English Liverpool and Spanish transfer tiles, as well as a limited selection of Minton and Art Nouveau pieces.

Send a SASE when requesting a brochure.

Helen Williams/Rare Tiles
12643 Hortense St.
Studio City, CA 91604
(818) 761-2756

Other Suppliers of Architectural Decoration

Consult List of Suppliers for addresses.

Glass

Architectural Antique Warehouse
Architectural Antiques Exchange
Architectural Salvage Co.
Art Directions
The Canal Co.
Great American Salvage Co.
Nostalgia, Inc.
Ohmega Salvage
Pelnick Wrecking Co.
Vintage Wood Works
Wooden Nickel Antiques

Ornamental Metalwork

Architectural Antiques Exchange
Architectural Salvage Co.
Ohmega Salvage
Schwartz's Forge & Metalworks
Steptoe & Wife Antiques Ltd.
Stewart Manufacturing Co.

Plaster, Composition, and Polymer Ornamentation

Nostalgia, Inc.
The Old Wagon Factory
Pagliacco Turning and Milling
Steptoe & Wife Antiques Ltd.

Applied Wood Ornamentation

Aged Woods
Architectural Antique Warehouse
Architectural Antiques Exchange
Architectural Salvage Co.
Central Kentucky Millwork Inc.
Great American Salvage Co.
The Joinery Co.
Kenmore Industries
Kentucky WoodFloors
Maurer & Shepherd Joyners Inc.
Ohmega Salvage
Pelnik Wrecking Co.
San Francisco Victoriana
Vintage Lumber & Construction Co.,
    Inc.

Cabinetry

Aged Woods
Alexandria Wood Joinery
Curvoflite
Dovetail Woodworking
Smith Woodworks and Design

Paneling

Art Directions
Central Kentucky Millwork Inc.
Cumberland Woodcraft Co., Inc.
Curvoflite
Dovetail Woodworking
The Fireplace Mantel Shop
Robinson Lumber Co., Inc.
San Francisco Victoriana
Silverton Victorian Mill Works
Somerset Door & Column Co.
Vintage Lumber & Construction Co.,
    Inc.

Tile Ornamentation

The Canal Co.
New York Marble Works

3.

Floors and Flooring

Beautiful floors are admired in any kind of house—new or old. But there is a special appeal in a sturdy, mellow random-width pine floor or an imaginatively laid oak parquet. Flooring in an older building has usually had a chance to age. Of course, it can also have become gouged, scraped, and otherwise disfigured. Today's remedy is most often a bath of polyurethane. This is not much better than the once popular method of scraping a floor—a technique akin to sand-blasting holes into a masonry building in an attempt to clean it. The problem with most synthetic finishes for floors is that they merely coat the surface—and with too high a sheen. The coating thus prevents the wood from "breathing," which it must do if it is not to rot over time.

For minor treatments of old wood flooring, a mixture of a fine butcher's wax and stain may suffice; surfaces which have had heavy use may require light sanding. If the wood has deteriorated to the point where it is no longer secure, replacement is the only solution. High-quality planks or strips are available from specialty dealers for entirely new floors or for patches. There are also commercial types of flooring which might serve your purposes if these include an all-new floor in either an old building or a new period-style structure. For the most part, it is best to stay away from the adhesive types and to opt for ¾" or thicker flooring which is nailed to the joists.

Wood has always been so plentiful in North America that other types of flooring such as stone, ceramic tile, or brick have never become very common. Marble and slate have usually been restricted to entryways; this is also the case with Victorian tiles. Today these materials, along with brick, are increasingly found in the kitchen as well as in bathrooms. Their cost is now little more than that of quality solid vinyl substitutes, the only synthetic with texture and durability. Sheet vinyl—which took the place of linoleum after World War II—is not satisfactory for use in old-style interiors. Linoleum, though hard to find today, is worth the search; it is like the wallpaper and the oilcloth of the past, a flowery, colorful medium.

We learn more each year about the ways in which floors used to be covered. Canvas floorcloths are among the most recent re-discoveries, and are rapidly becoming as popular as the old colonial-style standbys—the hooked rug and rag rug. Fortunately, today such rugs are being produced by hookers and weavers who use 100% wool and other traditional materials rather than double-knit yarns or acrylic throw-aways. The flood of floor coverings from the Far East will surely continue, but traditional skills are being re-learned here.

Re-milled heart-pine flooring and decorative woodwork by The Joinery Company, Tarboro, North Carolina.

Flooring

Aged Woods

Unfortunately, some lovely old buildings are neglected for so long that they cannot be salvaged. However, they can serve a purpose, as Aged Woods has shown. Carefully dismantling old houses and barns, most of them between one and two hundred years old, the company selects the finest salvaged wood and prepares it to be used again. The result is a selection of strong, dry antique wood flooring with beautiful colors and a wide range of sizes. Available woods include antique yellow pine, poplar, hemlock, fir, and white pine. The last, which varies in color from off-white to dark gray, is a heavily knotted soft wood with a wide grain, which should be used only for interior flooring. Also available are distressed or milled antique American chestnut, a rare species because of its decimation near the turn of the century; yellow cypress aged for twenty-five years, (a good wood for damp areas); and milled wormy chestnut. The floorboards come in two thicknesses. The ¾"-thick boards are available in random widths from 3" to 16"; the widths of the 1½"-thick boards range from 18" to 20". On occasion, boards as wide as 24" may be obtained. Constant widths for a more regular look are also sold.

Aged Woods recently introduced a new line of flooring called River Wood, consisting of pine, oak, hemlock, fir, and chestnut which had been submerged in cold running water since circa 1840. Only recently removed from the river, these faded woods have an appealing rusticity.

Brochure available. Wood samples, $10, refundable with order.

Aged Woods
Division of First Capital Wood
  Products
147 W. Philadelphia St.
York, PA 17401
(800) 233-9301

American Olean Tile

In addition to its many contemporary tile designs, American Olean is known for its Primitive tiles, including an 8" hexagonal shape. Their many surface and glaze combinations, as well as their slip-resistant surfaces and traditional colors, have made them popular with old house enthusiasts.

Now American Olean has released a collection of ceramic mosaics sure to please renovators even more. Available in 1" and 2" hexagons, 1" and 2" squares, and 1" by 2" rectangles, they come in

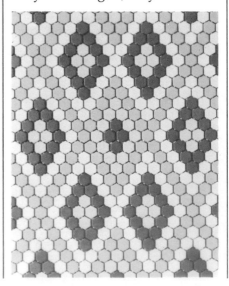

twelve stock colors, with thirty others available as special orders. The color is present throughout the tile, and the surface is unglazed. With a moisture absorption of less than one-half of one percent, these tiles are perfect for almost any surface. The 1" hexes are mounted on flexible 1' by 2' sheets for efficient, accurate setting. Several patterns are available; some are shown here. The overall patterns feature flowers, dots, and geometric figures, and the border styles are distinguished by clean, bold design.

Brochure on hex tiles, 25¢.

American Olean Tile
1000 Cannon Ave.
Box 271
Lansdale, PA 19446
(215) 855-1111

Laura Ashley

Designers from Laura Ashley are noted for their expertise in historic house decoration. Recent period projects included a Federal home on Long Island and a Georgian house in Wales, each one dazzling in the attention paid to every detail.

Italian tiles form a classic floor surface for bathroom or kitchen. The pavillion pattern of squares, octagons, and triangles—or any other of the Laura Ashley tiles—can be bordered with plain, nar-

row (4" by 8") color ways, available in packages of 25, for a decorator finish.

Home furnishings catalogue, $4.

Laura Ashley
Dept. B117, Box 5308
Melville, NY 11747
(800) 367-2000

Carlisle Restoration Lumber

If you're not prepared to pay the high prices that antique wood floors often command, but you love the look of pine or oak, you might want to consider newly milled timber. Dale and Carol Carlisle sell 8'- to 16'-long boards of new oak, square-edged pine, and ship-lapped pine that come with a no-waste guarantee. All three types of wood are available in ⅞" and 1" thicknesses and match the floor-board depths in most old buildings. The Carlisles will ship anywhere in the United States and offer on-site restoration consulting and designing from Maine to Maryland.

Literature available.

Carlisle Restoration Lumber
Rte. 123
Stoddard, NH 03464
(603) 446-3937

Craftsman Lumber

Colonial builders planed wide boards from Eastern white pine that is rare today. Craftsman Lumber devotes its efforts to providing kiln-dried pine boards that allow authentic reproduction of colonial woodwork. Flooring varies in width from 12" to 24" and from 8' to 16' in length. Random widths of 12" to 18" are used most often. Allow for approximately 20% waste when ordering pine boards.

Wide boards of red oak generally vary from 4" to 9", although choice widths of 10" to 16" can be had. Plan on 30% waste when requesting these tongue-and-groove boards.

Craftsman Lumber
R.R. 1, Box 65
Ashby, MA 01431
(617) 386-7550

Diamond K

Dismantled structures, mostly tobacco sheds, get a new life in the form of wide plank flooring from Diamond K. Twenty-five years of experience have made the company's president, Bill Krawski, an expert when it comes to antique woods. His 1"-thick floorboards are planed on one side and can be installed with either the rough or the smooth side facing upward. The smooth side can be stained. The boards come in two grades, which differ only in width. Select grade A boards range from 12" to 20" in width; grade A wood from 6" to 12".

Brochure available.

Diamond K Co., Inc.
130 Buckland Rd.
South Windsor, CT 06074
(203) 644-8486

Glen-Gery

Four shapes, fifteen sizes, and a palette of reds, browns, pinks, buffs, and grays make it easy to find a type of paving brick to suit you home. Glen-Gery's wire-cut and machine-molded bricks work equally well indoors or outdoors and for mortared or mortarless installation. The company suggests using them in running bond, basketweave, or herringbone patterns. The bricks shown, light

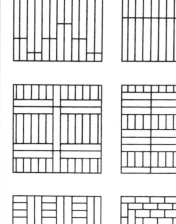

brown in color, measure 2¼″ high by 3⅝″ wide by 7⅝″ long.

Literature available.

Glen-Gery Corp.
Drawer S
Shoemakersville, PA 19555
(215) 562-3076

Hartco

Create your own patterned oak flooring with elements from Hartco and your own inventive formula. The Pattern-Plus system features modules in four themes: parallel, combination, parquet, and heringbone and basketweave. Variations include staggered pieces and perpendicular arrangements. The standard 4½″ widths of oak come in lengths of 9″, 18″, 27″, or 36″, combined using ¼″ slats to form units. Tongue-and-groove edges allow any combination of patterns. Stain and acrylic permeate the wood for lasting color and durability in flooring that stands up even to heavy kitchen use. Sanding and satin sealing finish the flooring, which is available in three shades: dark brown nutmeg, neutral ginger, and pale curry.

Special adhesive allows installation on a variety of surfaces. Hartco also markets floor care products to shield, shine and clean its flooring. Contact the firm for the name of the distributor nearest you.

Brochure available.

Hartco, Inc.
300 S. Main St.
Oneida, TN 37841
(615) 569-8526

Heart-Wood

Most of North Florida's pine forests, dense with trees three to six centuries old, fell to lumbermen sometime between the mid-1800s and 1920. Logs were floated downriver to sawmills, but many sank before reaching their destination. Heart-Wood has reclaimed much of this choice pine from ponds and rivers in Florida and Georgia and makes it available as both flooring and paneling. Future plans call for some of the lumber to be pre-cut for furniture kits. Other fine

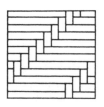

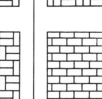

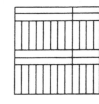

woods available from Heart-Wood include cypress and red cherry.

Wood sample and price list, $5.

Heart-Wood, Inc.
Rte. 1, Box 97-A
Jasper, FL 32052
(904) 792-1688

The Joinery Company

So strongly coveted was Colonial America's pine lumber that King George II once declared all straight pine trees over 24" in diameter to be the property of the crown. The reasons for the King's edict are the same reasons that today's old house restorers prize antique heart pine: it's strong and it's beautiful. Yet it's not always easy to find. The Joinery Company's straightened, re-milled heart-pine flooring is among the best to be found anywhere. It is available in five grades. Prime grade wood may be square-edged or tongue-and-groove and is ninety-five to one hundred percent heartwood. Available in 1" or 1¼" thicknesses, it comes in 3' to 16' lengths and random widths ranging from 3" to 12". The company's quartersawn and clear grades also come in 1" and 1¼" thicknesses and 3' and 16' lengths. Both have tongue-and-groove profiles and random widths of 4" to 7". The quarter-sawn wood is new, not antique; the clear grade contains only wood without knots or imperfections. The antique resawn pine has square edges and a thickness of 7/16". It's precisely milled and requires little cutting or sanding. Available in 2' to 8' lengths, its widths range from 3" to 7½".

The Joinery Company also sells wood in an antique original grade. The bottom and sides are re-milled for uniformity, but the top is merely cleaned and its surface left intact. The availability of the wood in this grade varies. The company is happy to give advice about installation and finishing for any of its flooring.

Brochure, $5.

The Joinery Co.
Department OHC
Box 518
Tarboro, NC 27886
(919) 823-3306

Kentucky Wood Floors

Kentucky offers several types of ready-to-install wood floors as well as custom flooring. Its solid plank floors are available in random or specified widths with either bevelled or square edges. Plugs of matching or contrasting wood are also available. The firm's pre-finished parquet is sealed and finished with either wax or polyurethane. The squares glue

down for easy installation. For more affordable parquet flooring, Kentucky sells unfinished parquet which the do-it-yourselfer can sand and finish on site. Kentucky flooring is available in a variety of woods, including oak, walnut, cherry, teak, and ash. Shown here is the firm's award-winning Citation pattern in burl and figured walnut with oak pickets.

Catalogue, $2.

Kentucky Wood Floors
4200 Reservoir Ave.
Louisville, KY 40213
(502) 451-6024

Moravian Pottery and Tile

In 1900, Henry Chapman Mercer founded the Moravian Pottery and Tile Works in an attempt to safeguard what he saw as a special American art form from the obsolescence threatened by assembly-line techniques. Tiles produced by Moravian craftsmen today use methods approximating Mercer's own: all are hand formed and coal-fired, guaranteeing that no two will ever be exactly alike. Glazes are mixed according to Mercer's original formulas. Among the various offerings of Moravian Pottery and Tile are quarry tile patterns ranging from 2¾" square to 4" square; a choice of cornices and borders, and countless decorative tiles, measuring 4" square, which can be arranged in any pattern you choose.

Catalogue, $4.

Moravian Pottery and Tile Works
Swamp Rd.
Doylestown, PA 18901
(215) 345-6722

Mountain Lumber

Mountain Lumber specializes in reclaiming prized heart-pine walls and flooring, some of it several centuries old, from historic buildings that are no longer habitable. The firm's selection of flooring includes both prime- and cabin-grade planks. Prime grade, quarter-sawn and knot-free, comes in a variety of sizes. Each plank is guaranteed to be at least 97 percent heartwood. The rustic look of cabin-grade wood includes hairline cracks, large knots, and greater grain variations. Mountain Lumber kiln dries each piece to reveal cracked or warped wood; all defective planks are discarded, insuring high quality.

Brochure available.

Mountain Lumber Co.
Rte. 2, Box 43-1
Ruckersville, VA 22968
(804) 985-3646 or
(804) 295-1922

Saxe Patterson

Geometry is somehow more appealing in Saxe Patterson's stoneware tiles than it ever was in the textbook. A sampling of patterns includes the smooth arcs of the raindrop (Gota) design, the rhombuses that alternately seem to form stars or baby's blocks, and the patented Penrose Parallelogram (random or regularly organized). The possibilities for interlocking rhombuses, squares, triangles, and hexagons are virtually unlimited.

Saxe Patterson creates its own glazes. Matte finishes in subdued colors like salmon, gray, and apricot are especially appropriate for high-traffic areas.

Brochure available.

Saxe Patterson
Box 15
Salazar Rd.
Taos, NM 87571
(505) 758-9513

Rising & Nelson

In 1869, Simeon M. Rising III and Camillus H. Nelson became partners in acquiring a slate quarry. The company's early advertisements extolled the merits of the slate they extracted—noncombustible, waterproof, durable, easy to maintain and available in an array of colors. Those qualities hold to this day. Natural slate comes in thicknesses of ¼" to 1" and has a non-slip texture unchanged by water or wax. Rising & Nelson cuts its slate in rectangles and squares, and in random patterns. The natural colors of the stone include purple, gray, green, mottled green/purple, and red.

Brochure available.

Rising & Nelson Slate Co., Inc.
West Pawlet, VT 05775
(802) 645-0150

Robinson Lumber

Rich, clear, antique longleaf heart pine is prized for its warm beauty. Robinson Lumber converts timbers saved from old warehouses into several grades of flooring. The highest quality is 95% heartwood, mostly quarter sawn, admitting just a scattering of tiny knots and a rare nail hole. "Rustic" boards have more sapwood, knots, and some nail holes. "Nail hole grade wood" comes from the outer layers of the antique lumber. Stair tread is also offered.

Brochure available.

Robinson Lumber Co., Inc.
Ste. 202
512 S. Peters St.
New Orleans, LA 70130
(504) 523-6377 or
(504) 523-6370

Vermont Cobble Slate

Weathered for decades in the roofs of old buildings and subsequently salvaged, Vermont Cobble Slate's antique tiles have acquired rich brown and buff colors. The old slate is cleaned and brushed by the company's staff and hand-cut to one of two different thicknesses. Flooring tiles are ¼" thick and are attractive anywhere in the house, but perhaps especially useful on the hearth or greenhouse floor. Veneer is ³⁄₁₆" thick and is designed for walls, countertops, and shower stalls.

Standard colors are green, gray, brown, purple, and black. The slate is shipped in random sizes and colors, although the company will do its best to obtain special colors or to cut custom sizes. Slate floors may be left untreated and washed with soap and water, but if you want a darker color, you can finish the slate with stone or slate sealer, polyurethane, or a mixture of one part linseed oil to two parts turpentine.

Literature available.

Vermont Cobble Slate
Smid Inc.
Sudbury, VT 05733
(802) 247-8809

Vintage Lumber

Vintage Lumber offers antique boards of American chestnut, oak, southern longleaf heart pine, and white pine, and newly milled cherry, oak, poplar, walnut, and white pine—any of which can be transformed into handsome tongue-and-groove flooring. The firm salvages wood from 19th-century buildings, removes nails, saws and kiln dries the planks, and then mills them. A wide range of lengths and widths is offered.

Literature available.

Vintage Lumber
9507 Woodsboro Rd.
Frederick, MD 21701
(301) 898-7859

Floor Coverings

Canvas Carpets

Popular in New England throughout the 18th century and until the mid-19th century, canvas floorcloths were known as "poor people's rugs." The qualities that made them practical then still apply today. Inexpensive, they are made of long-lasting, finely woven heavy cotton canvas. Once they have been stenciled with traditional or contemporary designs, they are varnished to a flat, satin, or gloss finish and are easy to maintain, requiring only periodic waxing and damp mop-

ping. Canvas tape or a thin non-skid pad will keep the floorcloths from slipping.

Marilyn Orner, the owner of Canvas Carpets, welcomes orders for custom sizes, designs, and colors. She also offers a number of standard floorcloth designs, including the intriguing Russian Block, shown here. It is based on a folk-

art pattern. Her Diamond Squares design is typical of the attempts of early floorcloth makers to imitate expensive parquet, tile, or, as in this case, marble. Orner offers ten standard background colors, including cream, deep blue, Turkish red, rosetone pink beige, light gray, and lilac, along with twelve stock sizes.

Catalogue, $1.

Canvas Carpets
Box 26
S. Egremont, MA 01258
(413) 528-4267

Folkheart Rag Rugs

Pure, pre-shrunk cotton, woven by hand in the Amish tradition, is used for Folkheart's hand-stenciled rugs. Heat-set fabric paint decorates the rugs with rustic silhouettes of horses, apples, baskets, tulips, and hearts.

Order a standard design, in stock rug sizes of 3' by 5', 2' by 4', or 2' by 3'. Or specify a larger pieced rug, of cotton and wool, custom stenciled and dyed to match any decor. Folkheart's rugs clean easily—machine wash in cold water, or dry clean.

Brochure, $1.

Folkheart Rag Rugs
18 Main St.
Bristol, VT 05443
(802) 453-4101

Good & Co.

Good & Co.'s floorcloths, decorated with coats of high-quality oil paint and varnish on heavy, wrinkle-free canvas, are durable and easy to clean, making them especially attractive for high-traffic areas.

A range of designs, attractively executed on the matte surface, includes a flower and feather pattern that mimics a hooked rug. The more stylized "Mont Vernon" shows a braided design framing diagonal rows of teardrops and diamonds. The checkerboard patterns, crisp and clear, are simple classics.

Good & Co. makes floorcloths in custom sizes and matches colors to your fabric, paint chips, or wallpaper. Order these tough, colorful cloths for rooms, halls, or staircases.

Catalogue available.

Good & Co.
Salzburg Sq.
Rte. 101
Amherst, NH 03031
(603) 672-0490

Import Specialists

Woven cotton rugs are just some of the folk art reproductions available from Import Specialists. The pastel blocks and stripes of the Tacoma rope weave rug or the regular green and red squares in a Spingfield twill can enrich a variety of decors. Old-fashioned cotton stencil rugs in a Texas Star design, an orderly Lincoln Log pattern, showing a weathervane with cantering horse, or edged with a parade of duck decoys, are guaranteed brighteners for any

room. Tough and attractive woven squares of rice straw, maize, and seagrass come in a range of sizes to cover any space in comfortable natural fiber.

For information on local distributors, contact:

Import Specialists Inc.
82 Wall St.
New York, NY 10005
(800) 334-4044
(212) 709-9633 (NY)

Linoleum City

Tough, colorful linoleum may be just the thing for your period home. Linoleum City imports such flooring from Taiwan, Japan, Portugal, and other parts of Europe. Selections range from cork floor tiles and traditional marbleized battleship linoleum to solid-color linoleum with a smooth surface or sheet vinyl in black-and-white, blue-and-white, or red-and-white checks. Solid,

⅛"-thick vinyl or asphalt tile comes in different colors and in 9" or 12" squares. Graining and color tend to vary, so ask for a sample of your particular favorite before placing an order.

Samples sent upon request.

Linoleum City
5657 Santa Monica Blvd.
Hollywood, CA 90038
(213) 469-0063

Scalamandré

This firm's extraordinary collection of 19th-century reproduction carpets was described at length in previous *Catalogues*. They have been used in restorations from coast to coast. The Wiltons are made in England, and the ingrains at Scalamandré's own Long Island City mill. These designs—all documented meticulously—can be seen in such places as Independence Hall, the Smithsonian Institution, and the Metropolitan Museum.

Scalamandré products are available only through interior designers or the design department of select retail outlets. For information on such sources, contact Scalamandré.

Scalamandré Silks, Inc.
950 Third Avenue
New York, NY 10022
(212) 980-3888

Victorian Collectibles

Four designs from the Brillion Collection of wallpapers have been adapted into rug patterns by Victorian Collectibles. This one, called Nouveau Fleur, is taken from a 9" border paper. Hand-woven from pure wool, it is executed in several shades of blue and rose with a cream-colored background. A similar style features poppies in red and green on an open field of brick red.

Two Victorian-style rugs are also available. One has a border of lavender and blue grapes surrounded by bands of moss green, wine, and brown. The background is cream, and the border colors are echoed in a center medallion. East Lake Victorian Frosted Lily combines rose tones, soft blues, deep reds, and golds in a floral border and center medallion.

Two standard sizes are sold: 6' by 9' and 9' by 12'. Custom colors are available to match your decor.

Brochure, $2.

Victorian Collectibles Ltd.
845 E. Glenbrook Rd.
Milwaukee, WI 53217
(414) 352-6910

Other Suppliers of Floors and Floor Coverings

Consult List of Suppliers for addresses.

Flooring

The Canal Co.
Central Kentucky Millwork Inc.
Whit Hanks
Jerard Paul Jordan
Maurer & Shepherd Joyners Inc.
M.J. May Antique Building
   Restoration
New York Marble Works

Floor Coverings

The Canal Co.
Partridge Replications
Schumacher

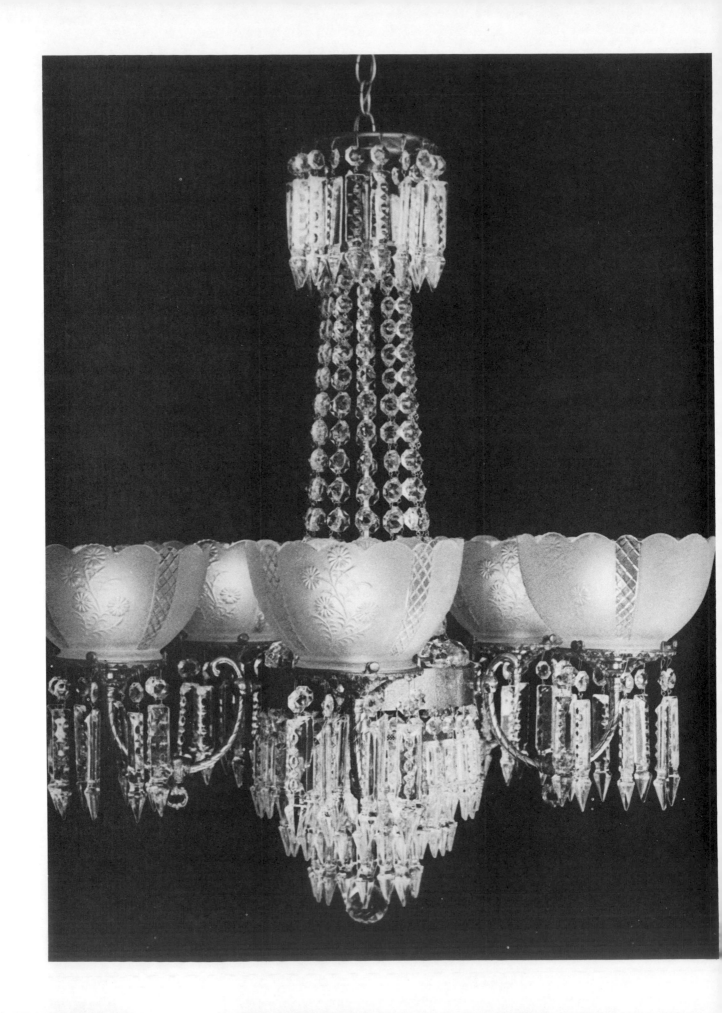

4.

Lighting

Period lighting devices used today are almost all reproductions. And why not? The attempt to regress to the technological dark age is absurd, a false type of historicity. And old fixtures—intended for candles, whale oil, benzene, kerosene, gas—are copied so well that they blend without trouble into almost any period setting.

Antique fixtures *are* still available and the majority of them are converted for electrical usage. As in the field of antique clocks, however, there is a great deal of parts switching. A completely original lighting fixture is a rarity indeed. Anyone seeking such a device—of almost any vintage or style—should buy from only a very well-established dealer.

The reproduction lighting industry is well established and is perhaps the largest of the crafts in the old house field. There are wood, brass, tin, and crystal chandeliers galore; this form remains the most glamorous of all. Lanterns, both for indoor and outdoor use, are very popular period appointments. Painted glass Victorian hanging lamps and Tiffany-style fixtures have also gained popularity. Unfortunately, the level of quality achieved in this last area is abysmally low. What may be appropriate for a roadside fast food parlor or steakhouse is not suitable for most period homes or offices.

The fixtures that we find the most pleasing and interesting for period rooms are those affixed to a wall. There are sconces and wall fixtures of all sorts to choose from. Beware, however, of the "solid" brass which is paper thin and the Taiwanese glass shade which has all the glow of a dead mackerel. Avoid, if you can, running cords down the wall or using any swag-like contraptions. Lighting wall areas can be a pleasant, indirect means of illuminating a room. Wall lamps can't be used for reading, of course, but that is why table and floor lamps exist.

If natural gas is abundant in your area, you may wish to make use of this source for at least some lighting fixtures. Gas provides a pleasant, and as used today, a very safe means of illumination. It is, of course, increasingly employed outdoors in historic neighborhoods. All of the early fixtures that one could possibly use for gas alone or combined with electricity—as they were for several decades—can be had in reproduction form today.

The Charleston, a six-light brass and Venetian crystal gasolier, by King's Chandelier Co., Eden, North Carolina.

Chandeliers

A chandelier can be an object of ostentatious showmanship or a silent testament to good taste. The key to both is an unerring sense of correctness and of scale. Before selecting what's right for your living room or parlor, study both the architectural style of your house and the proportions of the room. A late-Victorian gasolier, obviously, looks preposterous in a Georgian room; and a fixture designed for a ballroom would be all but suffocating in a small sitting room. The suppliers that follow stock handsome antiques or handcraft reproductions of museum pieces of virtually every style covering a 250-year period.

A.J.P., Coppersmith

Anthony J. Pietrafitta (A.J.P.) began crafting lighting fixtures almost half a century ago, and the Boston showroom of A.J.P., Coppersmith & Co. continues his work today. The firm brings tradition that dates from the birth of the state of Virginia alive in the present. Polished brass against handblown crystal, the Virginian lights a foyer with three branches. Measuring 15" wide and 28" from finial to finial, this unusual hanging fixture is topped with a crystal canopy and includes a 22" matching chain.

Catalogue available.

A.J.P., Coppersmith & Co.
34 Broadway
Wakefield, MA 01880
(617) 245-1223

Art Directions

In the opulence of brass, bronze, and crystal, Art Directions brings you restored and reproduced lighting fixtures gathered throughout the United States. Among its many offerings is a set of antique iron chandeliers (diameters range from 15" to 40") with art glass shades and inserts around slim iron patterning—diamond-shaped badges that ring these fixtures. Tiny, round bulbs

stud another chandelier, this one brass and brass-plated iron, trimmed with small, curving leaves.

The firm's St. Louis showroom displays it all, and inquiries will earn you a place on the mailing list.

Catalogue available.

Art Directions
6120 Delmar Blvd.
St. Louis, MO 63112
(314) 863-1895

Authentic Designs

Authentic Designs celebrates the wedding of solid Vermont maple and unalloyed brass, cut, bent, shaped, and hand turned according to the processes used by colonial and early American craftsmen. Made-to-order fixtures include a wide range of exquisite chandeliers. Two ranks of candles cluster around a smoothly flowing and lipped wood turned center.

The five branches of a simpler fixture dip at sharp angles from a near-spherical center. Bare elegance, ten separate tapers, molded to resemble those used in colonial times, form a ring around a stylized center.

Maple pieces receive a brown stain—or voice your own preference. Hand-rubbed paste wax protects the stain. Pick any paint, if you like, and Authentic Designs will apply it and a coat of antique glaze and grain. Brass parts arrive burnished and unlacquered to gain a patina of age, halted at the desired point by a simple coating of paste wax. If you like, select pewter or gunmetal plating, or choose the bright lacquered finish.

Catalogue, $3.

Authentic Designs
The Mill Rd.
West Rupert, VT 05776-0011
(802) 394-7713

Authentic Lighting

The circa 1910 solid-brass reproduction of an ornate chandelier with electric porcelain candles is just one of Authentic Lighting's fine products. The firm boasts an extensive selection of high-quality reproduction lighting. Although no catalogues are available, Authentic Lighting welcomes specific requests accom-

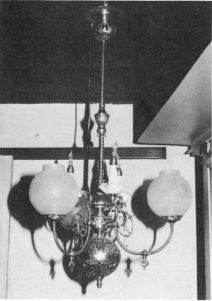

panying pictures, blue-prints, or other guides to aid them in assisting you.

Authentic Lighting
558 Grand Ave.
Englewood, NJ 07631
(201) 568-7429

Brass Light Gallery

Simple and graceful, the Sun Prairie (model 751) and the Oak Park (model 758) are part of the Goldenrod Collection of solid-brass Mission/Prairie-style light fixtures which promises to be expanded soon to include at least ten more pieces. The Sun Prairie chandelier, based on a 1910 design, has two lights with straight-edged glass shades and is

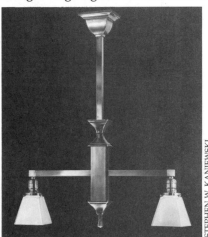

STEPHEN W. KANIEWSKI

STEPHEN W. KANIEWSKI

available in 18", 27", and 33" lengths. The Oak Park has four lights with curved-edged shades and may be 28" or 35" long. Both chandeliers are 22" wide when the glass shades, which are included with the fixture, are in place. Both are also available in satin antique or nickel-plated chrome finishes.

Brochure, $2.

Brass Light Gallery
719 S. 5th St.
Dept. 5
Milwaukee, WI 53204
(414) 383-0675

Brasslight

The clamor for class—lighting fixtures to suit the most stately of period homes—sparked Brasslight's production of singular, first-rate items almost fifteen years ago. Demand only increases for the firm's solid-brass chandeliers, and Brasslight has expanded its range, proffering a limited number of its best-loved styles.

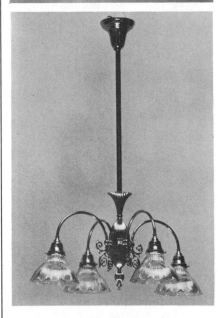

The 40" by 34" Caledonia's spiraling design of either four or six arms is set off by handsome floral print shades, both gas and electric. The four-armed Brookfield, 38" by 31", has a smooth-ribbed body crowned by a fountain spray of brass. Ruffled holophane shades complete the dazzling effect. The Turnhouse, five arms

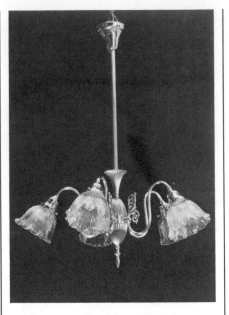

with steep, double arches, is more compact, 37" high and spanning just 26", but includes fancy ornamentation that makes it an uncommon centerpiece for a period room. All Brasslight fixtures are polished and lacquered, or can be left to darken naturally.

Catalogue, $3.

Brasslight, Inc.
90 Main St.
Nyack, NY 10960
(914) 353-0567

City Lights

Order the catalogue as a guide, imagine the lighting fixtures you'd love to own, and send a request to

City Lights. City Lights helps satisfy specific requests by sending Polaroids ($3. per photo) of its antique items, like the various gas and electric fixtures in its collection. City Lights has wired the original gas units of these turn-of-the-century pieces for electricity. The six-light fixture (24" wide, with a minimum length of 24") shows abundant coils and scrolls across its surface, with finials at every possible point. Ribbed loops and plentiful filagree distinguish the complicated eight-light fixture, and shades of antique etched glass accent both. Most of City Lights' antique fixtures are solid brass, polished and lacquered.

Ask about these beauties, or request the one that's "exactly right" for your home.

Catalogue available.

City Lights
2226 Massachusetts Ave.
Cambridge, MA 02140
(617) 547-1490

Classic Illuminations

Handcrafted reproduction lighting fixtures from Classic Illumination come with a stamp of approval from Underwriters Laboratories, Inc., and a tradition of fine work behind them. A six-armed American Victorian gasolier (30" by 30"), comes alive in solid brass

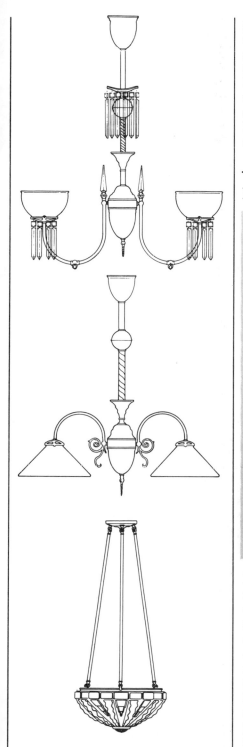

glass to illumine the room. An assortment of finishes includes glossy polished brass, polished and lacquered brass, lacquered brass plating, lacquer over slightly darkened brass, lacquer over deeply darkened brass, blackened brass with a lacquer coat, and chrome-plated brass.

Brochure available.

Classic Illumination Inc.
2743 9th St.
Berkeley, CA 94710
(415) 849-1842

Hammerworks

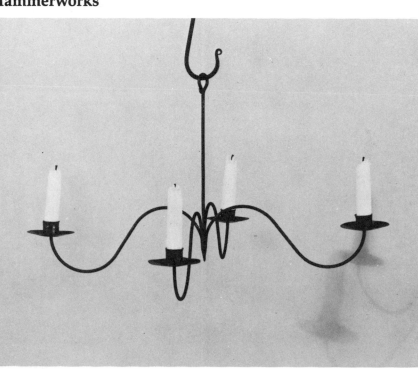

If your taste in chandeliers runs more to the primitive than to the ornate, Hammerworks has several models with smooth, simple designs. Some have only two arms, while others have four, five, or six. The model shown here (CH104I) has a gray-black antique iron finish. It can be designed to accommodate either electric power or wax candles and is ideal for an 18th-century room.

All Hammerworks pieces are hand-crafted by the company's tinsmiths and blacksmiths, and all the electrical parts are U.L. ap-

proved. Prices include bulbs, candles, and chimneys. Hand-spun brass or 7"mercury reflectors are available for the firm's sconces. Hammerworks also makes lanterns and other hanging fixtures. Although all are made with clear glass, seedy glass can be substituted at an extra charge.

Catalogue, $3.

Hammerworks
75 Webster St.
Worcester, MA 01603
(617) 755-3434

and prisms and spears of crystal. A less formal electric chandelier (30" by 30"), modeled on a turn-of-the-century fixture, sheds light on a tabletop and spreads a glow throughout the room. Or select the dish chandelier, so typical of the early 1920s but increasingly difficult to locate. With a classic revival shade suspended from three stems, this elegant, enclosed fixture shines through opaque

King's Chandelier

The King family has been designing and building their elaborate crystal chandeliers, sconces, and candelabra for three generations,

and the pieces pictured here are only a small sampling. The two Charleston models (10+5 and 6S) have decorative gas cocks on the

98

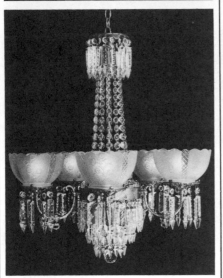

Brochure, $2.

King's Chandelier Co.
Dept. OHC-1
Eden, NC 27288
(919) 623-6188

M-H Lamp & Fan

This lovely reproduction of an early twentieth-century electric pendant comes with the pressed glass center bowl and three bell-shaped shades shown here. The metal parts, with the exception of the chain, are solid polished lacquered brass. The fixture measures 22½″ in diameter with a standard length of 27″ and a

arms for authenticity, frosted etched shades, and Venetian spear-point crystal prisms and buttons. The 10+5 is a fifteen-light fixture that measures 46″ wide and 50″ long; the 6S is 26″ wide and 29″ long.

The other two fixtures shown are part of King's series of chandeliers made of costly Strass crystal. The six-light model (Strass 6-R-8) has a standard and bobeches of leaded crystal and hanging drops of Austrian Strass. It is 22″ wide and 30″ long. The eighteen-light Schonbrunn is 44″ wide and 60″ long; all its crystals are Strass. It has stunning twisted rope crystal arms and is available in solid brass, although King's recommends a silver finish to enhance the beauty of the crystal.

For extra length, all chandeliers come with a foot of steel chain; additional chain may be ordered at a nominal cost. All the crystal in King's chandeliers is imported; the metal used in the U.L.-approved fixtures is available with brass plate or what the company calls a "silvery" finish created by nickel or chrome plating. The lights are electric and designed to be installed into a standard-size ceiling outlet, but any of them can be designed to accommodate candles at no extra charge. Hurricane shades or candelabra tapers (shown on the Strass 6-R-8) are available, although one may cost more than another on some models. Durward F. King, the manager, recommends a visit to his store to appreciate the full beauty of these fixtures and to see some of the unique pieces not featured in the catalogue.

minimum length of 18″. More chain can be ordered at a slight additional cost. Up to 60-watt bulbs can be used in this fixture and the many other reproductions made by M-H Lamp & Fan using methods of production developed before the turn of the century.

Catalogue, $3.

M-H Lamp & Fan Co.
7231½ N. Sheridan Rd.
Chicago, IL 60626
(312) 743-2225

Nowell's

Nowell's dares you to stroll through San Francisco's de Young Museum, the Haas-Lilenthal or the Louise Boyd Mansion, and to distinguish its elegant reproductions from the antiques it restores.

The Pacific Club chandelier is a

faithful copy of a native San Francisco Victorian fixture. Exquisitely scrolled details and ruffled glass bells enhance this fixture, available at a standard height of 42" (minimum height, 36"), 36" wide. The Embarcadero, a modern version of another Victorian fixture, is resplendent with twelve intricately patterned globes that light a grand room. At least

54" high, it is generally built to reach 60", and it spans 70", glass included. Both chandeliers allow the choice of a polished, lacquered, or antique finish. Many parts of these lighting fixtures interchange, and Nowell's welcomes specific requests and pictures.

Catalogue, $3.50

Nowell's, Inc.
490 Gate 5 Rd.
Sausalito, CA 94965
(415) 332-4933

Period Lighting Fixtures

As Period Lighting Fixtures points out, lighting has made rapid and beautiful progress after 3000 years of torches, grease lamps, and firebaskets. Among its many fine reproductions in tin and iron, Period Lighting Fixtures includes an eight- or ten-branch chandelier with a smooth, tubular center and delicately fluted bobeches.

All Period Lighting chandeliers come in pewter, aged tin, or painted or distressed tin finishes. Hand-dripped sheaths hide sockets, and wires are concealed within the fixtures. The chandeliers can be electrified or made for candles only. They are indispensable in 18th- or early-19th-century rooms.

Catalogue, $3.

Period Lighting Fixtures
1 Main St.
Chester, CT 06412
(203) 526-3690

Price Glover

The fine, the few—Price Glover imports select English reproduction lighting fixtures. 18th- and 19th-century styles are meticulously cast, finished by hand.

An eight-branch brass chandelier features an uncommon centerpiece with waves of gadrooning. A dove with outspread wings can rest on the 33½" by 35" fixture, or the chandelier can be requested unadorned for simpler tastes. Price Glover sconces and chandeliers may be lacquered if you wish. Although the fixtures are equipped to use candles, you may request that they be wired for electricity.

Brochure, $1.50.

Price Glover, Inc.
817½ Madison Ave.
New York, NY 10021
(212) 772-1740

Rejuvenation House Parts

Lighting fixtures made by Rejuvenation House Parts are often selected for restoration projects, and a look at these chandeliers explains why. Model CV4E (the Irvington) is a four-arm pool table light, also available with two or three arms. When the shades are in place it measures 26" in diameter, with a standard length of 40" and a minimum length of 19". Model CY4E (the Wilshire), also available in a two-armed version, is part of Rejuvenation's new Craftsman Collection, a group of replicas of early 20th-century

Mission-style fixtures noted for their authenticity. It measures 22" in diameter with a standard length of 36" and a minimum length of 20". The shades are sandblasted on the interior.

Both fixtures are made of solid polished brass, which can be lacquered on request. Rejuvenation warns that although lacquer preserves the shine, it can yellow and deteriorate, in which case stripping, polishing, and relacquering will be necessary. If left

unlacquered, the brass will acquire its own patina—just be sure to wipe it with brass polish after installation to remove fingerprints, and the piece can be spray-lacquered at any point during aging. Both fixtures take 60-watt bulbs and are U.L. listed.

Catalogue, $3. Craftsman Collection brochure available.

Rejuvenation House Parts
901 N. Skidmore
Portland, OR 97217
(503) 249-0774

Roy Electric

Advertising "fixture art in its finest form," Roy Electric has spent twenty years collecting,

restoring, and reproducing lighting fixtures from a rich historical past. In the Roy

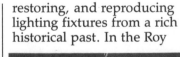

showroom, an imposing reproduction chandelier extends its two tiers of bulbs to illumine with elegance. A more angular chandelier has three layers—four bulbs each—that alternately aim downwards, up, and down again to fill a room with light. Yet another gorgeous piece spills light to the floor in a wide, looped platform of thirteen separate bulbs. Pure brass, silver soldered, fitted with superior wiring, polished, and lacquered by hand—every

lighting fixture here has the ingredients of high quality. Fixture sizes vary according to specification, and shafts, arms, and central supports are available in plain, reeded, or ribbed styles.

Catalogue, $3.

Roy Electric Co., Inc.
1054 Coney Island Ave.
Brooklyn, NY 11230
(718) 339-6311 or
(718) 761-7905

(darkening occurs without hand polishing), or antiqued and lacquered (patinaed, with satiny highlights).

Catalogue, $3.

Victorian Lightcrafters Ltd.
Box 350
Slate Hill, NY 10973
(914) 355-1300

Lt. Moses Willard

Lt. Moses Willard uses many of the same forms and tools whitesmiths used two centuries ago to produce fixtures that are still beautiful and of high quality, and are often endearingly uncommon. Among chandeliers with wood center turnings of carved pineapples, strawberries, acorns, or apples, as well as less whimsical designs, there is the Santa/Animal chandelier. During the year, tin animals—cow, hen, horse, lamb, pig, and rooster—circle the center. At Christmastime, three trees and three Santas replace them for more festive decor. Lt. Moses Willard offers a spectrum of painted finishes for wooden elements of the lighting fixture. Stained finishes include light distressed pine and medium walnut. On metal parts, the firm

Victorian Lightcrafters

The president of Victorian Lightcrafters, Ltd. pledges never to ship anything he wouldn't want to use in his own home. Crafted-to-order, cast, spun, and stamped from solid brass, superb lighting fixtures result.

Beautiful brass traceries ornament a gasolier, available with two, three, or four arms. Length ranges from 30" to 58"; width is a standard 28". In another Victorian Lightcrafter reproduction, opalescent teardrop shades highlight an electric chandelier with curving tendrils of brass joining each of two to six arms to the central ball.

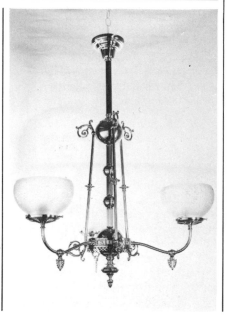

recommends the dark, artificial rusting of a distressed tin finish. Antique tin and natural pewter finishes are also available.

Set of catalogues, $2.
Color chart, $1.50.

Samples of tin finishes, $1.

Lt. Moses Willard, Inc.
1156 U.S. 50
Milford, OH 45150
(513) 831-8956

Catalogue available.

Art Directions
6120 Delmar Blvd.
St. Louis, MO 63112
(314) 863-1895

Hanging and Ceiling Fixtures

Generally less ambitious in design than chandeliers, hanging lamps are ideal choices for dim hallways or smaller rooms where multibracketed chandeliers would be overwhelming. Ceiling fixtures, of course, are good selections for low-ceilinged rooms. Yet their more utilitarian nature is not an excuse for inferior design and workmanship, since there are handsome, well-made reproductions available to complement any decor.

Art Directions

Art Directions offers "lighting to build a room around." Genuine antiques or reproductions with authenticity on any scale, masterworks often of brass, bronze, and crystal, they complement residences and commercial areas with uncommon grace. Two of Art Directions' more unusual Art Deco hanging fixtures are an aluminum, copper, and brass spun rim reproduction with a wide, luminous dome of glass, 28" in diameter, with a 42" drop; and a custom spun-aluminum reproduction with circle upon circle of gleaming metal.

Classic Illumination

Classic Illumination can provide you with reproduction lighting fixtures in almost any style. Model 1921-1, a pan fixture with a dish shade (not included), is 8" high and 12" in diameter; the shade has a panel design on the bottom and a ribbed rim interrupted with sprigs of foliage. The metal is solid brass, available in four finishes—polished, polished and lacquered, darkened with acid and lacquered, and chromium plated. Available in the same finishes, model 1922-1 is an inverted ceiling fixture which hangs from a gentle brass curve and which can be fitted with a

variety of ribbed dome, bell, and cone-shaped shades. It is 13" high and 12" in diameter. Model 1924-1 comes with an unusual fish shade and measures 14" high and 13" in

diameter. It is not available in chromium plate. Representative of Classic Illumination's Art Deco-inspired fixtures is model 1936-1, 12½" high and 12" in diameter,

which includes an etched geometric shade.

Brochure available.

Classic Illumination, Inc.
2743 9th St.
Berkeley, CA 94710
(415) 849-1842

Price Glover

Price Glover imports a select number of antique English fixtures in pure brass. An 18th-century hanging lantern, scrupulously reproduced, reveals a single candle encased in hand-blown glass with folded edges. Beaded details show off the molded brass fittings. The chain adjusts the height of this fixture, which is

available in 22" or 27" sizes with corresponding smoke bells of 8½" or 12".

Brochure, $1.50.

Price Glover, Inc.
817½ Madison Ave.
New York, NY 10021
(212) 772-1740

Washington Copper Works

Call proprietor Serge Miller for directions and take the pretty drive through the Berkshire foothills to visit the Washington Copper Works. Do call—Miller explains that he and his apprentice "are often out at craft fairs, doing our daily running, or just 'gone fishing.'" The planning pays off when you get to choose from the Washington Copper Works' superb fixtures. The slender Santa Fe has two racks of four candles each. Open and airy, with a framework of narrow bars and no bottom, it illuminates a stairwell beautifully. An exercise in appealingly simple geometry, another hanging fixture is a hand-wrought hollow cube of copper around a perfectly spherical bulb, all roofed by a tent of triangles. A compact octagonal ceiling fixture shines

down, reflecting light from its own copper panels, and allows a glow through side-sections of specially treated opaque glass. The Washington Copper Works' hanging fixtures, generally used indoors, may be weatherproofed to withstand outdoor use. Fixtures come unshined, "clean and ready to age." The Washington Copper Works recommends two finishes: either untreated or stained copper.

Catalogue, $3 (refundable with any order).

The Washington Copper Works
South St.
Washington, CT 06793
(203) 868-7527

Lt. Moses Willard

Early Colonial, 18th century, and Williamsburg tin reproductions, both handsome and useful, attract admiring approval, executed by Lt. Moses Willard with excellence in mind, using many of the same tools workmen gripped 200 years ago.

Four candles glow in a hanging hall fixture, 15" high by 9" wide. Simple angles and arcs, suspended from a circle of tin, the fixture

shows the contrast of styles available from Lt. Moses Willard, maker of sophisticated crimped, pierced, and patterned lights as well. The final touch on pieces like these is a finish of natural pewter; dark, old distressed tin; or antique tin.

Set of Catalogues, $2.
Color chart, $1.50.
Samples of tin finishes, $1.

Lt. Moses Willard, Inc.
1156 U.S. 50
Milford, OH 45150
(513) 831-8956

rooms, as does many of the firm's wall fixtures. All A.J.P. sconces come in finishes of antique copper, antique brass, or terne, a satiny lead-coated steel that looks and darkens like antique tin, yet won't rust.

Catalogue available.

A.J.P. Coppersmith & Co.
34 Broadway
Wakefield, MA 01880
(617) 245-1223

Authentic Designs

Along a backroad stretch in southwest Vermont stands a re-constructed mill where the craftsmen of Authentic Design re-create light fixtures with scrupulous attention to colonial and early American models. A single-candle wall sconce of unmistakably high quality has a tulip shaped mount,

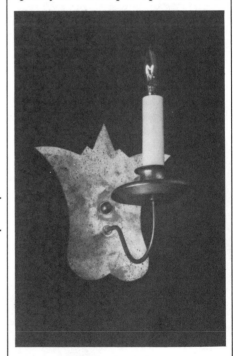

a rounded bottom that wells up to crest in five graceful points. This fixture, 7½" high by 7" wide by 7" deep, and other equally distinctive creations come hand burnished and unlacquered, with instructions simply to coat with paste wax when a pleasingly deep patina has darkened. Other options for Authentic Designs' many sconces include blue-black gun metal plating or the traditional polished shine with lacquer.

Sconces

These simple wall fixtures provide a pleasant source of light in hallways, above fireplaces, or in the dining room above a sideboard. Most common are the flat tin candleholders that do not project very far from the surface of the wall. These are most often found with straight or crimped brackets which serve as reflectors of the light and deflect the heat from the wall itself. Sconces can also be rather elaborately designed. The type to be used depends on the basic decor of the room in which it is to be used. Most reproduction sconces are fitted as electric fixtures. They can be ordered, however, as plain candle-burning pieces.

A.J.P., Coppersmith

Colonial craftsmen stuck shards of mirror together with mud and reflected candles in them for a dazzle of light indoors. A.J.P., Coppersmith, recasts their ingenuity in modern times with electricity or the original wax candle against a backing of fitted mirror panels for unusual sconces, 10½" tall and 7¾" wide. Crimped mirror sconces, 12½" by 5", have graceful pressed arches and a pattern of crisscrossed ribs against mirrored backings. A 17" by 12" oval ballroom sconce diffuses light throughout large

Catalogue, $3.

Authentic Designs
The Mill Rd.
West Rupert, VT 05776-0011
(802) 394-7713

The Brass Knob

The Brass Knob displays architectural antiques from the country's capital, often with their own particular historical tales. Among marble, ironwork, stained glass, and hand-carved wood, The Brass Knob also stocks brass hardware and solid-brass lighting fixtures.

Typical of the firm's antiques is a double-candle wall sconce with a medallion mount, beaded along the rim, a floral center, and a plume on top. Another wall fixture hangs from a classic circular mount, its bulb shaded by several draped petals of glass.

The Brass Knob supplies consultants for installation, planning, and design. Although no catalogue lists the constantly changing inventory, the Brass Knob is glad to respond to written requests or photographs.

The Brass Knob
2309 18th St. N.W.
Washington, D.C. 20009
(202) 332-3370

Brasslight

Since 1972, Brasslight has been producing excellent pieces such as the oval sconce pictured here.

This model has a 4″ by 6″ wall plate and is 7″ deep, with a turn knob socket and holophane shade. It can accommodate up to 60 watts. Brasslight makes a variety of both single- and double-armed sconces with hand-blown shades; all shades are installed facing downward unless otherwise specified. All Brasslight fixtures are made of solid polished lacquered brass. Variations in the finish will be made for an additional fee. Brasslight accepts custom orders.

Catalogue, $3.

Brasslight, Inc.
90 Main St.
Nyack, NY 10960
(914) 353-0567

City Lights

One-of-a-kind antique lighting fixtures is the City Lights specialty, and virtually every fixture shows this firm's potential for providing the unusual. For example, the double-swinging gas wall light shifts and extends, a splendid way to pan light into a room—luxurious lighting over the pages of a good book. Seven inches high, extending a full 24″ from its wall mounting, this antique dates from just before the turn of the century and is representative of

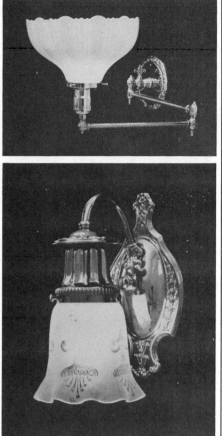

the high-caliber selections at City Lights. Solid brass, polished and lacquered, the fixtures from City Lights have been completely rewired or converted from gas, and come with original period glass shades from a warehouse selection of over one thousand choices.

Catalogue available.

City Lights
2226 Massachusetts Ave.
Cambridge, MA 02140
(617) 547-1490

Classic Illumination

Several unusual wall fixtures can be obtained from Classic Illumination. Model 1935-1 is a Deco-inspired sconce and would be appropriate in either contemporary or traditional homes. The shade ripples gently outward to a width of 9½″; the fixture measures 9″ high by 12″ deep. If you prefer sharper lines, take a look at model 1937-1, which measures 6″ high by 12″ wide by 6″ deep. Model 1933-1, a French Deco wall sconce with a frosted, etched shade, is

106

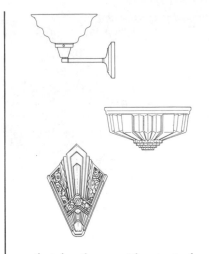

perfect for those with a taste for what the 1930s called "the modernistic". It is 12½" high, 9" wide, and 5" deep.

Brochure available.

Classic Illumination, Inc.
2743 9th St.
Berkeley, CA 94710
(415) 849-1842

Hammerworks

Hammerworks makes a variety of heart-shaped sconces such as the one shown here (W107). Some of the sconces accommodate two candles; others hold one. They're for purists only, though—they aren't adapted for electricity. All Hammerworks pieces are hand-crafted by the company's tin-smiths and blacksmiths. Hand-spun brass or 7" mercury glass reflectors are available, and all the heart sconces are made of iron.

Hammerworks also makes lanterns and hanging fixtures, and although all are made with clear glass, seedy glass can be substituted for an extra charge.

Catalogue, $3.

Hammerworks
75 Webster St.
Worcester, MA 01603
(617) 755-3434

Hurley Patentee Lighting

The proprietors of Hurley Patentee, Steve and Carolyn Waligurski, take pride in reproducing 17th- and 18th-century lighting fixtures as exactly as possible. They hand-turn wooden center posts and shape metal with simple hand tools. By using methods of craftsmanship appropriate to the period of the piece, they produce extremely good replicas. Finishes give the wood and tin an aged look. Electrified fixtures are fitted for candle bulbs and come with dripped wax sleeves and 15-watt bulbs unless other wattage is requested.

The sconces pictured here are some fine examples of Hurley Patentee's work, although literally scores of additional models are available. Those shown are made

of tin. The Primitive Oval sconce (SC301) is a copy of a very early piece and measures 16" high by 12" wide by 7" deep. It also comes in one and two-light sizes. The Sunset sconce (SC302) is 12" high, 18" wide, and 4" deep. The Perched Eagle sconce (SC326) features a large, unusual backplate and also comes in a three-light version. It measures 17" high by 9" wide by 4½" deep. A punched design distinguishes model SC332, whose backplate represents a pineapple, the symbol of hospitality. It is 15" high, 7" wide, and 3″ deep. Hurley Patentee accepts custom orders and also makes a wide variety of early-American chandeliers, floor lamps, and table fixtures.

Catalogue, $2.

Hurley Patentee Lighting
R.D. 7, Box 98A
Kingston, NY 12401
(914) 331-5414

M-H Lamp & Fan

Some of M-H Lamp & Fan's most attractive pieces are combination gas-and-electric-style wall fixtures. Model 8303 measures 15″ high by 7½″ wide by 14″ deep; model 8324 is 11″ high, 15″ wide, and 15″ deep; and model 8347 is 15″ high, 21″ wide, and 15″ deep. All three have fitter sizes of 2½″ and 4″ and accept up to 60-watt bulbs. The metal parts are made of solid polished lacquered brass. Shades for these models must be ordered separately. Ken Horan, the manager of M-H Lamp & Fan, is proud of his company's attention to authenticity in its reproduction

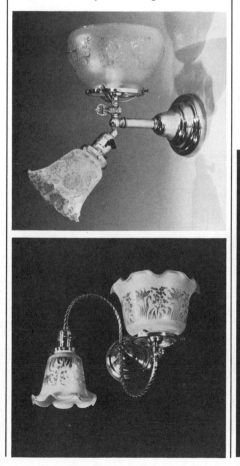

of period lighting fixtures. All gas-style arms are wired for electricity; there are switches on most electric-style arms, none on gas. A turn knob or pullchain canopy switch can be installed for an additional charge.

Catalogue, $3.

M-H Lamp & Fan Co.
7231½ N. Sheridan Rd.
Chicago, IL 60626
(312) 743-2225

Saxe Patterson

Saxe Patterson's tiered ceramic ziggurat sconces come in seven styles, ten colors, and a choice of smooth or stucco finishes. Model PZ1111-3, 11″ high by 10¾″ wide by 5⅝″ deep, is shown; all ziggurat lights are U.L. approved and come with mounting brackets. The fixtures are a must for Art Deco aficionados. Samples of the colors, which include sandstone,

dove grey, twilight blue, mauve, and heather, are available for a fee on a 2″ by 2″ ceramic square.

Brochure available.

Saxe Patterson
Box 15—Salazar Rd.
Taos, NM 87571
(505) 758-9513

Rejuvenaton House Parts

Sturdy and simple, this cast-iron porch sconce (the Alsea, model WPCA) from Rejuvenation House Parts is finished with a black oil-base enamel and is U.L. listed for damp locations. It takes a 60-watt bulb and measures 12″ high by 6″ wide by 8″ deep, with shade. The

Alsea is part of Rejuvenation's new Craftsman Collection, a group of replicas of early 20th-century Mission-style fixtures noted for their authenticity.

Catalogue, $3. Craftsman Collection brochure available free of charge.

Rejuvenation House Parts
901 N. Skidmore
Portland, OR 97217
(503) 249-0774

Roy Electric

Eschewing the often chintzy results of modern mass production, Roy and Roz Greenstein of Roy Electric restore and reproduce

108

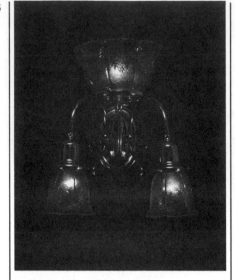

old lighting fixtures in "the proper way," enhancing the workmanship of high-quality antiques with today's technical advances. Top-of-the-line wiring and silver soldered joints trim Roy Electric's solid brass fixtures. One elegant reproduction fixture mounts on a wall with concentric ovals of brass flanked by small scrolls of ornamentation. A center bulb opens ceilingward, while two smaller bulbs, which may be encased in delicately ribbed glass shades, arch down on your choice of plain, reeded, or ribbed arms. This fixture and scores of others are highly polished and lacquer-dipped.

Catalogue, $3.

Roy Electric Co., Inc.
1054 Coney Island Ave.
Brooklyn, NY 11230
(718) 339-6311 or
(718) 761-7905

Washington Copper Works

Serge Miller, proprietor of the Washington Copper Works, has an apprentice to help him build (and initial, and date) every lighting fixture that leaves his shop for a new home. The firm offers modeled fixtures in the style of pub lights, mill house lanterns, and gunnery wall lights. Shown is a simple and attractive wall fixture with a pagoda top. Bowed ribs surround the lit globe in a more elaborate wall model,

crowned by a frilly, crimped copper accent. For a proper finish choose natural copper, which forgoes lacquer or polishing for a clean surface that will acquire the greenish-brown verdigris tone, or select stained copper in any hue from a pale brown to near-black.

Catalogue, $3 (refundable with any order).

The Washington Copper Works
South St.
Washington, CT 06793
(203) 868-7527

Table and Floor Lamps

There are few more difficult decorative chores than finding suitable table and floor lamps for the period home. Most commercial products look ridiculously out of place or are such obvious fakes (butter churns with gingham shades; miniature force pumps with milk-glass globes) that the home owner resorts to occasionally dubious conversions of his own (5-gallon crocks and turn-of-the-century grocery tins equipped with harps and shades). What to do? We've recommended in the past the use of old kerosene lamp bases converted to electricity with adapters available at most hardware stores. We still think this a fine idea. But several of the suppliers listed in this book are coming up with ideas of their own. Some of them, we think, have missed the mark. "Paul Revere" lanterns with lamp shades growing out of the peaks look pretty silly to us, and we've rejected them even though they are produced by one of the most reputable firms we know. We offer here a couple of the better ideas, but acknowledge that the problem of locating suitable electric table and floor lamps will be with us for at least a while longer.

Baldwin Hardware

A set of silver English candlesticks manufactured circa 1886 by Hawksworth, Eyre & Company was the inspiration for this 27"-high Victoria lamp (model 7619).

Available with a white pleated shade, a natural pleated shade, or an opaque black shade with a hand-rolled gold edge, it uses a three-way bulb and is made of solid polished brass. Its classical columnar shaft and stepped base give it the ability to blend with many styles and decors. The brass is coated with a clear baked enamel for easy care and durability, and the bottom is felt-covered to prevent scratching.

Literature, 75¢.

Baldwin Hardware Corp.
841 Wyomissing Blvd.
Box 82
Reading, PA 19603
(215) 777-7811

Brasslight

Brasslight's line of classic desk and table lamps is represented here by the Kirk model, which stands 22" high and swivels at the top of the 10" holophane cone-shaped shade. The lamp has a turn knob socket and can accept a maximum of 60 watts. Its metal parts, like those of all Brasslight fixtures, are solid polished lacquered brass; variations can be made in the finish for an additional fee. Brasslight accepts custom orders.

Catalogue, $3.

Brasslight, Inc.
90 Main St.
Nyack, NY 10960
(914) 353-0567

Federal Street Lighthouse

Federal Street Lighthouse specializes in handcrafted reproductions of antique lighting fixtures, although the company also produces a few new designs. This table lamp (model ATL1 KC2) has an unlacquered brass base which can be finished with pewter if desired; it stands 11" high and 5" wide. The shade, which is available in off white, gray, or tan, is made of hand-cut paper. It is trimmed with velvet and cord which may be moss green, wine, navy, dusty blue, rust, or beige. Federal Street Lighthouse also makes chandeliers, ceiling lamps, sconces, and lanterns in a number of finishes. Proprietor Cheryl B. Smith welcomes inquiries.

Catalogue, $3.

Federal Street Lighthouse
38 Market Sq.
Newburyport, MA 01950
(617) 462-6333

Renaissance Marketing

The heart of Renaissance Marketing's collection of Tiffany and Art Nouveau reproductions is represented by this twelve-light lily table lamp (TL-12), which stands 20½" high. The stems are bronze, and the lilies are made of hand-blown favrile glass. Several adaptations of this lamp are available, including two floor

high, 16" wide. Finishes include a shiny polished and lacquered surface, a polished but unlacquered exterior that darkens or can be polished by hand, or an antiqued and lacquered look. While not table lamps per se, a pair of these newel post lamps would look just fine (and quite authentic) on the ends of a Victorian sideboard.

Catalogue, $3.

Victorian Lightcrafters Ltd.
Box 350
Slate Hill, NY 10973
(914) 355-1300

Victorian Reproduction Lighting

High-caliber reproductions of over a century's worth of designs come to you from Victorian Reproduction Lighting. Styles of table lamps vary from the simple models covered by glass shades that display painted farm scenes to distinguished curves, curls, and crimpings of a four-branched Victorian lamp. Tall, slender, spiraling or ribbed, beautifully crafted bodies of these floor lamps sup-

models and table versions with seven or eighteen stems. Renaissance also features serpent lamps in which a snake stands erect except for a small coil near the top which holds a glass shade. The firm's line of reproductions will soon include wall sconces, sculptured lighting, and ceiling fixtures as well.

Catalogue, $2.

Renaissance Marketing, Inc.
Box 360
Lake Orion, MI 48035
(313) 693-1109

Victorian Lightcrafters

Interest is sharp and antiques are in short supply—hence the demand for top-notch reproductions of Victorian light fixtures. Victorian Lightcrafters has matched that demand for the White House and can do the same for you. A gas and electric style solid-brass newel post fixture has a triplet of frilly shades curling downward from the dainty center support. A larger shade blooms upward at the top of the lamp. The fixture can be cast to stand 23" to 28"

port dainty cloth shades or more substantial glass versions. Victorian Reproduction Lighting provides an appealing selection of glass shades in frosted, floral, opalescent, etched, and cut designs. The firm takes custom and modified orders, as well.

Poster brochure, $1.50.
Catalogue, $4.

Victorian Reproduction Lighting Co.
1601 Park Ave. S.
Minneapolis, MN 55404
(612) 338-3636

Lanterns

After the chandelier, the lantern is the most popular form of period lighting fixture in North America. It might even be called a poor man's chandelier since this relatively simple device was and is often used in place

of something fancier. A lantern can be employed in a number of different ways—mounted on a post, hung from a chain, fixed against the wall, carried from place to place, or simply left as a table lamp. The lantern is most

properly a candle-burning fixture or at least one that imitates such a source of light. Aside from the railroad lantern, it does not have a reservoir for fuel and thus it cannot employ oil or gas.

A.J.P., Coppersmith

A.J.P., Coppersmith, patterns the octagonal Constitution lantern on a fixture from Captain Hull's quarters on the U.S.S. Constitution. The lantern's open bottom spills extra light into hallways, onto tables. The series of Culvert lanterns, airy and bright, have double-rounded tops designed originally to let smoke escape from oil or candles. Both types of open-bottomed, hanging lanterns, with "X" or "H" crossbar patterns, range in height from 16" to 23", and vary from 6" to 9" in width, with a depth of 8" to 10½". Lanterns come finished in antique brass, antique copper, or lead-coated copper. A.J.P., Coppersmith, will provide the antique green verdigris finish on copper lanterns at no extra charge.

Catalogue available.

A.J.P., Coppersmith & Co.
34 Broadway
Wakefield, MA 01880
(617) 245-1223

Heritage Lanterns

It's easy to see how the globe lantern became a classic, and Heritage Lanterns does a splendid job of reproducing it. This version (B225 medium) comes in rust-proof brass or copper and can be mounted inside, outside the front door, or a foot or two from the top of a post. It comes in four sizes -- small (22½" high by 12½" wide by 13½" deep), medium (24½" by 14¾" by 15½"), large (29" by 17" by 18½"), and extra large (35" by 18" by 20½"). The small and medium sizes have a socket at the top of the globe which will accommodate up to 100 watts; the large and extra large are socketed at the globe bottom, and Heritage recommends a 75 or 100-watt large chimney bulb.

pewter and will not rust. Heritage lanterns are not lacquered or polished, thereby encouraging natural aging. Most are appropriate for indoor or outdoor use.

Brochure, $2.

Heritage Lanterns
70A Main St.
Yarmouth, ME 04096
(207) 846-3911

Hurley Patentee Lighting

If you prize authenticity in a reproduction and you're looking for a colonial lantern, Steve and Carolyn Waligurski at Hurley Patentee may be able to help. They take great care to make their replicas as close as possible to the original antique fixtures, even using methods of production appropriate to the period of the piece. Electrified fixtures are fitted for candle bulbs and come with dripped wax sleeves and 15-watt bulbs unless other wattage is requested. The tin lanterns illustrated here provide samples of Hurley Patentee's variety—the company also produces chandeliers, table lamps, floor lamps, and wall fixtures.

Model L130, the Hall Lantern, is hexagonal, with a hinged door and three lights, and measures 17" in height and 8" in width. Model L126, the Welcome Lantern, is an outdoor fixture painted black, with a pierced design on the front and sides and a shaped apron. It measures 21" high by 13" wide by 7" deep and mounts on a wall. The Waligurskis accept custom work.

Catalogue, $2.

Hurley Patentee Lighting
R.D. 7, Box 98A
Kingston, NY 12401
(914) 331-5414

Period Lighting Fixtures

Period Lighting Fixtures prides itself on its catalogue of early American lighting. A rich history inspires the classic designs, including a range of solid-copper lanterns. The rugged New England Barn Lantern, 17" high by 8½" wide, can use a circular pewter reflector if desired. A handsome bracket lantern has a wall mount that can include graceful 42" wings. Soldered along each seam, the sturdy lanterns are never polished or lacquered, but come in an oxidized green verdigris, a flat painted black finish, or a natural copper that weathers to rich bronze. For

Heritage also makes a distinctively shaped Triangle Double Top lantern (W127 small), which comes in copper and brass. Seedy or plain glass is availalbe for either size—small (13½" by 12" by 8") or large (18" by 13¾" by 12").

The company is justly proud of its lanterns, which are produced largely by hand with double-thickness flat glass. Most are available in both copper and brass; some also come in solid copper coated with a dull pewter that matches well with antique

Antique Lighting Devices

A surprising number of antique lighting devices from the 19th and early 20th centuries have survived the march of technology. There is little or nothing from earlier times—save candle-holders—which has withstood the test of time. Lighting was one of the first fields to be tackled by reproduction craftsmen in the post-World War II period, and since then there has also been a gradual re-awakening of interest in the restoration of lighting devices. Few of them have emerged entirely unscathed from use. Like antique clocks, most of the devices require one new part or another, and all call for some sort of refurbishing. In the hands of a qualified craftsman, such as those covered in the write-ups that follow, the antique can become as useful as the new.

Architectural Antique Warehouse

Restored antiques and faithfully crafted reproductions—all of the Architectural Antique Warehouse's lighting fixtures are solid brass. Use these quality items, including table and floor lamps, hanging lanterns, wall fixtures, and chandeliers, to accent your favorite period room. It's obvious from the filled floor (and ceiling) of the showroom that the Architectural Antique Warehouse can satisfy numerous unusual requests. Ask for information about consultation and renovation services and supervision.

The Architectural Antique Warehouse
1583 Bank St.
Ottawa, Ontario, Canada K1P 6H6
(613) 526-1818

smaller post lanterns, Period Lighting Fixtures makes a welded lamppost of iron piping, a collar, and crossbar.

Catalogue, $3.

Period Lighting Fixtures
1 Main St.
Chester, CT 06412
(203) 526-3690

Authentic Lighting

It's difficult to top the elegance of a circa 1840 bronze chandelier, gilded in 24-karat gold. Complete with its original glass, this gas fixture is typical of the lighting devices available from Authentic Lighting. The firm features an ex-

tensive selection of original gas, early electric, and Art Deco lighting, as well as plating, polishing, and general repair services for lamps and fixtures. Authentic Lighting is happy to mail photographs to its customers in response to any requests.

Authentic Lighting
558 Grand Ave.
Englewood, NJ 07631
(201) 568-7429

Gaslight Time

Between 1860 and 1930, talented lighting craftsmen honed their art to masterpiece status. The work they produced has reached the showroom of Gaslight Time, where restored fixtures feature an extensive collection of Victorian gas chandeliers. A wide selection of original and reproduced glass lampshades enhance the handsome fixtures themselves. Gaslight Time restores and also reproduces antique lighting fixtures. Custom work is also offered.

Photographs, $1 each.

Gaslight Time
823 President St.
Brooklyn, NY 11215
(718) 789-7185

Greg's Antique Lighting

Greg's Antique Lighting specializes in one-of-a-kind antique lighting fixtures. Most of these restored antiques are American, spanning styles and ages from the mid-1800s to the first decades of the 20th century. The changing inventory precludes literature or catalogues, although particular requests garner appropriate photographs. A trip to Greg's Antique Lighting is well worth your time—the firm boasts the largest stock of antique lighting fixtures on the West Coast.

Greg's Antique Lighting
12005 Wilshire Blvd., W.
Los Angeles, CA 90025
(213) 478-5475

Half Moon Antiques

Half Moon's proprietors, Lee and Lynne Roberts, specialize in locating and restoring antique lighting fixtures. Their pieces are rewired and the brass polished and lacquered to create beautiful fixtures such as those shown. In order, they are: a combination gas-and-electric style chandelier with the original matte silver-plated brass finish; a Louis XV style brass and onyx gas style chandelier with original gilding and etched shades; and a brass gasolier chandelier with etched "crown" shades.

Lee and Lynne Roberts can be reached through their Red Bank showroom, which is open seven days a week from eleven to five. Because this showroom is

operated by several antique dealers and because Half Moon exhibits at antique shows periodically, appointments are strongly recommended. Half Moon does not issue a catalogue but will send photographs in response to a brief description of the fixture desired.

Half Moon Antiques
c/o Monmouth Antique Shoppes
217 W. Front St.
Red Bank, NJ 07701
(201) 842-7377

Illustrious Lighting

If you're in search of authenticity, take a look at Illustrious Lighting's selection of antique fixtures. Dating from 1800 to 1940, the company's stock can meet a variety of needs, and each piece has been fully restored. Early gas fixtures and gilded candelabra suit older homes, but the newer ones haven't been forgotten; Illustrious Lighting usually has a number of craftsman-style and French and American Art Nouveau chandeliers on hand. Other items often available include gas-and-electric chandeliers with two to twelve arms, electric chandeliers, table and floor lamps, Emeralite desk lamps, French billiard table lights, carbon lamps, Eastlake and Renaissance Revival fixtures, kerosene pull-down lights, and silver and brass sconces in a variety of styles.

Since the company's stock varies, the best way to find a suitable fixture is to send Illustrious Lighting some idea of your price range and a description of the room or rooms. Include dimensions, ceiling heights, and the types of furnishings present. Photographs of individual fixtures can be obtained for a fee.

Illustrious Lighting
1925 Fillmore St.
San Francisco, CA 94115
(415) 922-3133

London Venturers

London Venturers is one of the few antique lighting firms that offers a catalogue. The catalogue is periodically updated, and items that have been sold are marked as such. If you want a piece that's marked as sold or that doesn't appear in the catalogue, the company may still be able to help, so give them a call.

Most of London Venturers' pieces are made of solid brass and are wired and ready to install. They can accept bulbs of up to 60 watts, but 25-watt or 40-watt bulbs are recommended. The variety of the company's stock is impossible to describe briefly—it includes gas, electric, and combination fixtures; Mission style, Gothic Revival, and Art Deco; chandeliers, pendants, sconces, and articulated wall arms; and fixtures ranging from

the 1860s to the 1920s, with a special emphasis on the 1890s and the turn of the century. For a full appreciation of the selection available, take a look at the catalogue.

Catalogue, $2.

London Venturers Co.
2 Dock Sq.
Rockport, MA 01966
(617) 546-7161

Watertower Pines

Take delicate antique designs—Art Deco shades, Victorian chandeliers—that have fallen on tough times, and restore them to light

SUZANNE STOHLMAN

SUZANNE STOHLMAN

116

up houses and lives again. Display them in a two-story carriage barn that dates from 1867, and you've got Watertower Pines. Besides the exceptional finds in the firm's showroom, Watertower Pines will also repair fixtures and can furnish or special order reproductions and other supplies. Fixtures are carefully restored to allow owners to return to the original fuel source if desired. A range of unique items bars cataloguing, but Watertower Pines sends replies and photographs in response to inquiries.

Watertower Pines
Box 1067
Kennebunk, ME 04043
(207) 985-6868

Yankee Craftsman

Every piece that emerges from Bill Sweeney's workshop is special. Sweeney and his sons will tackle almost any project, from repairs and parts replacements to custom lamp design and restoration of antique fixtures. Recently, Yankee Craftsman restored Nathaniel Hawthorne's astral lamp and the chandelier under which Henry Wadsworth Longfellow was married. Although a bearskin, stuffed birds, and a menagerie of animals outside (including a wild boar) make Sweeney's workshop unusual, and while he has received commissions from as far away as Saudi Arabia, it's the simple things that make Yankee Craftsman noteworthy. The staff's skill and dedication result in pieces of first-rate quality, and Sweeney gives his customers the attention they deserve.

In this photograph of the workshop, Sweeney (*right foreground*) is working on a desk lamp reproduction that his shop will be producing soon. It's so close to the original that it's fooled antique dealers.

For information, call or write Sweeney's workshop.

Yankee Craftsman
357 Commonwealth Rd. (Rt. 30)
Wayland, MA 01778
(617) 653-0031

Outdoor Lighting Fixtures

Among the ugliest of modern artifacts to be seen along our streets and roads today are lighting fixtures. They often appear to stand as alien creatures and even neighborhood dogs are reluctant to pause along their trail. Yet, outdoor lighting, as many homeowners have discovered in rural and suburban areas, needn't be so forbidding and unattractive. Graceful standards are availalbe for both municipal and home lighting purposes, and these are capped with similarly handsome lanterns.

A.J.P., Coppersmith

The first Windsor lantern appeared in England almost a century ago, and the distinguished style charmed its way to become one of the most popular post lanterns ever. A.J.P., Coppersmith, provides the graceful lantern in two sizes, 14" by 30" and 16" by 35", with a four-arm "frog" that attaches the lantern with a 3" post fitter, adding 8" to reach an overall height of 38" or 43". The Windsor Post Lantern comes in either a polished and lacquered copper finish that should darken slowly after a couple of years or an antique copper finish. A.J.P., Coppersmith, can supply rustproof cast-aluminum posts in heights of 6' or 9'.

Catalogue available.

A.J.P., Coppersmith & Co.
34 Broadway
Wakefield, MA 01880
(617) 245-1223

A/S Noral

A/S Noral's lanterns are designed to stand the test of weather in harsh, coastal Norway, and now the appealing, tough designs are available to the North American public. The hand-finished, diecast aluminum fixtures arrive finished in your choice of matte black, white, or a weathered copper appearance of patinated green, each protected by a polycarbonate of

acrylic glaze. Noral's lanterns have panes of the substance used in bulletproof windows, and the firm promises its lanterns are proof against corrosion for two decades, showing the way to the "many illuminating years ahead."

Brochure available.

In North America, Noral lanterns are distributed by:

F.P. Architectural
379 Eglinton Ave. W.
Toronto, Ontario, Canada M5N 1A3
(416) 483-4085

Silver Dollar Trading

For classic design, it's hard to beat the Silver Dollar Trading Company's four-arm street lights (models 1550, 1551, and 1552). All these models are made of cast aluminum and are available in black, white, medium dark green, or chocolate brown. 12" globes with 4" necks must be ordered separately. Model 1550 is 9' high and 3' wide with an 18"-high base; 1551 is identical, except that its base measures 6". Model 1552 stands over 11' high with globes in place and has an 18" base and a slightly altered column.

Silver Dollar also makes aluminum outdoor globe sconces and a number of other street lights which range in height from 8' to 13' and may have from one to five globes. Some lights are designed to be fitted with acorn-shaped rather than round globes. Also available are indoor electric ceiling and wall lights made of solid polished brass, which are based on some of the earliest electric light designs.

Catalogue, $2.

Silver Dollar Trading Co.
Box 394
San Elizario, TX 79849
(915) 851-3458

D.W. Windsor

When London's Covent Garden Market needed craftsmen for its unusual pineapple lanterns, D.W. Windsor took the job—and contributed to a restoration project that won a 1981 Civic Trust Award. Windsor trains the craftsmen it employs. They number each lantern produced and are

skilled in restoring lanterns and lampposts. Windsor's exterior lighting products include hand-made brass and copper lanterns in natural, polished and lacquered, or painted black finishes. Special glazing resists vandalism, and the lanterns can accommodate automated photoelectric switching gear and economical sodium lamps.

Brochure available.

The North American Supplier of Windsor Fixtures is:

F.P. Architectural
379 Eglinton Ave. W.
Toronto, Ontario, Canada M5N 1A3
(416) 483-4085

Supplies and Services

Anyone who has ever looked for a replacement part for a favorite lamp has probably been driven wild at the local home center supermarket searching through row after row of teeny plastic bags for something even vaguely similar to what is sought. Chances are that the victim of today's impersonal hardware emporium has given up and simply bought a new lamp. But rejoice. There is hope. The following firms should solve your spare parts problems with no trouble at all.

Brass Light Gallery

If you're looking for glass shades to complement a lighting fixture in the angular Mission/Prairie style, Brass Light Gallery offers two styles—a straight-edged (model 761) and a curved-edged shade (model 762). Both are 4⅛" high with a 2¼" fitter opening and feature glossy exteriors, frosted interiors, and clear edges. The straight-edged shade is 4" wide; the curved-edge, 3½".

Catalogue, $3.

Brass Light Gallery
719 S. 5th St.
Dept. 5
Milwaukee, WI 53204
(414) 383-0675

Burdoch Silk Lampshade

Few lighting accessories evoke a sense of the Victorian more than elaborately embroidered, long-fringed lampshades of the type made by Burdoch Silk Lampshade. The company stocks over four-hundred shades, and thirteen colors are available, including burgundy, white, honey beige, and ivory. All fringe is 5½" long. The shade pictured here, Victorian Joy, has a lower width of 18" and a height of 15½". It can come as shown, with the sides and center embroidered, or with plain sides. Burdoch also sells bases for lamps. *Nota bene:*

Because of the tendency of silk to yellow and fade, Burdoch makes its lampshades of satinized polyester.

Brochure, $2.

Burdoch Silk Lampshade Co.
11120 Roselle St.
San Diego, CA 92121
(619) 458-1005

The Cobweb Shop

For historic authenticity and the softness of candlelight, order a lighting fixture that takes real wax tapers. Find a candle mold or dip your own—the Cobweb Shop will meet your traditional requirements with pure beeswax by the pound. Manufacturers of hardware as well, the Cobweb Shop will help you fuel the period lighting fixture you've selected.

Catalogue, $2.

The Cobweb Shop
N 3956 North U.S. 2
Iron Mountain, MI 49801
(906) 774-6560

Federal Street Lighthouse

Sometimes the most difficult things to find are the small objects that make a room complete—like decorative lamp finials. The right one may be hard to locate when a replacement is necessary. Cheryl B. Smith's Federal Street Lighthouse makes seven types of finials. Models CF1 (tree of life), CF3 (pineapple), CF4 (Chinese ideogram), and CF6 (urn) are

Elcanco

Elcanco specializes in electric candle products—electric wax candles, beeswax candle covers, and flame-like bulbs. The firm's most unusual candle is the Starlite, which uses Elcanco's handmade Candlewick bulbs to produce a special one-candlepower light. The bulbs require an adapter, which is included, in order to reduce normal voltage to the six-volt limit. All of Elcanco's electric wax candles are covered in gold or ivory-colored beeswax which is thick enough at the base to allow the candles to be shaved to fit most holders. Extra wax is included and can be melted around the candle base for an especially authentic look.

Brochure available.

Elcanco
60 Chelmsford St.
Chelmsford, MA 01824
(617) 256-9972 or
(617) 256-8809

brass; model CF2, shaped like one of a number of Netsuke gods, is made of soapstone. Model CF5 is a disc of cinnabar with an Oriental design, and CF7 is made of painted porcelain.

Catalogue, $3.

Federal Street Lighthouse
38 Market Sq.
Newburyport, MA 01950
(617) 462-6333

Paxton Hardware

In search of frills and fittings for your favorite lighting fixtures? Odds are that the rare antique find has lost a finial or two over the years, so Paxton Hardware supplies those finials plus glass chimneys of varying size, brass shell sockets, steel or brass pipes

and nuts, candle covers, chains, and canopies. Particularly attractive are Paxton's glass ball lampshades. The versatile style of etching on a satin backing complements many decors. On a nature theme, the opaque ball with flycatchers feathered in blue,

brown, and white, and the delicate pattern of roses on cream are choices that will please.

Mini-catalogue available. Full catalogue, $3.50.

Paxton Hardware, Ltd.
Dept. OHC
7818 Bradshaw Rd.
Upper Falls, MD 21156
(301) 592-8505

Victorian Lightcrafters

Fifteen years ago, Victorian Lightcrafters began restoring antique Victorian lighting fixtures. A few years later, with demands outstripping supply, the firm began building its own—solid-brass designs based on originals and illustrations from vintage catalogues. To complement the large array of fixtures, Victorian Lightcrafters provides glass fitter shades of various sizes. Opalescent, engraved, lipped in cranberry or amber . . . the choice is wide and includes many appealing selections.

Catalogue, $3.

Victorian Lightcrafters Ltd.
Box 350
Slate Hill, NY 10973
(914) 355-1300

Other Suppliers of Lighting

Consult List of Suppliers for addresses.

Chandeliers

The Antique Hardware Store
Architectural Antiques Exchange
Robert Bourdon, the Smithy
Federal Street Lighthouse
Heritage Lanterns
Hippo Hardware and Trading Co.
Hurley Patentee
Period Furniture Hardware Co., Inc.
St. Louis Antique Lighting

Hanging and Ceiling Fixtures

A.J.P., Coppersmith
The Antique Hardware Store
Architectural Antiques Exchange
Brass Light Gallery
Brasslight, Inc.
Federal Street Lighthouse
Hammerworks
M-H Lamp & Fan Co.
Period Furniture Hardware Co., Inc.
Rejuvenation House Parts
Silver Dollar Trading Co.
St. Louis Antique Lighting
Victorian Lightcrafters, Ltd.

Wall Fixtures

The Antique Hardware Store

Architectural Antiques Exchange
Robert Bourdon, the Smithy
Brass Light Gallery
Federal Street Lighthouse
Heritage Lanterns
Hippo Hardware and Trading Co.
King's Chandelier Co.
W.F. Norman
Nowell's, Inc.
Period Furniture Hardware Co., Inc.
Price Glover Inc.
Silver Dollar Trading Co.
Victorian Lightcrafters Ltd.

Table and Floor Lamps

The Antique Hardware Store
Robert Bourdon, the Smithy
Hurley Patentee
King's Chandelier Co.
M-H Lamp & Fan Co.
Nowell's, Inc.
Period Furniture Hardware Co., Inc.
Period Lighting Fixtures
St. Louis Antique Lighting
Washington Copper Works
Lt. Moses Willard & Co.

Lanterns

Federal Street Lighthouse
Hammerworks
Period Furniture Hardware Co., Inc.
Sunflower Glass Studio
E.G. Washburne
Washington Copper Works

Antique Lighting Devices

City Lights
Whit Hanks
London Venturers Co.
Roy Electric Co. Inc.
Wooden Nickel Antiques

Outdoor Lighting Fixtures

Federal Street Lighthouse
Hammerworks
Heritage Lanterns
W.F. Norman
The Old Wagon Factory
Period Furniture Hardware Co., Inc.
Period Lighting Fixtures
E.G. Washburne
Washington Copper Works

Services and Supplies

Hammerworks
Heritage Lanterns
Hippo Hardware and Trading Co.
Hurley Patentee
M-H Lamp & Fan Co.
W.F. Norman
Period Furniture Hardware Co., Inc.
Period Lighting Fixtures
Rejuvenation House Parts
Renaissance Marketing, Inc.
Roy Electric Co. Inc.

5.

Heating and Cooking

Beating the high cost of energy is a game which is not only profitable but enjoyable. The ways in which our ancestors coped with the extremes of hot and cold can provide some useful lessons for us as well. Now that the hoopla over the burning of wood rather than oil (or as a supplement to oil or gas) has died down, however, one can study the alternatives a bit more dispassionately *and* profitably.

There is no doubt that alternative, old-fashioned ways of heating a building can be effective. A supply of coal or wood or kerosene, however, must be close at hand. If these fuels are not naturally plentiful in your area, their cost will not be much less than modern equivalents. In most areas of North America, alternative heating devices must be seen as supplemental systems and not as the primary source of heat. (In the extreme South, of course, coal or wood or kerosene may be all that is needed year-round.)

There are many individuals who would disagree with this pronouncement concerning supplemental use, but we are addressing the average homeowner and not the super-resourceful or Spartan citizen. Sweaters and thermal underwear will take a lot of the chill out of the air; kerosene heaters can perform miracles of efficiency in offices, workrooms, garages; even the much maligned open fireplace, if supplied with a fireback and a good damper, can throw out a surprising amount of heat. But when it gets really cold, there is nothing quite like a central heating system.

The old house purist has a particularly difficult time with heating. Should the fireplace be closed up—at least during the winter months? Not necessarily. As suggested previously, it can be fitted up with several devices—a decent damper and a fireback will make it a more efficient "instrument." By the mid-1800s, the fireplace was disappearing as it was no longer needed for cooking or heating. Of course, stoves were frequently fitted into the fireplace opening in the 19th century. It is by no means inappropriate, therefore, to install a stove in a fireplace. We would be reluctant, however, to recommend ever closing up a fireplace. A room without such a central feature always seems particularly heartless and unfocused.

Most of the heating stove models made today are singularly unattractive. There has been little attempt to copy some of the classic types of the past. A few, however, are available and might be tried. Cook stoves and ranges have changed little in design in this century. Their use by the Amish and Mennonite communities in the East and Midwest, as well as in Canada, has made these devices more accessible to others as well.

The Glenwood Gold Medal, a restored kitchen range with both gas and wood ovens, from Good Time Stove Co., Goshen, Massachusetts.

Stoves

The choice of wood as an alternative fuel source in recent years has rescued many an old cast-iron monster from the junkyard. But before you buy one of these originals, beware. While an antique can be equally as warming as a reproduction, make sure that it has been expertly refurbished. A stove that isn't airtight can be just as great a fuel thief as that oil burner down in the basement, and a hundred times as dangerous.

Many companies have capitalized on the recent demand for wood-burning stoves by mass-producing reproductions in record numbers. It's therefore easy to find one; what's difficult is to locate one that's handsome as well as utilitarian. The manufacturers listed in the following section have not sacrificed style for the sake of utility or profit: they offer many attractive models, some based on 19th-century originals, in a variety of sizes and styles to suit every need.

Aetna

Founded in 1890 and still operated by the Markowitz family, Aetna provides antique, reproduction, and modern stoves and accessories. The company's four-story building, located in one of Philadelphia's historic districts, is the repository for a large inventory of replacement parts, including stove pipes, hot air registers, and flue stops for coal and wood stoves. The firm routinely buys out foundry inventories to maintain its stock, included in which is a good selection of both new and reconditioned cast-iron and porcelain-enamel stoves.

Brochure available.

Aetna Stove Co., Inc.
S.E. Corner 2nd and Arch Sts.
Philadelphia, PA 19106
(215) 627-2008 or
(215) 627-2009

Barnstable Stove Shop

Located in a restored horse barn once used for cranberry processing, Barnstable Stove Shop dis-

plays more than 300 antique kitchen ranges and parlor stoves. Each stove is completely sandblasted and rebuilt; all seams are cemented and spray painted. Doug Pacheco, owner of Barnstable, guarantees the quality of his nickel plating and foundry work. His selection of period stoves includes Mica Baseburners made from 1880 to 1920, turn-of-the-century Glenwoods, and Crawfords made by Walker and Pratt Co. beginning in the 1850s. If you have a prize behemoth that needs refurbishing, Barnstable will do it for you, or will trade it

in on a model more suitable for your needs.

Brochure, $1.

Barnstable Stove Shop
Rte. 149, Box 472
West Barnstable, MA 02668
(617) 362-9913

Bryant Stove Works

There's a reason that so many modern stoves have been based on 19th-century patterns—old stoves work. They're efficient, and they have a beauty that modern ones can't match. At the Bryant Stove Works, a family business located on a 100-acre farm, old stoves are appreciated. Joe and Bea Bryant sandblast and restore antique stoves, using new parts, nickling, grates, and liners. About 150 are kept in stock at all times, and searches for particular stoves are undertaken willingly.

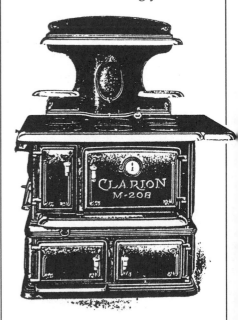

One stove usually available is this 208 Clarion M, a cabinet-style unit with a shield-elevated shelf. It's part of the Clarion collection, produced since 1839, and stands 54" high. Clarion stoves are available with a variety of options, including water tanks and removable ash pans. The 208 is coated with a special heat-resistant paint. Bryant also offers parlor heaters, including the Glenwood wood-burning model shown here. It was produced in three sizes and two

styles: direct, with a straight-run flue; and indirect, with a cabinet base enclosing a divided flue for extra heating. If you can visit the company, Joe and Bea recommend seeing their stoves in person to appreciate their beauty and solid construction. If you can't, write or give a call. Bryant Stove Works will crate and ship stoves anywhere in the world.

Brochure and catalogue available.

Bryant Stove Works, Inc.
Box 2048 Rich Rd.
Thorndike, ME 04986
(207) 568-3665

Good Time Stove

Richard "Stove Black" Richardson, proprietor of the Good Time Stove Company, has been restoring and selling antique kitchen ranges and parlor stoves for more than a decade. His shop, located in the Berkshire Hills, a heavily wooded rural area of western Massachusetts where such stoves have been *de rigueur* for over 200 years, displays a variety of models, each painstakingly and lovingly restored to peak efficiency. The Glenwood Gold Medal features both gas and wood ovens; the Gold Coin is festooned with flowers, leaves, and shields, while the Atlantic Queen is a sleeker, less ornate model. Richardson scours the countryside in search of old stoves to restore and generally has a wide selection available to choose from.

Brochure available.

Good Time Stove Co.
Rte. 112, Box 306
Goshen, MA 01032-0306
(413) 268-3677

Lehman Hardware

Modern electrical stoves and microwave ovens are certainly convenient, but they don't have the even cooking, the heating capacity, or the aesthetic appeal of wood or coal-burning cookstoves. Lehman sells several models of stoves that heat, cook, and please the eye, including the Jotul 8 shown here. Its design is based on that of a hand-crafted colonial cabinet, and its glass front lets you watch the fire. The flue outlet vents from the top or the rear, and although the Jotul 8 is designed for freestanding installation, it can be adapted for most fireplaces. The Jotul accommodates logs up to 20" in length (or will burn coal) and comes in four finishes—black paint, blue/black porcelain, almond porcelain, or red porcelain.

Every stove sold by Lehman has its own special features. The Cawley 800 is equipped with an extra-deep firebox to prevent logs from rolling out, dual air controls, and four loading doors that allow it to hold logs up to 24" in length. The Waterford Stanley wood cooking range has a heat control that makes it easy to keep the stove burning overnight; a convenient warming shelf is an extra bonus. One of Lehman's finest stoves is this Elmira Oval cookstove, which has been produced by a Canadian manufacturer for

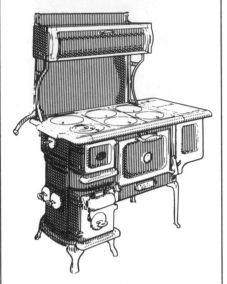

eighty years. It features a cast-iron and firebrick-lined firebox that is 20" long, 9" wide, and 11" deep, six square feet of cooking surface, and a ten-year limited warranty. The oven, 11½" high by 18" wide by 20" deep, has a three-position rack and a door thermometer. Options include almond or black porcelain finish, a solid copper water reservoir, coal grates, and a water jacket for heating running water. The cooktop height is 32"; overall measurements are 62" high by 41" wide by 29½" deep.

Catalogue, $2. Brochure on Oval cookstove, no charge.

Lehman Hardware & Appliances, Inc.
Box 41, 4779 Kidron Rd.
Kidron, OH 44636
(216) 857-5441

measurements are 32¼" high to the range top, 52" wide, and 30" deep. A six-gallon water reservoir can replace the end shelf, as shown here, increasing the total width by 5". Another available option is the replacement of the high shelf with a warming oven. The Queen Atlantic can be manufactured to burn either wood or coal.

If you prefer something a little less grand, Portland also makes a reproduction of the Atlantic Box Stove, a simple rectangular heater with Gothic side panels that add efficiency as well as decoration. Recessed side panels inside the stove eliminate the need for liners or firebrick, and the 28½"-long firebox can be loaded from the side or top and is capable of burning whole logs. An extra-wide hearth assists cleaning, and there's a cooking surface on top to make the unit as useful as possible. Overall, it measures 26¾" high by 22¾" wide by 41¼" long.

Literature, $2.

Portland Stove Co.
Box 377
Fickett Rd.
N. Pownal, ME 04069
(207) 688-2254 or
(207) 775-6424

Portland Stove

Some old stoves are like bulldogs—so ugly that they're lovable. Portland Stove's reproduction of the 1906 Queen Atlantic is no exception. It's squat, fat, and black in the grandest tradition and has more character than any modern stove. Fine cast-iron construction makes it dependable, and attention to detail makes it an accurate reproduction. Its six lids and roomy oven (11" high by 18¼" wide by 19¾" deep) provide ample cooking space. Overall

Woodstock Soapstone

Although most antique and reproduction wood stoves are made of cast iron, there is an alternative, and a more efficient one, according to spokesmen for this Vermont firm. Soapstone produces gentle, even heat without the temperature fluctuations of metal; warms efficiently at low heat output; and holds coals long after the fire has died down, so rekindling from the coals is quick and easy. Woodstock Soapstone manufactures its handsome stoves with iron castings and double soapstone walls, in three models: the Woodstock, patterned after a century-old New England piece; the Classic, with its solid front and glass door; and the Fireview, with a glass front and solid door. Every model has cast-iron baffles and a cast-iron bottom, lined with firebrick. An optional catalytic combuster adds efficiency and cuts pollution.

Brochures available.

Woodstock Soapstone Co., Inc.
Airpark Rd.
Box 37H
West Lebanon, NH 03784
(603) 298-5955

Mantels

If you're fortunate enough to have one or more working fireplaces, good period mantels will be of interest to you. Every fireplace should be properly "framed," in much the same way you would set off a treasured painting. The companies listed in the following section can supply antique and reproduction mantels in a variety of styles, materials, and sizes to meet every need and to suit every period decor. Other suppliers can be found in chapter 1, Structural Products and Services.

Architectural Antiques West

Mantels from Architectural Antiques West, faithfully reproduced in kiln-dried solid Honduras mahogany, are designed to draw attention. Six styles are kept in stock: ornate Victorian, simple Country English, exotic Spanish Colonial, flowery French Rococo, perfectly proportioned Neoclassical, and fluid Art Nouveau. They range in size from 3'9" high by 5'2" long with a 3' by 4' opening to 4'6" high by 6' long with a 3'2"-long by 4'3"-wide opening. Because the mantels are hand-crafted, however, there may be slight variations in the dimensions from one piece to another. They are shipped unfinished to allow you to match the stained or painted mantel to your decor. Any of the designs can also be executed in oak; custom sizes may be specified.

Architectural Antiques West has distributors in many parts of the country; to find out which is nearest to you, contact:

Architectural Antiques West
3117 S. La Cienega Blvd.
Los Angeles, CA 90016
(213) 559-3019

Bay Waveland Woodworks

Bay Waveland's craftsmen are specialists in fine woodworking: using the drawing or photo you supply, they can create a custom mantel to your exact specifications, or you might elect to order one of the stock models, such as this one, usually on display in their Waveland, Mississippi, retail shop. Crafted of red cypress, it is also available in oak, mahogany, and walnut. In addition to its own custom mantels, Bay Waveland stocks Victorian brackets, mantels, and trim, and usually has a supply of turn-of-the-century porch swings and benches on hand.

Brochure available.

Bay Waveland Woodworks
1330 Hwy. 90 W.
Waveland, MS 39576
(601) 467-2628

Mailing address:

Rte. 4, Box 548
Bay St. Louis, MS 39520

Dalton-Gorman

If you are trying to refurbish a period home or decorate in a particular historic style, you may find it difficult to procure an antique marble mantel to finish off the parlor or master bedroom. Dalton-Gorman can probably help: the firm specializes in accurate re-creations of period mantels, each available in a number of different variegated marbles—from whites and pinks to beiges, golds, greens, and blacks. Illustrated are two of the styles the company offers: the ornate Louis XV and the gracefully arched Victorian. Each has attached, grouted side returns, a separate mantel shelf and hearth, and a complementary firebox. Most Dalton-Gorman mantels are freestanding, so that they can embellish a plain wall or a working hearth with equal ease. Marbles are finished in either high gloss or matte; the natural material resists staining and can be buffed using any transparent household wax.

Brochures available.

Dalton-Gorman
1508 Sherman Ave.
Evanston, IL 60201
(312) 369-5575

Fireplace Mantel Shop

Fore more than thirty-five years The Fireplace Mantel Shop has specialized in manufacturing architectural woodwork, including moldings, panels, valances, staircases, and more than a dozen styles of decorative mantels. One of its most flexible mantel designs, the Multee, can be used with either a flush fireplace or a projected facing and is available in a choice of three styles: with bed molding, bed and dentil molding, or bed and dentil molding finished with an oval casing. The Chestertown features a bull-nose shelf; the Metropolitan, squared-off columns and handsome vertical detail; and the Shipwright, a gracefully curved breast board and delicate proportions. Each mantel can be ordered in custom sizes to fit your exact specifications, and each is crafted of kiln-dried pine, sanded but left unfinished so that you can add your own decorative paint or stain.

Brochures available.

The Fireplace Mantel Shop, Inc.
4217 Howard Ave.
Kensington, MD 20895
(301) 564-1550

Remodelers' & Renovators' Supply

Odd-shaped windows and other surprising architectural details are part of the charm of a vintage home. Among the most important architectural focal points of a room is the mantel, and if your historic or reproduction house doesn't have the proper one, Remodelers' & Renovators' Supply can provide it. Measure the brick area and firebox of your hearth, and the company will build a clear pine mantel to complement any period style.

Catalogue, $2.

Remodelrs' & Renovators' Supply
512 W. Idaho St.
Boise, ID 83702
(208) 344-8612 or
(208) 344-8613

Spiess Antique Building Materials

Formerly named Spiess Stained and Leaded Glass, this company has turned its attention to antique woods. Spiess usually has some antique mantels available, along with other wood architectural

elements. Shown here is an elaborately carved foliage design. It and more classical styles are typical of the pieces Spiess has on hand at any given time. Call for an appointment before visiting the office.

Spiess Antique Building Materials
228-230 E. Washington St.
Joliet, IL 60433
(815) 722-5639

Sunshine Architectural Woodworks

Not every mantel is right for every room, so finding the perfect one can be difficult. Sunshine Architectural Woodworks makes the search a little easier by supplying ten mantel styles. Most can be adjusted to meet your room's special requirements. Some are available with an optional raised oval center panel which can be plain or carved with one of five designs—rose and ribbon, wheat and straw, grapes and vines, bells and cockles, or acorns and boughs. The standard wood is kiln-dried poplar in two grades—paint grade and stain grade. However, all mantels can be manufactured in walnut, cherry, mahogany, oak, white pine, birch, maple, and a host of other domestic woods. Mantels are shipped unassembled. A sample of wood, consisting of a raised panel and frame and measuring about 8" by 11", is available and can be returned for a full refund of its purchase price.

Some examples of Sunshine's work are illustrated here, including model 232HW and the more ornate 213HW. Both stand 57¼" tall and 74" wide with an 83"-long shelf. The opening on

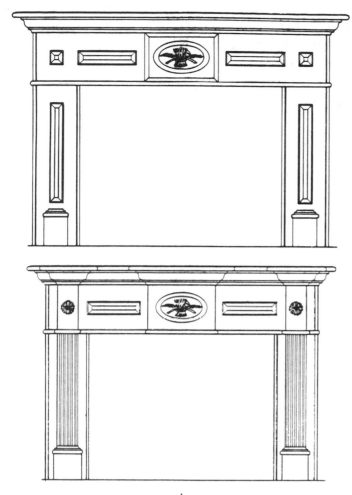

Crete's inflatable forms, guaranteeing preservation of historic structures.

Brochure available.

Insul-Crete
4056 Bailey N.W.
Massillon, OH 44646
Canton: (216) 478-5751
Akron: (216) 376-1899

Superior Clay

each is 39¼" high by 50" wide, and each is available with or without a raised center panel. The return sides can be modified to wrap projecting chimneys, and height or width can be altered.

Catalogue, $4.

Sunshine Architectural Woodworks
Rte. 2, Box 434
Fayetteville, AR 72701
(501) 521-4329

Maintenance and Design

While most owners of conventional heating systems include regular cleaning and maintenance checks in the cost of those systems, many of the same people balk at the expense involved in keeping fireplace chimneys and wood stoves in good working order. And that's unfortunate. Proper liners and clean flues are essential for efficient operation—not to mention safety; ignoring them can be very costly in the long run. Your local phone book can supply the name of a good chimney sweep; for more complicated maintenance work, you may wish to contact one of the following specialists.

Insul-Crete

The poured refractory concrete recipe used by Insul-Crete protects against chimney leakage, staining, creosote odor, and fire. By reflecting virtually all heat toward the fire again, the Insul-Crete lining cuts down on heat transfer and creosote. Its pores allow it to expand and contract without breakage. Use Insul-Crete to reinforce old unlined chimneys or to repair a chimney damaged by fire. Even the most uneven old chimney can be lined using Insul-

Formed of selected ceramic materials fired to a temperature of 2,000 °F., the flue linings available through Superior can be molded in square, rectangular, or round acid-proof sections. In addition, Superior offers twenty different styles of handmade chimney tops ranging from 12" for the petite Essex to 45" for the Magnum. Corresponding weights range between 25 and 420 lbs. These durable tops function to keep out damaging wind and water while providing unobstructed venting of smoke and dangerous gases. Even sulphuric acid, the most corrosive of the combustible gases, cannot damage or corrode these linings and tops. The clay products are thus virtually maintenance free. Among the more interesting styles of top offered are the Sentry, Trinity, Cathedral, Beacon, and Diamond.

Brochures available.

Superior Clay
Box 352
Uhrichsville, OH 44683
(800) 848-6166
(800) 282-6103 (OH)

Thermocrete

Unlined or inadequately insulated chimneys, though picturesque adjuncts to a period house, can be dangerous. Without suitable liners, chimneys can overheat to the point of setting a house on fire. Less spectacular results are still serious: creosote and condensation produce acids that eat away at mortar, sometimes to the point of letting sparks and fumes into the room. Thermocrete specializes in poured chimney linings of cement and volcanic ash, a mixture that adapts itself to any chimney shape, filling cracks and breaks and allowing future cleaning to be done with ease. The Thermocrete lining won't rust or corrode and doesn't require expensive installation. It is suitable for coal, gas, oil, or wood-burning systems.

Brochure available.

Thermocrete Chimney Systems
7111 Ohms Lane
Minneapolis, MN 55435
(800) 328-6347
(612) 835-1338 (OH)

Fireplace Accessories

If you've just taken possession of the old house of your dreams and are about to purchase the first accessories for a fireplace, you'll probably want to begin with andirons, tools, and a screen. There are hundreds of styles and sizes to choose from: some of the best and most attractive are described in the following listings. After you've taken care of those necessities, you might consider additional pieces. How about a wood box? Or a swinging crane from which to hang a copper pot? Or a cast-iron fireback? Any of these pieces, if selected with an eye to design and workmanship, can increase your enjoyment of the fireplace for years to come.

Bona Decorative Hardware

If you're looking for accessories to complement your fireplace, Bona may have what you need. The company stocks an array of useful tools, including grates, brass andirons, firewood holders, tool and tong brackets, wood tongs, and bellows. Complete sets of tools like the one shown here (model 100) are also available. The set is made of polished brass and mounts easily near your fireplace.

Catalogue, $2. (Supplement available at no charge.)

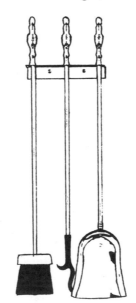

Bona Decorative Hardware
3073 Madison Rd.
Cincinnati, OH 45209
(513) 321-7877

Robert Bourdon, The Smithy

What began as a hobby for Robert Bourdon became The Smithy, a

full-time business. Bourdon is willing to produce just about anything that can be made from forged iron; the andirons and fireplace crane that appear in his brochure are only a few examples of his work. Most of his work is custom, so if you need something special, write or give him a call. If you send a stamp along with a request for his brochure, he'll send it free of charge.

Brochure available.

Robert Bourdon, The Smithy
Box 2180
Wolcott, VT 05680
(802) 472-6508

Hearth Realities

If you have a rare metal-fronted, coal-burning fireplace that needs

a replacement grate, Hearth Realities has a variety of hanging basket grates to choose from. This round grate comes in eleven sizes and is made of gray iron formed in a complex sand-casting process. The bars extend 2" into the room to provide efficient heating. The grate comes complete with a top lug hook and a 2½" channel on each side to allow it to fit frames with lugs spaced anywhere from 1½" to 5" apart. Hearth Realities' selection of original replacement parts for coal-burning fireplaces is unequaled; the company cautions that great care must be taken with measurements to insure proper fit.

Brochure available.

Hearth Realities
Box 38093
Atlanta, GA 30334
(404) 377-6852

Kayne & Son

If you aren't satisfied with the ordinary, Steve Kayne can provide you with one-of-a-kind fireplace accessories. Each piece he forges has its own distinctive personality, like that of the elaborate fireplace enclosure shown here. A small, beautifully shaped Moravian heart forms a handle at the top of the screen, and the design is echoed in the long hinges. At their centers are graceful Renaissance twists. Kayne will make any piece illustrated in his catalogue in any size that suits your needs. It's best to order as far ahead of time as possible, though, because all of his work is custom and therefore takes longer than assembly-line products to make. Restorations, repairs, and reproductions are common projects at the forge, so don't throw away a treasured old grate, andiron, or

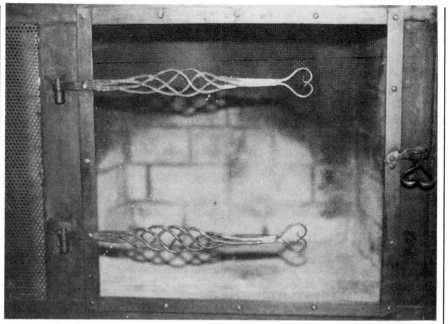

fireplace crane just because it's broken.

Kayne works primarily in steel, which he will finish in one of five ways. He can merely wax it to prevent rust, polish it so that it looks like pewter, burn oil on it to create a slightly rust-resistant black matte finish, black it, or paint it with fire-resistant flat black paint.

Catalogues available.

Kayne & Son
76 Daniel Ridge Rd.
Candler, NC 28715
(704) 667-8868

Nostalgia

Historic old Savannah is a treasure trove of 19th-century architecture, most of it located in the central historic district, one of the largest landmark areas in the country. Housed in a Victorian building, Nostalgia is perfectly situated to capitalize on the architectural heritage of its neighborhood. All of the company's reproduction iron fire screens and surrounds are cast from originals found in Savannah homes. Most are available in either cast iron or aluminum; dimensions vary with the particular style selected.

Catalogue, $2.50.

Nostalgia, Inc.
307 Stiles Ave.
Savannah, GA 31401
(912) 232-2324

Pennsylvania Firebacks

First introduced in late-15th-century Europe, the fireback

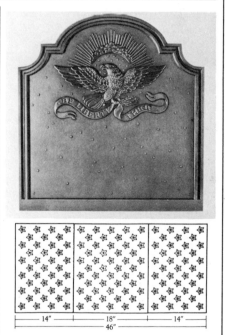

quickly became popular because of its heat-saving design and later, its decorative qualities. Pennsylvania Firebacks offers 9 different original designs by J. Del Conner, each molded of durable cast iron. Shown are the American Eagle and the Field of

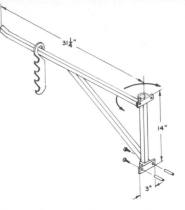

Stars, the latter designed to be installed either horizontally or vertically. The Field of Stars is available in standard 21½" by 18" size or in a more flexible 14" by 21½" model so that several can be combined to fit a variety of fireplace sizes. You may wish to mount the fireback with strong steel anchors and bolts (available from the company), or merely to prop it at the back of the hearth.

Pennsylvania Firebacks also offers hand-painted fireboards designed by Carol Nagel. She will create a unique pattern to your specifications, or you may choose from her Shaker Tree of Life or Virginia Plantation styles, as shown.

Catalogue, $2. (refundable with purchase)
Brochure, 10¢.

Pennsylvania Firebacks, Inc.
1011 E. Washington Lane
Philadelphia, PA 19138
(215) 843-6162

withstand years of use and is easy to install. Mounting hardware is included, as is the serrated pot hanger.

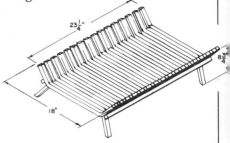

Rustic makes a variety of gratings which vary in size, bar spacing, and price. This model, 50-D, has the densest grating and the greatest size. It pairs nicely with Rustic's curved andirons, (model 49-D), reproductions of one hundred-year-old originals.

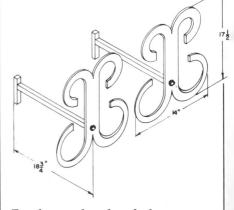

For those who already have fireplace tools, but nowhere to hang them, Rustic makes this sturdy accessory hook (model 147-C-1), and once the fire's going, an auxiliary tripod (model 62-C)

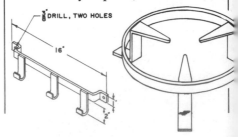

Period Furniture Hardware

Even Period Furniture's voluminous catalogue cannot list each and every item offered by the firm. Among the items it does list, however, are iron and brass andirons in a variety of styles; brass fenders; tempered glass fire screens; and custom spark guards, made to measure. Cast-iron firebacks and coal grates are also available; most fireplace hardware is constructed of solid brass or brass and cast iron and can be ordered in your choice of finishes.

Catalogue, $3.50.

Period Furniture Hardware Co., Inc.
123 Charles St.
Box 314, Charles St. Sta.
Boston, MA 02114
(617) 227-0758

Rustic Home Hardware

Most of Rustic Home Hardware's fireplace equipment is made of heavy-duty welded steel which is finished with a durable flat black paint. This is the case with the pieces pictured here. The fireplace crane (model 52-D) is built to will enable you to keep the tea kettle or coffee pot on the boil.

Catalogue, $5.

Rustic Home Hardware
R.D. 3
Hanover, PA 17331
(717) 632-0088

Schwartz's Forge & Metalworks

Joel A. Schwartz takes a personal hand in the design and execution of every item that leaves Schwartz's Forge and Metalworks. Schwartz says he seeks "lyrical qualities" in metalwork, and the beautifully designed gates, grates, and even cheese-cutters from this forge reflect his efforts. Interlocking stars and clovers pattern one 3' by 4' firescreen, while another (35" by 38") links decorative bars and circles for an arresting accent piece. Use Schwartz's own designs or ask him to bring one of your ideas to fruition.

Portfolio available.

Schwartz's Forge & Metalworks
Forge Hollow Rd.
Box 205
Deansboro, NY 13328
(315) 841-4477

Helen Williams

Helen Williams's interest in antique Dutch artifacts has led her to collect an unparalleled selection

of wall tiles dating from the mid-17th century to 1800. All are 5" square, and colors range from Delft blue and manganese to polychrome, tortoise shell, and antique white. She is especially fond of those designs which picture stories from the Old and New Testaments. In addition to her antique tiles, Williams generally has a finite number of 17th-century Dutch firebacks, such as the one illustrated, available. Elaborately decorated with shields, crowns, trumpets, and lions, this fireback measures 30" by 18".

Send SASE for brochure.

Helen Williams/Rare Tiles
12643 Hortense St.
Studio City, CA 91604
(818) 761-2756

Heating and Cooking Supplies

Anyone who makes use of an old-fashioned wood-burning stove for heating or cooking should have the best possible accessories on hand. These may range from the practical tools necessary for tending a fire to specialized instruments such as oven gauges. There are also cast-iron and steel utensils which make cooking easier as well as more enjoyable. Many of these accessories have the extra bonus of being handsomely formed and, when not in use, serve a decorative function not without value in a period setting.

Bryant Stove Works

If you have an old stove that just needs a few parts to work again and you can repair it yourself, or if you're looking for some accessories to complete your period kitchen, take a look at the supplies available from Bryant Stove Works. Among the parts and accessories usually in stock are hot water plugs, oven gauges, scrapers for cleaning ash under the oven and between the covers and top, stove polish, mica, isinglass, ash pans, iron liners, lids, racks, and grates. Call or write Joe and Bea Bryant for more information.

Brochure and catalogue available.

Bryant Stove Works, Inc.
Box 2048, Rich Rd.
Thorndike, ME 04986
(207) 568-3665

Pat Guthman Antiques

There's something reassuring about the solidity and strength of iron cookware. Most of the pieces sold by Pat Guthman Antiques have the additional recommendation of having existed for more than one hundred years. Although Guthman also sells antiques for the hearth and kitchen which are made of brass, copper, stoneware, and pewter, 18th- and 19th-century iron forms the bulk of the stock. Items commonly available include porringers with or without white enamel lining, hearth toasters, meat hooks, standing rotating broilers, bird spits, and kettles. Surrounded by such utensils, it's easy to imagine yourself transported back to colonial times.

Guthman exhibits at antiques shows in a number of cities and towns during the year. Feel free to call and find out if one near you will be attended. If so, Guthman will be happy to bring specific items for your examination.

Brochures available.

Pat Guthman Antiques
342 Pequot Rd.
Southport, CT 06490
(203) 259-5743

Kayne & Son

Steve Kayne has been a blacksmith since the age of eight, and the experience shows. His forged cooking utensils have individual personalities that reflect their custom design and Kayne's expert craftsmanship. A catalogue of sample items is available; all of them can be ordered in any size,

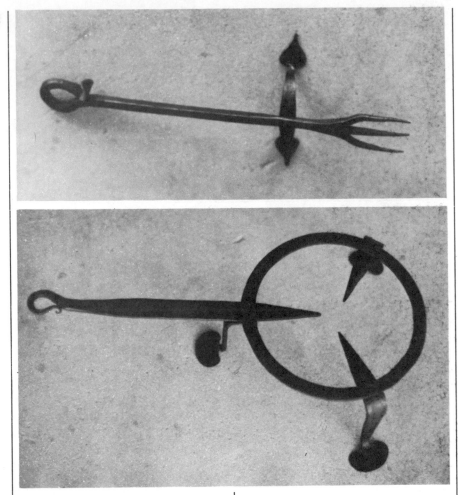

Small touches like stamped tin flue-hole covers or cast-iron pipe dampers will make a room look more authentic. The hole covers have coppered steel spring holders; pale yellow rims surround assorted stamped designs. The covers measure 9⅝" in diameter and fit 5" to 9" holes. The damper has a steel pivot rod and a handle that stays cool. Six sizes, ranging from 3" to 9" in diameter, are available.

Some of Lehman's products might be hung on the walls of a period kitchen as well as used on the stove or in the oven. The company's cast-iron cookware selection includes kettles ranging in size from one pint to forty-five gallons and skillets from 6½" to 20½" in diameter. The cornstick pan (model 19-27C2), which also

comes in a nine-stick version, can be used as a decoration as well as a utensil. The same is true of the two-loaf French bread pan (19-2FB2) and the eight-slice cornbread skillet (19-8CB2). A five-

quart Dutch oven from Lehman measures 10¼" in diameter and 4" deep. Properly seasoned, it will last a lifetime.

Catalogue, $2.

---

and repairs, reproductions, and restoration are frequently undertaken. Most items are made of steel, although copper and brass are sometimes employed.

Some of Kayne's products are perfect for old-fashioned hearth cooking. The toasting fork allows you to use the flames for cooking while keeping your hands away from the heat, and the broiler's legs keep it at an appropriate height above the coals.

Catalogue available.

Kayne & Son
76 Daniel Ridge Rd.
Candler, NC 28715
(704) 667-8868

Lehman Hardware

It's hard to beat a product that both adds to a room's beauty and to its efficiency, and at Lehman Hardware such products abound. Among them are practical accessories for wood stoves, including shovels, grate shakers, pokers, lid lifters, soot scrapers, mica, and stove black. Many of them are ornamental as well as useful. The Lehman wood tongs (model WT) are constructed of

steel with steel rivets and have a handy 24" reach and a 28" overall length. They're also an attractive adjunct to the stove. The same is true of coal hods, available in galvanized steel with an optional antique black finish. They feature twelve-quart capacity, dust-tight folded seams, and reinforced edges.

Lehman Hardware & Appliances, Inc.
Box 41, 4779 Kidron Rd.
Kidron, OH 44636
(216) 857-5441

Newton Millham

No two pieces of handcrafted iron hardware which issue from Newton Millham's one-man forge are exactly alike, but each reveals the painstaking work of a skilled artisan. Select a custom design from your own books or sketches, or choose a model from Millham's collection of 18th- and 19th-century designs. Among the more unusual are pancake flippers and spatulas (6" to 15" long), a 15" ladle inspired by 18th-century New England, and a 6" pot lifter that safely removes dinner from the flames. An elaborate, 30"-long adjustable bird spit and meat roaster is attractively decorated, finished top and bottom in brass or turned steel. Any one of these pieces, hand-filled and fitted and protected with a beeswax and linseed oil veneer, would show to advantage beside your period hearth.

Brochure, $1.

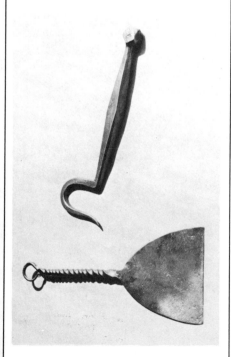

Newton Millham
672 Drift Rd.
Westport, MA 02790
(617) 636-5437

Other Suppliers of Heating and Cooking

Consult List of Suppliers for addresses.

Mantels

Architectural Antique Warehouse
Architectural Antiques Exchange
Marion H. Campbell
Central Kentucky Millwork Inc.
Classic Architectural Specialties
Curvoflite
Great American Salvage Co.
Whit Hanks
Ideal Co.
The Joinery Co.
Jerard Paul Jordan
Nostalgia, Inc.
Ohmega Salvage
Pelnik Wrecking Co.
Sheppard Millwork, Inc.
Somerset Door & Column Co.

Maintenance and Design

William H. Parsons & Associates

Fireplace Accessories

Ball and Ball
Whit Hanks
Newton Millham
Robinson Iron

Cooking Utensils and Stove Accessories

The Country Loft
Newton Millham
Portland Stove Co.
Woodstock Soapstone Co., Inc.

6.

Hardware

It is difficult not to love hardware—yes, really love it. You may not share our enthusiasm for bits and pieces, tools, and various kinds of devices that make things work. But we know there are millions of others like us "out there" who are similarly passionate about visiting old-fashioned hardware stores, or perusing the latest copy of a colorful mail-order hardware catalogue. There is, perhaps, a bit of the tinkerer in each of us. We want to know what makes something tick, to put it together and to take it apart again. At the same time, there is an aesthetically appealing element about such useful mechanical objects. And nowhere is this more the case than in the old house field.

The typical restored house is a gold mine of locks, latches and bolts, pulls, and various kinds of utensils and gadgets. In a time before everything was machine-stamped or sealed with a synthetic, it was necessary to fashion many objects by hand out of the most durable and affordable material available—iron, tin, and brass being most common. Today there are many metalsmiths who will create new hardware with the same artistry as the old. The demand for quality period hardware is great, and increasing numbers of young men and women have taken up the old crafts of blacksmithing, tinsmithing, and fine metal working.

One of the best ways to examine good period hardware is to visit restored houses open to the public or museum complexes such as Williamsburg, Old Deerfield, Greenfield Village and the Henry Ford Museum, and the Winterthur Museum. There one can see the very best in antique and reproduction pieces. Curators are always willing to share information regarding skilled craftsmen. Without leaving your own home, however, you can start on a tour of the best sources for period hardware in the pages of this book.

Handmade custom *cire perdu* hardware by Cirecast, San Francisco, California.

136

Architectural Hardware

At the beginning of the 19th century the term "hardware" meant chiefly mechanics' tools and builders' hardware, but it soon came to mean all small metal articles used in the construction of houses or for household purposes, tools of mechanics' trades, furnishing goods for kitchen and dining room service, tin plate, sheet iron, nails, screws, fence wire, etc. By the beginning of the 20th century it was not uncommon for a large hardware house to have in its catalogues nearly

100,000 kinds and sizes of articles. Given the quantity and variety of hardware hand made and mass produced in America, it's no wonder that most old houses still have original pieces intact. Guard and preserve these artifacts from the past, but, if you need to seek replacement parts, collect some of the excellent catalogues of reproduction pieces that follow. We haven't counted, but we think that you'll come close to the quantity available at the turn of the century.

original. The stock of early American items includes strap hinges, latches, bolts, doorknobs, drawer pulls, and a range of accessories for the bath. A lustrous black finish with forged edges is standard, but numerous selections come in antique copper, Old English brass, or pewter. Acorn gladly responds to requests for further information.

Catalogue available.

Acorn Manufacturing Co., Inc.
Mansfield, MA 02048
(617) 339-4500

A-Ball

Is there a damaged or missing heating grate in your old house? If so, A-Ball can replace it with one of eight stock styles or custom cast one from your original. The grates are aluminum reproductions of Victorian pieces; choices include the curving, spiky design of model GG108 and the more

geometric pattern of model GG104. Model GG108 is 13½" long and 10¾" wide; GG104 measures 16" by 16". A-Ball's grates can also be used as imaginative boot scrapers, table tops, plant stands, trivets, or wall decorations. A-Ball carries an extensive line of hardware and plumbing supplies.

Catalogue available.

A-Ball Plumbing Supply
1703 W. Burnside
Portland, OR 97209
(503) 228-0026

Arden Forge

Peter A. Renzetti's Arden Forge, established in 1970, is notable both for its collection of antique hardware and for its highly accurate reproductions. Renzetti works in wrought iron, cast iron, steel, copper, lead, tin, pewter, zinc, and wood using anvil, forge, and assorted power and hand tools and machining equipment. Arden Forge is often chosen to do restoration and reproduction projects for museums and historical societies. Hardware from the 18th and 19th centuries is an Arden specialty, although the company does just about everything from hand-making nails to restoring and appraising antiques. No catalogue is available, but calls and letters are welcome. Renzetti can reproduce any piece in Albert

Acorn Manufacturing

Acorn stocks hand-crafted hardware for use indoors and out. Each piece is a scrupulously executed reproduction of a period

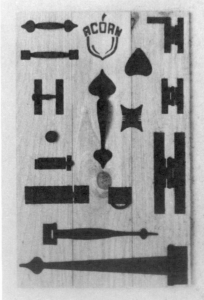

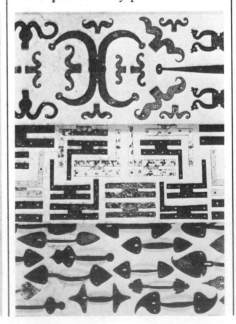

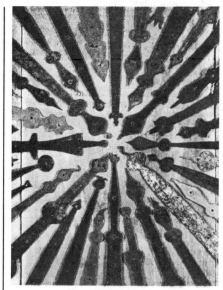

H. Sonn's *Early American Hardware* —just specify plate and page numbers—but if you'd like something custom made, he will be glad to accommodate you. The photographs here illustrate a small portion of Arden Forge's vast selection.

The Arden Forge
301 Brinton's Bridge Rd.
West Chester, PA 19382
(215) 399-1350

Baldwin Hardware

Baldwin Hardware's selections include an array of brass doorknobs, door trim, hinges, and name plates. Equip French doors that have the slimmest of stiles with solid brass cremone bolts. Either design—knob or slender lever—hides bolt guides beautifully. A solid brass rim lock, coated with transparent enamel, outfits metal-clad doors in elegance.

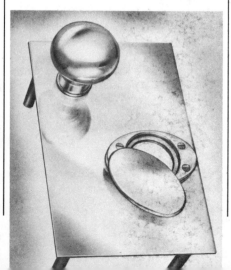

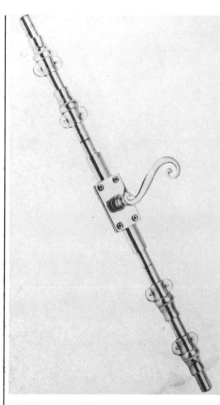

Color pamphlets, 75¢.

Baldwin Hardware Corp.
841 Wyomissing Blvd.
Box 82
Reading, PA 19603
(215) 777-7811

Blaine Window Hardware

Blaine Window Hardware is a treasure trove of resources—but take your stamina along when you set out to make your choice from over 20,000 replacement parts at Blaine's. Offering to furnish "any part for any window," as well as hardware for closets and patio doors, lockers, and more, Blaine will custom design, cast, or copy rare hardware. Unusual items include various

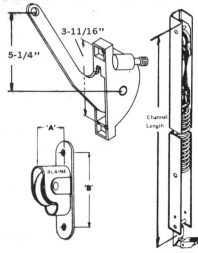

awning operators equipped for pole or chain operation. Blaine's one piece replacement window channels cut air leakage when you substitute them for old styles. Blaine's sash pulleys—steel axles with cast aluminum wheel and housing—are also available in brass and bronze.

Catalogue, $2.

Blaine Window Hardware
1919 Blaine Dr.
Hagerstown, MD 21740
(301) 797-6500

Bona

A solid brass letter slot may not be *de rigueur* for a period front door, but it can be a useful, and handsome, addition. Bona offers several different styles, including the very simple and very ornate models shown here. Complementary back plates and numerals are also available, each made of solid brass.

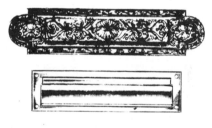

Catalogue, $2.

Bona Decorative Hardware
3073 Madison Rd.
Cincinnati, OH 45209
(513) 321-7877

Circecast

Circecast specializes in handmade custom hardware, focusing on Victorian and Edwardian pieces of cast iron, bronze, and stamped steel. The firm supplies architects and designers with custom reproductions, a process which often requires it to locate appropriate models for a specific historic project. The lost wax method of casting employed by Circecast allows the company to replicate exceedingly intricate designs, including those which grace keyplates and hinges from the Ekado, Lily, and Columbian collections.

Catalogue available.

Cirecast
380 7th St.
San Francisco, CA 94103
(415) 863-8319

Elephant Hill Ironworks

Working from books, drawings, antique pieces, and custom designs, Kenneth H. Parrot of Elephant Hill Ironworks strives for authenticity and durability in his hand-forged reproductions. Readers of previous *Old House Catalogues* may remember Elephant Hill as Strafford Forge of South Strafford, Vermont. Parrot's specialty is 17th- and 18th-century colonial hardware. An informative catalogue is available, and some items are kept in stock, but it's best to order as far ahead of time as possible, especially if you're on a strict building schedule. Most of Elephant Hill's pieces are made to order. Forged nails or screws are supplied with orders on request.

The 18th-century square plate spring latch pictured here displays Parrot's skill and attention to detail. The brass handle is of an unusual stirrup shape, and the sliding bolt is tipped with a gleaming brass knob. Elephant Hill also manufactures a number of Dutch strap hinges (model 350), more ornate than ordinary strap hinges and available in rolled-eye or welded-eye configurations. The rolled-eye hinges come in 10″, 12″, and 16″ lengths; the welded-eye in 18″, 20″, and 24″ lengths. These hinges were most popular in New Jersey, Pennsylvania, and New York and were also found in New England, but they are appropriate for period homes outside the Northeast as well. The smaller sizes are perfect for shutters, cupboards, or lightweight doors.

Catalogue, $2.

Elephant Hill Ironworks
R.R. 1, Box 168
Tunbridge, VT 05077
(802) 889-9444

Federal Street Lighthouse

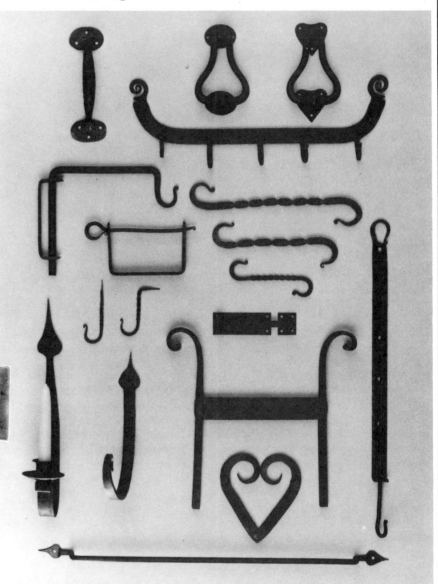

Building on a decade of experience with unusual hardware, the Federal Street Lighthouse continues to expand its array of period reproductions as it locates excellent craftspeople to forge them. Iron knockers, latches, hangers, hooks, boot scrapers, and towel racks are available. The inventory includes mostly hand-forged items,—and Federal Street Lighthouse will accommodate requests for custom pieces.

Catalogue, $3.

Federal Street Lighthouse, Ltd.
38 Market Sq.
Newburyport, MA 01950
(617) 462-6333

Kayne & Son

Kayne & Son takes pride in keeping costs low enough to let its customers ignore die-cast or flimsy steel stampings in favor of cast brass and bronze or hand-forged iron hardware. The authentic colonial styles offered are taken from antique models, and rare pieces make Kayne & Son a treasure cache for the most demanding old house enthusiast. Selections in-

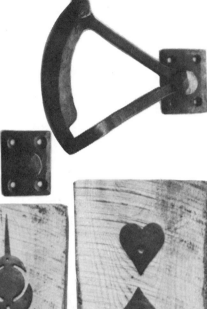

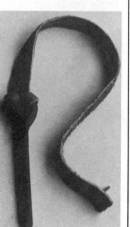

clude a weighty, rugged Dutch-door quadrant to secure upper and lower doors. Sleinder points, crescents, and circles adorn matching thumb-latch handles and thumb pieces. A heart-shaped keyhole cover is crafted of hand-forged iron. The firm found its inspiration for an unusual bean shutter dog in Charleston, South Carolina's, historic district. Early designs include leather-thonged locks and hand-wrought nails to secure window sash and a hand-forged iron or brass door knocker shaped like a musical note.

Catalogue available.

Kayne & Son
76 Daniel Ridge Rd.
Candler, NC 28715
(704) 667-8868

Newton Millham

Artisan Newton Millham hand forges iron hardware to custom order. Send him a photograph, measured drawing, or a reference from one of numerous books he recommends, and he can reproduce any number of unusual

early American iron pieces. The Community House of Bethlehem, Pennsylvania, furnished the 200-year-old models for Moravian latches with tulip-shaped ornamentation. Window sash hardware includes a leather and iron double-hung sash pin from the 18th century. Butterfly and strap hinges, andirons, and kitchenware all come from this blacksmith's shop. Millham forges and/or file finishes all of his work, and he applies coatings of beeswax and linseed oil. Pieces for outdoor use usually have a flat black finish with anti-rust primer; latches are coated with beeswax.

Catalogue, $1.

Newton Millham
Star Forge
672 Drift Rd.
Westport, MA 02790
(617) 636-5437

Omnia Industries

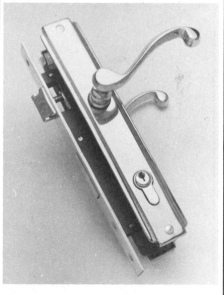

It's usually easy to find hardware for the front door, but what if your house has French doors, patio doors, or other doors with narrow stiles? Omnia Industries makes a variety of hardware for such doors, including the narrow stile backset mortise lock shown here. Standing 6¾" tall and trimmed in solid polished lacquered brass, it is available with a double profile cylinder or with the turnpiece on the inside. A selection of nine lever handles, four backplate styles, and four finishes—polished brass, polished chrome plated, satin chrome plated, or shaded bronze plated—makes it versatile enough to suit almost any door. Omnia also makes solid brass Cremone bolts for French doors. One of the firm's finest models (2057/CR) comes with two rods, five guides, and two strike plates. It is distinguished by an oval knob with a classical foliage design and beaded rim and by guides shaped like columns interrupted by wreaths. Omnia sells only to distributors, but will inform consumers of the dealer nearest them.

Omnia Industries
49 Park St.
Box 263
Montclair, NJ 07042
(201) 746-4300

Period Furniture Hardware

Plain-domed or decoratively shaped and beaded, Period Furniture Hardware's forged-brass doorknobs are typical of this reputable firm's high quality products. Among the wide array of offerings are handsome brass mortise locks available in a variety of attractive styles—some oval, some rectangular, some more elaborately shaped. Fanciful designs for solid-brass doorknockers include the whale, lion, fox, dolphin, shell, torch, anchor, and pineapple. Trivets, jamb hooks, thumb latches, offset icebox hardware, and even Chinese character pulls symbolizing long life and good luck — find all of them (and quite a bit more) at Period Furniture Hardware. All brass hardware sold by the firm is available in a darkened antiqued finish, unless the shiny "golden glow" finish is requested.

Catalogue, $3.50.

Period Furniture Hardware Co., Inc.
Box 314
Charles St. Sta.
123 Charles St.
Boston, MA 02114
(617) 227-0758

Remodelers' & Renovators' Supply

If you're looking for a late-Victorian doorbell, you'll appreciate the old-fashioned twist doorbells at Remodelers' & Renovators' Supply. In diameters

of 3" or 4", one model simply mounts on the outside of the door, and another has a bell indoors with the ringer outside. Both are rimmed by complicated curlicues of the same solid brass that forms their bodies. Remodelers' & Renovators' Supply can trim the rest of the door with ease, furnishing doorknobs, pulls, latches, plates, and more. The firm's catalogue is as varied as an old-style hardware store.

Catalogue, $2.

Remodelers' & Renovators' Supply
512 W. Idaho
Boise, ID 83702
(208) 344-8612 or
(208) 344-8613

Rustic Home Hardware

The handmade steel and iron objects forged at Rustic Home Hardware are miles away from the mass-produced pieces in other companies' catalogues. The firm's sturdy gate hinges, 18" long and built to last, are typical of the high

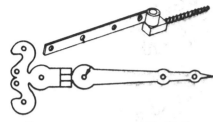

quality you can expect. Crafted from hot rolled steel ¼" thick, the flat hinge is of equal quality, but more decoratively formed. The firm also provides wine and utensil racks, meat and pot hooks, and an exhaustive selection of fireplace accessories. Rustic Home Hardware sprays every piece of steel or iron with black paint that retards scuff marks.

Catalogue, $5.

Rustic Home Hardware
R.D. 3
Hanover, PA 17331
(717) 632-0088

David Swearingen

Security, good looks, and authenticity combine in the locks and keys made by David Swearingen. Most of his locks are keyed differently, although many can be keyed alike, keyed alike in sets, or masterkeyed on request. Both locks and keys may be stamped with letters or numbers, and keys can be fit to antique locks. Swearingen's huge collection of antique and reproduction locks includes genuine 19th-century locks and keys, some in the original packaging, and reproduction Victorian and colonial bit key locks. The collection was recently augmented by the acquisition of all obsolete dies, patterns, and tooling from the country's oldest lock manufacturer. A limited number of reproductions have resulted, ranging in date of design from about 1835 to 1935. Also obtained from the manufacturer were some old

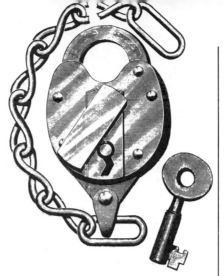

woodcuts illustrating the locks, one example of which is shown here. A small catalogue describes some of Swearingen's products, including wrought-iron padlocks, rim locks, mortise locks, and fancy keys. The full line contains thousands of items and is displayed in the company's "Block-buster Catalogue," available on a three-day loan for $5 plus a $35 deposit which is refunded if the catalogue is returned postpaid within thirty days.

The piece illustrated here, model 112, is a solid cast bronze reproduction of a railroad switch lock. It features a self-locking spring shackle, a spring keyhole cover, and a drain hole to prevent freezing. It comes with one bronze key and is 2½" wide. Available variations include a narrower 2⅛"-wide version and one without a chain.

Catalogue, $1.

David Swearingen, Bonded Locksmith
220 E. 6th St.
Jacksonville, FL 32206
(904) 356-5396

Tremont Nail Co.

For want of a nail . . . you needn't go farther than Tremont. The company makes twenty types of cut nails, which are fashioned according to old patterns. Tremont should know about the ways in which old nails were made—its establishment in 1819 makes it the oldest nail manufacturer in the United States. Samples of each of the varieties, as well as historical

background and a price list, may be obtained for $3.75 postpaid. A catalogue of wrought-iron hardware and household accessories is also available.

Tremont Nail Co.
Dept. OHC, 8 Elm St., Box 111
Wareham, MA 02571
(617) 221-5540

Williamsburg Blacksmiths

Located in the foothills of the Berkshires, Williamsburg has been a manufacturer of wrought-iron hardware since 1922. Experience is at least partially responsible for the high quality of the company's reproductions, especially those of door hardware. Norfolk laiches, first introduced around 1800 and widely used in the 19th century, come in six styles. Model 44 is a reproduction of an original piece owned by the company. Measuring 7½" high by 1⅝" wide, it can be made entirely of iron, or the three bulbs in the handle center can be made of pewter or brass.

Some of Williamsburg's locking devices provide an especially refreshing alternative to modern complexity. The 3" locking pin (model 603) rests above a latch bar

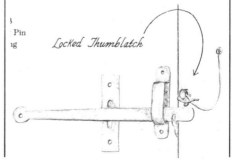

Locked Thumblatch

or through a double-hung window sash. When not in use, it hangs from a leather thong nailed to the wall. Another interesting locking device is the Cane bolt, designed to be used with double doors. Model 5260 is 12" long and 1½" wide; model 5270 is identical but larger, measuring 14" long and 1¾" wide.

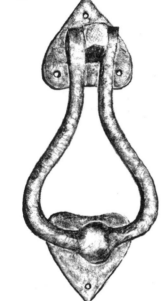

Williamsburg doesn't forget the front of the door, either. These door knockers catch the eye with fluid lines and sturdy construction. Bell-shaped model 35 is 7¼" high and 3¾" wide. The unique S-shaped curl of model 40 requires a 3" clearance, so beware—storm doors can't hang too close.

It's 6" high and 2½" wide. All items are coated with a phosphate compound and black lacquer to prevent rusting. Williamsburg encourages visits to its showroom.

Catalogue, $3.

Williamsburg Blacksmiths, Inc.
Rte. 9
Williamsburg, MA 01096
(413) 268-7341

Windy Hill Forge

The snowstorm that leaves your pitched-roof period home looking like a Currier and Ives winter print can spell trouble for weighted-down rain gutters and for the roof itself. Windy Hill Forge offers fanciful snow irons shaped like fans, leaves, acorns, eagles, or flowers. Steel bolts, brackets, and castings accompany all irons. Among Windy Hill Forge's other hardware selections, take note of twenty-one different kinds of decorative cast-iron brackets. A few simple hacksaw cuts will convert many of these designs to the scale that best suits the shelving in your home. A col-

lection of cast-iron washers shaped like diamonds, flowers, or stars (ranging from 7" to 14") is one of the most exceptional offerings from the firm. These are the decorative structural devices seen on the brick walls of old multi-story buildings that prevented the walls from bulging and spreading. They can also be ordered in brass or aluminum for indoor use on through bolts.

Brochures, 25¢.

Windy Hill Forge
3824 Schroeder Ave.
Perry Hall, MD 21128-9783
(301) 256-5890

Woodbury Blacksmith

If you live in a 17th- or 18th-century house and insist on the historical authenticity of all replacement hardware, then you require work hand-forged at the fire by Woodbury Blacksmith & Forge Co. Thumb latches, spring latches, strap and side hinges; H, HL, and butterfly hinges; bar latches and rat-tail hinges; bolts, hasps, and hooks; shutter dogs and Norfolk latches—all have been ordered from the Woodbury blacksmiths for impressive restoration projects throughout North America. Since the designs for each of these hardware types are representative of the differing styles favored in particular colonial regions, you can select with

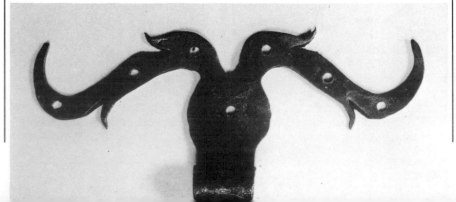

certainty the styles of hardware that are indigenous to the location of your house. Woodbury hardware is not die-stamped, cast, nor reworked commercial hardware. It is hand forged and faithfully copied from good originals. While the smiths prefer to forge from pure wrought iron, shortness of supply requires occasional substitution of soft steel. Shown here is a ram's horn side hinge, typical of Woodbury's stock output. The firm is more than willing to accept custom jobs and will work from excavated artifacts, drawings, or original hardware.

Catalogue, $2.

Woodbury Blacksmith & Forge Co.
Box 268
Woodbury, CT 06798
(203) 263-5737

Accents also supplies tasselled molding hooks with picture wire made of three-ply 60-pound cord. The hooks come in gold and ivory; picture lights are also available.

Brochure available.

Classic Accents Inc.
Box 1181
Southgate, MI 48195
(313) 282-5525

Household Hardware

The old house can greatly profit from attention to details. This does not mean we must slavishly attend to every particular in order to wipe out all traces of modernity. Such a task, aside from its great difficulty and cost, is quite impractical, especially in the selection of common household hardware. But by careful choice, many traditional objects can be put to

proper use to enhance the period decor and enrich the experience of the user. If the prospect of standardized household hardware depresses you, then the high quality of the selections that follow will illustrate how some history-minded manufacturers are pursuing the quest for excellence and helping to dispel the gloom of contemporary mediocrity.

Bona

Among the more unusual hardware items featured in Bona's catalogue are custom brass bar rails and fittings. The firm will cut and prepare rails to your order, so no matter the length of antique bar you are refurbishing, you should have no trouble in providing a rail to finish it.

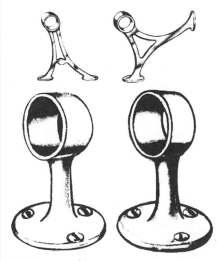

Catalogue, $2.

Bona Decorative Hardware
3073 Madison Rd.
Cincinnati, OH 45209
(513) 321-7877

Classic Accents

Modern plastic switch plates look awkward and out of place in a period room. Classic Accents has a plate in a floral design (model D220) that's more suitable. The solid brass fixture is a reproduction of an original from an old Michigan home, shown here with the S90 push-button light switch. The S90 is inlaid with mother-of-pearl and is easy to install. Classic

Conant Custom Brass

Nothing is more aggravating than trying to sweep that last bit of dust out of the corners on stairs or floors. You never quite feel that you've gotten it all. Conant Custom Brass presents an old solution that for some reason has been forgotten in recent years—the dust corner. Introduced in the 1890s, dust corners quickly evolved from wood to brass. They save time and give an ordinary

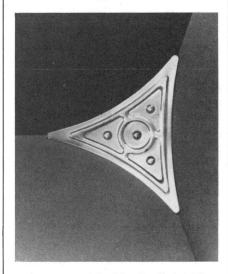

staircase a period look. Conant's solid brass corners come with an embossed surface (smooth surface on request). A minimum of ten corners must be ordered. They come with round-headed brass nails and a special steel punch for easy installation. Conant sells other types of brass hardware as well.

Literature on dust corners available.

Conant Custom Brass
270 Pine St.
Burlington, VT 05401
(802) 658-4482

| ## Country Loft

Small details add a subtle touch of authenticity to a period room. Among the charming household items offered by the Country Loft are a wrought-iron candle-keeper that holds a good supply of candles. It is meant to be secured to a beam with the hand-forged nail that Country Loft supplies. Primitive, hand-hammered iron holders to skewer Indian corn on each of ten spikes make a colorful dried display. A pierced-tin spice bin with a heart-shaped pattern would be an interesting accent on the wall of a country kitchen.

Seasonal catalogues available.

The Country Loft
South Shore Park
Hingham, MA 02043
(800) 225-5408

Hurley Patentee

Hurley Patentee is best known for its superb reproductions of colonial lighting fixtures, made from aged metal and 200-year-old wood. In addition, however, the firm offers hand-crafted reproduction hardware notable for its quality and its attention to authentic detail. Iron hooks and brackets and a colonial fire screen are among the items available. An elaborately ornamented foot scraper, 15″ high by 8″ wide, comes equipped with bolts, or can be secured in cement. Hurley Patentee can produce custom pieces to satisfy your most unusual request.

Catalogue, $2.

Hurley Patentee
R.D. 7, Box 98A
Kingston, NY 12401
(914) 331-5414

Remodelers' & Renovators'

A flimsy tin mailbox has no place beside a period front door. Remodelers' & Renovators' Supply offers a sturdy, ornate letter box which measures 12″ by 5″ and weighs five pounds. The firm says that the solid brass mailbox should last forever—a statement that's hard to disbelieve. More

suitable for a colonial home is the simpler model with newspaper rack. It measures 14″ by 5″. Other solid-brass hardware offered by Remodelers' & Renovators' includes a solid brass coat hook patterned with flowers, which measures 10¾″ by 4″ and projects a mere 2″ from the wall.

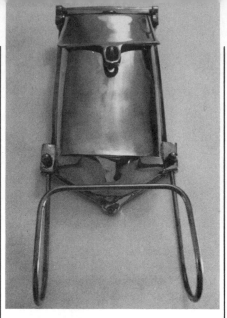

Catalogue, $2.

Remodelers' & Renovators' Supply
512 W. Idaho
Boise, ID 83702
(208) 344-8612 or
(208) 344-8613

Bath and Kitchen Hardware

The fixtures and fittings found in the kitchen and bath are those which are usually the first to go in any renovation. Careful thought, however, should be given to the replacement of sinks, tubs, and toilets. In many cases, it is possible to refinish these antique pieces. If that proves impossible, they can be replaced with fixtures that are at least old-fashioned in appearance. Specialty plumbing and salvage houses around the country regularly supply reconditioned and reproduction fixtures. Similarly, these dealers can supply reproduction old-style fittings such as faucet sets that can be substituted for the hopelessly corroded antique.

A-Ball

It's good, simple design and first-rate quality that have made A-Ball an *Old House Catalogue* favorite. Those elements are apparent in this cast-iron porcelain pedestal sink (model ER1011). The lines are pleasing, and it's a strong, durable piece. It's drilled for a 12″ widespread faucet and measures 30″ high by 24″ wide by 20″ deep. Another example is this solid oak high-tank toilet with a white china bowl. The hardware for it is available in brass or chrome, and each part can be ordered separately.

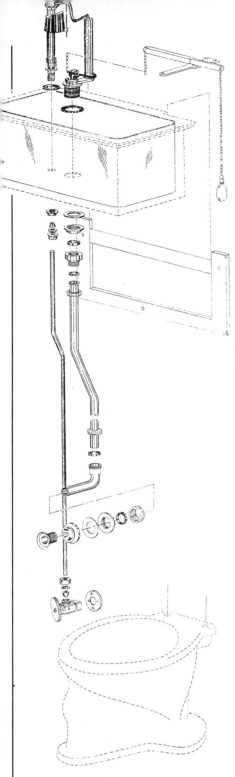

can measure from 5½" to 14" between the handle centers. Brass or porcelain spoke-style handles are available, and lever handles can be substituted (model BL3). Choose the finish you prefer—polished brass or chrome-plated brass. For more information, write to A-Ball.

Catalogue available.

A-Ball Plumbing Supply
1703 W. Burnside
Portland, OR 97209
(503) 228-0026

However, it's more than fine reproduction that makes A-Ball special; it's also the company's efforts to solve problems that occur frequently in the restoration of old houses. This exposed mixing faucet (BL2), popular in the 1930s and subsequently forgotten, is just one of A-Ball's solutions for old pedestal sinks that cannot be adapted for widespread faucets. Its gooseneck spout is 12" high, and its width is adjustable and

Barclay Products

What Victorian bathroom would be complete without a claw-foot bathtub? Barclay Products can supply a polished-brass-legged 5' acrylic/fiberglass reproduction in red, brown, white, bone, or platinum. This tub, model 5968, is shown with Barclay's useful brass and oak bath seat (model 3321) and a faucet and hand shower unit (model 4001B).

No less critical than the choice of a tub is the selection of a sink, and Barclay can help there, too.

The high rim and Classical columnar base of the Colonial sink (model 5818) might appeal to you, as might its generously sized (27⅝" wide, 23" deep) basin. It stands 36¾" high including the 3¾" back and is shown with Barclay's 795 faucet set. You may prefer the more delicate, fluted shape of the Shell pedestal sink (model 5828), shown with the

lever-handled 746 faucet set. It measures 35½" high, with a 20" wide and 16¼" deep basin. Either sink is well-suited to a period bathroom.

Catalogue available.

Barclay Products Ltd.
424 N. Oakley Blvd.
Chicago, IL 60612
(312) 243-1444

Besco

Expert in restoration, Besco has filled its Boston showroom with antique plumbing supplies and re-surfaced porcelain, and makes faucets and fittings to order. Besco stocks many fine reproductions and can custom-copy fixtures, as well. Solid brass (polished or satin finish), porcelain, or fluted china basins are also available.

Besco participates in a collector's network and can often accommodate orders for unusual items.

Besco Plumbing
729 Atlantic Ave.
Boston, MA 02111
(617) 423-4535

Brass Finial

The Brass Finial offers all kinds of period reproduction hardware, from a brass Chippendale pull or a porcelain cabinet knob to a clawfoot tub. Shown here is the company's reproduction of a turn-of-the-century pedestal sink, the Berkeley model, composed of vitreous china. As the company's name implies, most of its fixtures are made of polished brass, left unlacquered to achieve an attractive patina over time. Chrome finish is available, if you prefer.

Catalogue, $1.

The Brass Finial
2408 Riverton Rd.
Cinnaminson, NJ 08077
(609) 786-9337

The Broadway Collection

If you want to combine the beauty of the past with the efficiency of the present, The Broadway Collection offers twelve complete lines of bathroom hardware that blend well with period furnishings. Each line contains almost everything the well-equipped period bathroom might need—faucets, handles, levers, shower heads, pedestal lavatories, towel bars, robe hooks, soap dishes, shower rods, and drains. All the metal is solid brass and is available in several finishes—polished unlacquered, coated, or electro-plated.

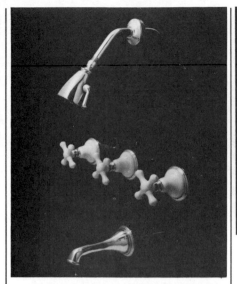

Model 19844-3 is a three-valve tub and shower set from Broadway's Colony White Suite. "HOT" and "COLD" lettering is available on the porcelain handles. The faucet is 5½" deep, and the centers of the outside valves are 8" apart. Brass fittings for Colony White hardware are available polished with clear lacquer, coated in a slightly darker finish that Broadway calls French bronze, or electroplated with pewter or polished chrome.

If you prefer all-metal fixtures to combinations of brass and porcelain, the Old Dominion Suite may suit your taste. Model 19230 is a faucet set available in polished unlacquered or polished lacquered brass, French bronze, or pewter on polished chrome electroplating. It is about 5" deep, with a maximum distance of 20" between the handle centers. All handles in this suite are lever style.

One of Broadway's finest lines is the Edwardian Suite. Model 19770 is a graceful gooseneck faucet that stands 11¾" tall with two spoke handles whose centers can be mounted a maximum of 20"

apart. The handles are topped by small white insets which bear the letters "H" and "C". Broadway's Edwardian fixtures range from the very simple—a smooth white pedestal lavatory (model 10070-3)—to the very complex—the exposed tub and hand shower wall mount (model 19797). The latter extends about 5" from the wall and features two spoke style handles whose centers are 8"

apart, a porcelain lever, and an elegant hand-held shower head resting in a delicate cradle. All of the Edwardian Suite fixtures are available in polished unlacquered or polished lacquered brass or electroplated with pewter or polished chrome.

Catalogue available.

The Broadway Collection
250 N. Troost
Olathe, KS 66061
(800) 255-6365
(913) 782-6244 (KS)
(800) 468-1219 (Canada)

D.E.A. Bathroom Machineries

D.E.A. restores old bath appliances and fixtures and creates faithful reproductions, as well. Choose a Victorian pedestal sink (32" high by 24" wide by 20" deep) in milky vitreous china, or an oak vanity in golden, brown, or natural finish. Shower heads in

porcelain, polished brass, and chrome come in fixed or hand-held, octagonal or low-flow designs. Brass or chrome towel warmers provide toasty towels on the energy it takes to illuminate a standard light bulb. D.E.A. can provide the smallest pieces to furnish a period bathroom—even soap dishes are available, all made of lacquered brass in pierced or solid styles and several different shapes.

Catalogue, $2.

D.E.A. Bathroom Machineries
495 Main St.
Box 1020
Murphys, CA 95247
(209) 728-3860

Kohler

Widely admired for its extensive line of sleek, modern bath fixtures and furnishings, Kohler also manufactures a number of faucets in its Antique series which replicate more classic styles. These faucets come in a choice of brushed, polished chrome, or gold finishes (and real gold, at that!). Ceramic-accented handles

are offered in a range of colors. For an unusual look, you might choose inserts of onyx, in tones which Kohler calls "Persian Chocolate" and "Turkish Pearl."

Catalogue, $3.

Kohler Co.
Kohler, WI 53044
(910) 264-3877

Lehman Hardware

With over thirty years of serving the local Amish and Mennonite communities, J.E. Lehman is an expert at producing things that

work simply and well. Through his mail-order catalogue, which features seven hundred items which use no electricity, he has made his merchandise available throughout North America. Lehman is the man to see if you're looking for products that are not only appropriate to your house, but also functional. The cast-iron pitcher pump, for example, is perfect for water levels under 20' and can pump up to 25' if necessary. It has a 4" stroke and stands 16" high; its machined cylinder is 3" in diameter, and 1¼" pipe will be required for it. Lehman also sells pump jacks which can be attached to a motor to convert the circular motion into the vertical stroking action

necessary to operate a hand pump. The jacks are adjustable and can accommodate 4½" or 6" strokes at a rate of forty strokes per minute. All gears are made of machine-cut steel and are bathed in oil for long life. The catalogue includes a chart which gives information on the number of gallons per hour that the jack can pump, taking into account the cylinder size, water depth, and the motor's horsepower.

Catalogue, $2.

Lehman Hardware and Appliances, Inc.
Box 41, 4779 Kidron Rd.
Kidron, OH 44636
(216) 857-5441

19th Century

Save space and create atmosphere with sugar and flour bins from 19th Century Hardware. Made of tin plate, these reproductions measure 11" high by 10" wide by 9½" deep and mount on the underside of a cabinet shelf. Slide them out to use them. The flour bin (model B-425) has a sifter and crank; the sugar bin (model B-430) has a lever dispenser. For a look at other Victorian-style hardware and one of the more interesting catalogues around, write 19th Century.

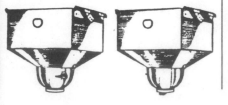

Catalogue, $2.

19th Century Hardware and Supply Co.
Box 599
Rough & Ready, CA 95975
(916) 432-1040

Saxe Patterson

Clay from Taos, New Mexico is formed into stunning ceramic art by the craftsmen at Saxe Patterson. Self-rimming basins are available in round (18" outside diameter, 15" inside diameter) or oval (15" by 19" outside diameter, 12" by 16" inside diameter) styles. Hand-finished vitreous porcelain, fired at white-hot temperatures, receives a coating of glaze at 2350° Fahrenheit. Saxe Patterson creates its own glazes, glossy and matte—many including local ingredients

—for a distinctive and durable formula. Glaze samples are available for varying charges, refundable with large orders.

Brochure available.

Saxe Patterson
Box 15
Salazar Rd.
Taos, NM 87571
(505) 758-9513

or illustrations in books, and most of his pieces can be altered to suit the buyer.

Remodelers' & Renovators'

This Idaho company is a specialist in the manufacture and distribution of quality reproductions for all areas of the period home. Samples include this oak low-boy water closet, its copper tank liner concealed by handsomely polished wood. A solid brass shaving mirror rotates to any convenient angle; its telescoping design is a space-saver in a small room.

Catalogue, $2.

This low-tank toilet is a good example of Rheinschild's fine work. Similar to the John Douglas model (which gave us the slang term "John"), this piece has a high-quality white china bowl and a tank and seat of solid oak. The tank is lined with stainless steel. If you like the looks of the oak, but already have a new or antique bowl that you prefer, you can purchase the tank and seat only, and hardware for customizing your bowl will be included.

Remodelers' & Renovators' Supply
512 W. Idaho
Boise, ID 83702
(208) 344-8612 or
(208) 344-8613

S. Chris Rheinschild

Just when it feels as if individuality and creativity have disappeared entirely, a craftsman like S. Chris Rheinschild reminds us that they still exist. Rheinschild began making his toilets and basins when he was restoring his 1905 Los Angeles home, and it's good news for old house lovers that he's still at it. Taking pride in the accuracy of his reproductions and also in their durability, he offers a limited warranty on his toilets for two years and on his faucets, made by a venerable Chicago firm, for one. All woods used in his pieces can be ordered in natural, light, medium, or dark finishes, and customers can voice a preference for highly figured or straight-grained wood. Rheinschild will be glad to work from custom designs

Cheap imitations or thinly cut ¾" modern marble have no place in a Victorian bathroom. Rheinschild's vanity top is far more appropriate. Carved from 1¼"-thick Italian marble quarried around the turn of the century, it is 30" wide and 20" deep. Holes are cut for the basin and faucets, and a ¾₆"recess is ground into the top to prevent spills. Changes may be made in size, shape, or faucet drilling.

Rheinschild's faucets are just as

impressive as the rest of his products—the two illustrated here are evidence of the wide range of styles available. The basin faucet with filigree is 6¾" tall with a spout projection of 4¼". It is solid brass with ornate cast-in details and is a reproduction of an early design. The Chicago tub faucet is manufactured by an Illinois company that has produced the same style for seventy-five years.

After perusing the catalogue, you may decide on one of Rheinschild's beautifully crafted basins to complete a period sink. The

round brass basin has a fluted interior and is powder-coated and oven-baked for a durable finish. Its 15" diameter includes a 1" lip. It is 6" deep, with no hole for overflow. The oval basin is made of white china with three overflow holes and measures 17" long by 14" deep; the lip is 1" thick and is unglazed. For more information, take a look at the catalogue or give Rheinschild a call.

Catalogue, $1.

S. Chris Rheinschild
2220 Carlton Way
Santa Barbara, CA 93109
(805) 962-8598

Sink Factory

When self-taught potter Michael Stringer could discover no manufacturers of Victorian sinks to suit him, he retired to his garage, mixed up a ceramic recipe that worked, and began casting, firing, and glazing. Pedestal lavatories offered by his Sink Factory include the Bentley, the Berkeley, the Whitney, and the Yardley. Vanity basins come in several sizes and shapes; vanity tops, in four sizes of a round style, three ovals, a scallop shape, a shallow kidney design, or the angular Wellington.

Catalogue, $3.

The Sink Factory
2140 San Pablo Ave.
Berkeley, CA 94702
(415) 548-3967

Steptoe & Wife

Specializing in the manufacture and distribution of quality architectural restoration products, Steptoe & Wife offers porcelain-handled brass faucets and basin cocks, ceramic and brass shower heads, reproduction pedestal sinks, and many other bathroom fixtures for period homes. If you have an old clawfoot tub that is perfect for a long, leisurely soak, but need to install a shower head, Steptoe suggests its Converto Shower. It comes complete with curtain rod and supports, can be assembled quickly by even a duffer, and won't ruin the period effect you are striving for. All Steptoe hardware is available in chrome-plated or polished brass finish.

Brochures available.

Steptoe & Wife
322 Geary Ave.
Toronto, Ont., Canada M6H 2C7
(416) 530-4200

Vintage Plumbing

Vintage Plumbing has amassed a huge library of appropriate manufacturing catalogues to guide its fine restoration work on rare, decorative turn-of-the-century bath fixtures. Inquire about the specifics and you'll receive color photographs and full descriptions of particular items including antique clawfoot tubs, pedestal lavatories, showers, pull chain toilets, and brass accessories.

Brochure available.

Vintage Plumbing and Sanitary
* Specialties*
17800 Minnehaha St.
Granada Hills, CA 91344
(818) 368-1040

Watercolors

Watercolors distributes a number of lines of bathroom fixtures,

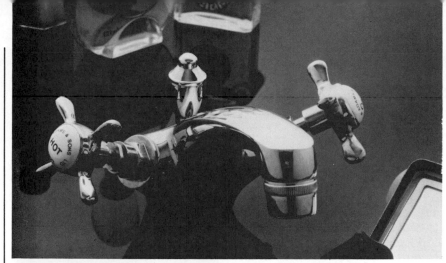

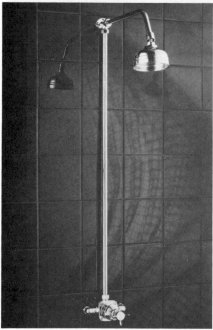

Robert Bourdon

Robert Bourdon started working with forge, hammer, and anvil because he found the blacksmith's art to be a relaxing and rewarding hobby; he's been at it full time now for more than twenty years. Most of his work is in the duplication of hardware and other iron pieces necessary in the restoration of old buildings and the construction of period reproduction homes. He will duplicate a piece to your specifications and offers a variety of other objects—from chandeliers to weather vanes—as part of his extensive repertoire.

Of particular interest to those in need of fine period furniture hardware is Bourdon's skill in reproducing even the most elaborate pieces. He is prepared to replicate almost any hardware illustrated in Wallace Nutting's *Furniture Treasury*.

Brochure available for SASE.

Robert Bourdon
The Smithy
Wolcott, VT 05680
(802) 472-6508

Phyllis Kennedy

The days when the ice man came and delivered the big crystal blocks that kept perishables cool have passed, but many of the now-charming iceboxes he filled remain. Phyllis Kennedy outfits those boxes in high quality and style, with antique and heavy-duty cast-brass latches, hinges, and door lifts. Kennedy even markets the cast-brass trademark labels of Columbia and White Clad, two of the more popular brands of icebox.

Included in Phyllis Kennedy's broad selection of Victorian and early 20th-century restoration hardware are replacement parts for Hoosier cabinets—from flour sifters and latches to knobs and cabinet rolls. Also available is a variety of period furniture hardware, including drawer pulls, bail sets, drops, backplates, knobs, and keyhole sets. The collection is so thorough that you'll even find

some of which would work well in a period bathroom. The Antique Regal collection of solid brass fixtures includes this angular one-piece sink faucet with a pop-up drain and the elongated wall-mount shower mixer. Both are available in chrome, gold plate, or a finish called "antique," which is a gold alloy.

The Edwardian line is represented by a pillar tap, available in basin or bath sizes of ½" and ¾". The spout of the basin version, which is illustrated here, can be obtained in an extended size for use with marble vanity tops. All fixtures in the Edwardian group are manufactured in England from brass and gun-metal. The handle insert is porcelain. Polished brass, chrome, nickel, and gold-plated finishes can be matched to your decor.

Brochure available.

Watercolors
Garrison on Hudson, NY 10524
(914) 424-3327

Furniture Hardware

Providing proper hardware for antique furniture is among the least important concerns of the owner of an old building. When the roof is leaking and the windows about to fall out, the question of whether or not a lowboy has its proper brass escutcheon is not likely to loom as a central issue. But there will come a day—we keep hoping—when we can worry about how the house is furnished as much as we do about how it is held together. The following suppliers are some of the best in the country for basic pieces, as well as specialty items such as finials and sockets.

replacement hardware for old steamer trunks.

Catalogue, $2 (refundable with first order).

Phyllis Kennedy
9256 Holyoke Ct.
Indianapolis, IN 46268
(317) 872-6366

19th Century

The 19th Century Company's catalogue is almost as interesting as the products it describes. Replete with Victorian-style line drawings and typefaces, it announces, "We are famous for our locks and keys." The company *should* be famous for its specialty locks, which include roll-blind locks, chest locks designed for any box with a hinged lid, and universal locks mountable on drawers, left-hand, or right-hand doors.

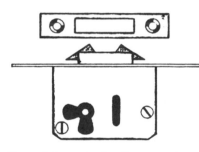

One of these is the Piano Lid lock, model F-38, a full mortise two-way lock for lift lids. It is steel with a face of solid brass and measures ½" high, 3" long, and 1¼ " deep, with a distance of ¾" from the pin to the lock face.

There's hardware to improve just about every piece of furniture in a Victorian home at 19th Century. Wardrobes, china cabinets, bookcases, and armoires can benefit from the combination escutcheons/door pulls. Intricate designs in solid brass give period pieces a new touch that looks old. Model ES-478 is 3" high by 1" wide.

Catalogue, $2.

19th Century Hardware and Supply
Co.
Box 599
Rough & Ready, CA 95975
(916) 432-1040

Paxton Hardware

At Paxton the range of historic reproduction furniture hardware begins with the 18th century (Chippendale, Sheraton, Queen Anne, and Hepplewhite) and ultimately encompasses the many styles of Victorian design (from Renaissance Revival to Eastlake and beyond). Shown here are just a few of Paxton's many fine pieces: Eastlake drawer pulls, a Victorian teardrop pull, a selection of mortise and roll-top desk locks, and wrought-brass Sheraton knobs. For the full array of Paxton's offerings, order the firm's mail-order catalogue.

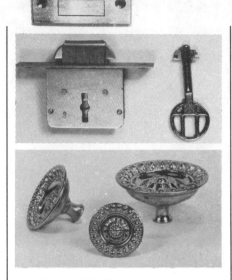

Catalogue, $3.50.

Paxton Hardware, Ltd.
Dept. OHC
7818 Bradshaw Rd.
Upper Falls, MD 21156
(301) 592-8505

Period Furniture Hardware

Among the thousands of items offered by this Massachusetts firm is a staggering array of furniture and interior hardware such as the drapery holdbacks and clock finials illustrated here. Period Furniture's 120-page catalogue will give you some idea of the exhaustive choices available; most pieces are made of solid brass and the company prides itself on the quality of all items it carries.

Catalogue, $3.50.

Period Furniture Hardware Co., Inc.
Box 314, Charles St. Station
123 Charles St.
Boston, MA 02114
(617) 227-0758

Prospect Products

How nice, in this age of plastic, to find escutcheons carved from oak or walnut. Choose the plain round or diamond-shaped models, or select the more elaborate leaf-studded designs. Prospect Products offers brass escutcheons as well. Wood and porcelain knobs, drawer pulls in oak and cherry, keyholes, and keys—page through the catalogue for the restoration hardware and supplies you need. The variety and quality are impressive, to say the least.

Catalogue, $2 (refundable with first order).

Prospect Products
8000 Rose Island Rd.
Box 70
Prospect, KY 40059
(502) 228-3493

Restoration Supply

Keep it all under lock and key—secure your home authentically with hardware from Restoration Supply. Wardrobe locks in plain steel range in size from ¾" by 1¾"

to 1½" by 3". Chest locks, also steel, come with a strike plate and

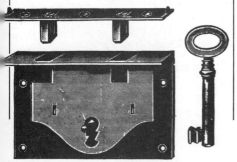

double set of keys. Restoration Supply can provide a variety of hardware for other uses, from several different lines. Antique door hardware and reproduction furniture hardware, all in brass, plus brass, porcelain, and wood casters, round out the selection.

Catalogue, $2.

Restoration Supply
Box 253
Hawesville, KY 42348
(502) 927-8494

Scott's Antiques

Brass bed parts, locks, keys, bails, pulls, drops, knobs, rings, handles, escutcheons, mirror movements (for mounting dresser, washstand, and shaving stand mirrors), kitchen cabinet and cupboard hardware—even an old wall-mounted Coca-Cola bottle opener—these are only a few of the reproduction Victorian and early 20th-century hardware treasures to be found at Scott's Antiques. The assortment of steamer trunk hardware is the largest we recall seeing and is, alone, worth ordering the firm's extensive catalogue.

Catalogue available.

Scott's Antiques
Rte. 9, Box 536
Springfield, MO 65804
(417) 866-6303

Williamsburg Blacksmiths

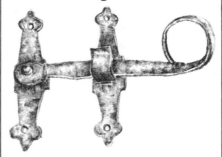

It's hard to resist this gently curving cupboard latch from Williamsburg Blacksmiths. Its shape makes it something more than an ordinary fastener, and its forged iron composition makes it far more than decorative. A phosphate coating and black lacquer protect it from rust. Standing

3½" tall and 5" wide, it's also suitable for closet doors, and it's only one of the many latches available from Williamsburg. Visit the showroom or write for the catalogue to see more latches, plus cabinet hinges, escutcheons, and other types of iron hardware.

Catalogue, $3.

Williamsburg Blacksmiths
Rte. 9
Williamsburg, MA 01096
(413) 268-7341

The Woodworkers' Store

The Woodworkers' Store was established to serve the needs of people who like to build and tinker. Just about everything you'd want for a woodworking project is to be found in the pages of its catalogue or within the walls of its retail stores in Minneapolis, Seattle, Denver, Boston, San Diego, and Columbus, Ohio. Furniture hardware is no exception—the Woodworkers' Store has a wide variety of hinges, handles, locks, escutcheons, and other pieces. Whether you're just replacing a knob or two on an old roll-top desk or building a wardrobe from scratch, it's worthwhile to take a look at what this company offers.

Catalogue, $1.

The Woodworkers' Store
21801 Industrial Blvd.
Rogers, MN 55374
(612) 428-4101

Antique Hardware

The pace at which old architectural America is being ripped down has increased rapidly. New building often means the loss of the old, even if it is only a barn or a decayed tenement. Wreckers, unlike those of the recent past, however, no longer scatter everything to the wind. More and more individuals are rushing in to save building materials and ornamentation before they are reduced to dust. It is not only valiant to do so; it is economically advantageous. The number of architectural antiques emporiums across North America is increasing—and they are having no problem in disposing of such items as old bricks, mantels, hardware, flooring, windows, and doors. These outlets are valuable sources of supply when the need arises. And the need—and the stock, of course—include choice bits of antique hardware and ancient plumbing fixtures. Remember, however, that stock constantly changes. The objects inventoried in such stores and warehouses are largely one-of-a-kind.

Architectural Antiques

An 18,000-square-foot showroom provides ample space for the wares of Architectural Antiques. Find rare antique hardware and plumbing here, or avail yourself of Architectural Antiques' locator service, whereby the firm will search for your specific needs. Photographs are available in response to specific requests. Architectural Antiques ships its finds anywhere.

*Architectural Antiques
121 E. Sheridan Ave.
Oklahoma City, OK 73104-2419
(405) 232-0759*

Canal Co.

Canal's architectural salvage yields rare prizes in authentic hardware. The firm's rotating stock includes most everything. Door hardware features brass, porcelain, and glass knobs; door stops, hinges, rim locks, thumb latches, letter slots, and skeleton keys. Choose from various guards, lifts, sash pulleys, and sash weights for windows. Ask for antique marble sinks and bathtub feet for the bathroom, or find the right andirons, screens, fenders, and log holders for the hearth. A computerized inventory guarantees quick answers to your design questions, and you can keep your purchases in fine condition with one of several cleansing products always available.

Stock listing available.

*The Canal Co.
1612 14th St., N.W.
Washington, D.C. 20009
(202) 234-6637*

Monroe Coldren & Son's Antiques

Specializing in unique authentic pieces may preclude a catalogue, but it hasn't stopped Monroe Coldren & Son from becoming one of the world's largest suppliers of original antique hardware. The firm will see you through all hardware requirements for any project. It skillfully repairs and restores antique pieces crafted from brass, copper, and iron, and if no antique from the extensive inventory of 18th- and 19th-century hardware suits your purpose, Monroe Coldren & Son will create a reproduction to your specifications.

*Monroe Coldren & Son's Antiques
and Restorations
723 E. Virginia Ave.
West Chester, PA 19380
(215) 692-5651*

Half Moon Antiques

Half Moon has rescued bath fixtures made between 1890 and 1940, skillfully preserving original nickel finishes on brass when possible, often stripping ravaged surfaces and polishing the brass underneath to a high gloss. Soap, sponge, and tissue holders, towel bars, shelves, racks, and hooks, incorporating materials such as enameled cast iron, glass, and porcelain fill out the wide selection of Half Moon Antiques. Make an appointment before visiting Half Moon's retail shop, part of a forty-member group shop, since continuing appearances in antique shows make for erratic schedules and keep Half Moon's proprietors on the road. No catalogues or brochures are available, but Half Moon will mail photographs of current stock items in response to specific inquiries.

*Half Moon Antiques
% Monmouth Antique Shoppes
217 W. Front St.
Red Bank, NJ 07701
(201) 842-7377*

Ohmega Salvage

Eight years of experience in antiques salvage have made Ohmega a good place to find just about anything, especially door hardware or bath and kitchen fixtures. The company has rebuilt a number of antique kitchen fixtures, claw-foot tubs, pedestal sinks, toilets, tub and shower sets, marble vanity tops, and bar fixtures. All carry a one-year plumbing guarantee that covers the costs of parts and labor. Ohmega also sells a variety of reproduction pieces.

*Ohmega Salvage
Box 2125
2407 San Pablo Ave.
Berkeley, CA 94702
(415) 843-7368*

Roy Electric

Under layers of colored coatings or old nickel and chrome plating, Roy Electric knows there are exquisite antique solid-brass bath fixtures to be had. The firm will provide beautifully restored ball and claw tubs, pedestal sinks, and more unusual plumbing items. Roy Electric polishes, lacquers, and epoxy bakes them, or the firm will ship them "as is" for the hardworking do-it-yourselfer.

As Roy Electric has expanded the range of its business, it has begun to fabricate solid brass to outfit antique plumbing fixtures. For ex-

Tennessee Tub

Antique tubs can be charming, but many show the sad abuse they've suffered over the years. Contact Tennessee Tub, and purchase a tub from the firm—or request restoration services of your own antique. Tennessee Tub will completely restore and reglaze a tub in white, shades of beige, pastels, dark blue, antique red, or a two-tone combination. For a touch of period elegance, request brass, nickel, or chrome plating on tub legs.

Flyer available.

Tennessee Tub, Inc. & Tubliner Co.
6682 Charlotte Park
Nashville, TN 37209
(615) 352-1939

Tools

Even if you are not a do-it-yourself craftsman in need of tools and special building and cabinetry supplies, you will find the catalogues of the major suppliers an unending delight. These publications range from the very simple offerings of the specialty toolmaker who supplies only one particular type of instrument to the glorious color publications of suppliers of thousands of items from all over the earth. Undoubtedly, even if you are all thumbs, you will discover something that you must have because it is not only handy to have around the house but is, in itself, a work of art.

Frog Tool Co.

Whether you're looking for a professional workbench, a woodcarving set, special veneer tools, scrapers, vises, or saws, you'll have a wide range to choose from in this Illinois firm's catalogue. Frog Tool is both a manufacturer of quality woodworking tools and a dealer in special items made by other manufacturers. It offers, for example, a handsome workbench made from fully cured red beech, which is hand-fitted in Germany and guaranteed, according to the company, to withstand several lifetimes of abuse.

Catalogue available.

Frog Tool Co., Ltd.
700 W. Jackson Blvd.
Chicago, IL 60606
(312) 648-1270

ample, large oval, round, or rectangular shower curtain rings are now available. Accessories include everything from shelves and hampers to toothbrush holders. Roy Electric will strip and refinish customers' antique finds, and nickel or chrome plating is available as well.

Catalogue, $5.

Roy Electric Co., Inc.
1054 Coney Island Ave.
Brooklyn, NY 11230
(718) 339-6311 or
(718) 761-7905

Garrett Wade

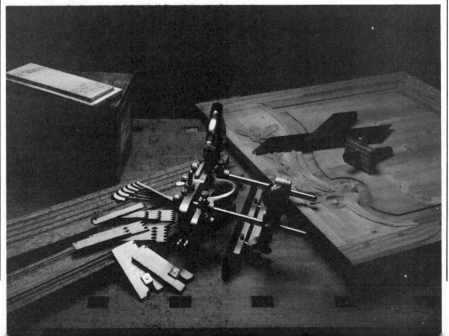

Even if your interest in do-it-yourselfmanship is only a passing phase, you'll want to order Garrett Wade's colorful catalogue. One look at the superb design, photography, and information contained therein and you'll be hooked. There's no doubt that it's an exceptional catalogue; no wonder it's been called a necessity for every woodworker. Its handsome pages are chock-full of supplies to suit both the home handyman and the professional. Among the new items in its over 2,500 listings are jigs, template guides, and inlay kits for routers, as well as an assortment of traditionally designed planes that deserve rediscovery. Precision saws, planers, and other power tools produced in Switzerland by INCA arrive for U.S. distribution solely through Garrett Wade. Devoted woodworkers will enjoy the firm's catalogue since it includes exhaustive information on tool use and care.

Catalogue, $4.

Garrett Wade
161 Avenue of the Americas
New York, New York 10013
(212) 807-1155

Lehman Hardware

If you have tall fruit trees or just a corner that could use an unusual decorative object, this fruit picker from Lehman Hardware may do the trick. It has a 105" reach and a padded basket to get to the tops of trees without bruising the fruit. The two-piece handle lets you use it for lower branches with convenience. Lehman also carries other garden implements, including scythes, hoes, and a garden plow, all of which are functional as well as attractive.

Catalogue, $2.

Lehman Hardware and
* Appliances, Inc.*
Box 41, 4779 Kidron Rd.
Kidron, OH 44636
(216) 857-5441

Mechanick's Workbench

You've seen wonderful displays of furniture made just the way colonial craftsmen did—but what happened to the tools those craftsmen used? The Mechanick's Workbench has preserved them—everything from an Archimedean drill to an invoice from Quackenbush, Townsend, & Co. Many of the tools are completely intact and in splendid condition. An eel spear, every delicate prong whole, is just one of the firm's novel prizes. An 1865 edition of a carpenter's and joiner's handbook and a carved bone pump drill suitable for a museum display show the hard-won quality and variety at the Mechanick's Workbench.

The Mechanick's Workbench has an ongoing research project chronicling New England planemakers of the 18th century. The firm has plotted out estimates of apprenticeship periods, marriages, and relatives who were planemakers as well. A Foster's patent turn-table iron smooth plane is a star example in the tool collection. Its use varies with the adjustable angle of iron to body. The single production run of this model, means that a scant number of these tools, dated January 29, 1907, remain. Pick up—and don't put down—a catalogue from the Mechanick's Workbench.

Catalogue available.

The Mechanick's Workbench
Box 544, Front St.
Marion, MA 02738
(617) 748-1680

PRG

Do your own woodwork and you'll know the smart satisfaction of quality craftsmanship that belongs fully to you. You'll also become intimate with the whims of the weather, and how they affect your work. To alert you to the dampness that may warp wood and damage finishes, PRG brings you top-notch moisture meters that will solve the problem. "From England, where moisture detection is a major industry," PRG (the Preservation Resource Group) imports the 7-oz. Protimeter H_2O Minor and the 6.5-oz. Protimeter Mini for wood, and the double-scale Protimeter Minor (6.5 ozs.) for both wood and brick, mortar, or plaster. Purchase a hammer electrode or a deep wall probe to enhance the meter's range. The U.S.-made Delmhorst meters come in pocket, compact, and standard sizes (the last detects moisture content within the widest range: 6% to 80%). Several different electrodes complement its design. PRG offers an excellent selection of other alarms, detectors, monitors, and tools, all designed to give you the edge in producing quality work.

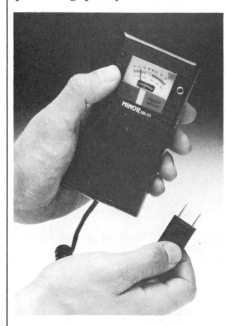

Don't forget the "Form-A-Gage" profile gauge previously featured in *The Old House Catalogue* and available from PRG. The rods are suspended in a uniform magnetic field and can be replaced when needed by the manufacturer.

Fliers available.

PRG
5619 Southampton Dr.
Springfield, VA 22151
(703) 323-1407

Other Suppliers of Hardware

Consult List of Suppliers for addresses.

Architectural Hardware

The Antique Hardware Store
Architectural Antique Warehouse
Ball and Ball
Robert Bourdon, the Smithy
Busy Bridge
Carolina Craftsmen
Cassidy Brothers Forge, Inc.
Classic Architectural Specialties
Colonial Furniture Refinishing and
    Stripping
Eighteenth Century Hardware Co.
Hippo Hardware and Trading Co.
Newton Millham
19th Century Co.
Ohmega Salvage
The Old Wagon Factory
The Settlers
The Shop, Inc.
The Woodworkers' Store

Household Hardware

The Antique Hardware Store
The Arden Forge
Ball and Ball
Robert Bourdon, the Smithy
Busy Bridge
Carolina Craftsmen
Classic Architectural Specialties
The Cobweb Shop
Colonial Furniture Refinishing and
    Stripping
19th Century Co.
Period Furniture Hardware Co., Inc.
Prospect Products
Remodelers' & Renovators' Supply
Scott's Antiques
Williamsburg Blacksmiths

Bath and Kitchen Hardware

Acorn Manufacturing
The Antique Hardware Store
Architectural Antique Warehouse
Baldwin Hardware Corp.
Robert Bourdon, the Smithy

Busy Bridge
Classic Architectural Specialties
The Cobweb Shop
Colonial Furniture Refinishing and
    Stripping
DeWeese Woodworking Co.
Buddy Fife's
Hippo Hardware and Trading Co.
Ohmega Salvage
Omnia Industries
Pelnik Wrecking Co.
Perma Ceram
Rustic Home Hardware
Tennessee Tub, Inc. & Tubliner Co.

Furniture Hardware

Acorn Manufacturing
The Antique Hardware Store
The Arden Forge
Ball and Ball
Busy Bridge
Carolina Craftsmen
The Cobweb Shop
Colonial Furniture Refinishing and
    Stripping
Hippo Hardware and Trading Co.
Omnia Industries
The Settlers
The Shop, Inc.
David Swearingen, Bonded
    Locksmith

Antique Hardware

Architectural Antique Warehouse
The Arden Forge
Vintage Plumbing and Sanitary
    Specialties
Wooden Nickel Antiques

Tools

The Arden Forge
19th Century Co.
Prospect Products
The Woodworkers' Store

7.

Paints and Papers

Painting a building, inside and out, remains the most common way to transform its appearance. Certain combinations are thought to be traditional for a period building. Mustard and barn red, for example, have become so commonly used for 18th-century-style houses that we have accepted these colors as traditional whether they are or not. Recent evidence suggests that the colonists usually painted only barns red and used many colors other than mustard for their houses. Regardless of what the textbooks tell us, however, paint is a sensible and economical way of cleaning up the past.

While a new coat of paint will renew a building in the eyes of the beholder, it may, in fact, be injurious. The build-up of layers prevents the original surface—whether of masonry or of wood—from releasing moisture that naturally accumulates in the building material. Proper preparation of a surface that is to be painted, especially on the exterior, will cut down on this problem. So, too, will the use of an oil-base paint rather than a latex formula. Oil nourishes wood or clay products and bonds more effectively.

Papers are enjoying a new popularity, as they should. They can dramatically change an interior space. There are all types of papers—for ceilings, cornices, that lower area of the wall below a chair rail known as the dado, and, of course, for whole wall panels. Paper borders can also be used around doors and windows and along a chair rail. There was a time when wallpaper was used with great abandon. Under the layers of paint inside your old house may be one or two of paper as well: printed papers were cheaper than paints until ready-mix formulas were introduced in the late 1800s.

Room size and amount of natural light will determine to a large extent how wallpaper is used. There is no reason why two or even three designs—complementary, of course—can't be employed in the same space. You will be better off staying with papers that are not pre-pasted or coated with a synthetic finish. There are papers of this type which are perfectly suitable for period rooms—and a few are included in the following pages—but, in general, the appearance of uncoated papers is superior and their installation not that much more difficult; some find them easier than the pre-pasted. Trying to reposition a paper that already has an adhesive coating can be a frustrating experience, especially when the material stretches.

Obelisk, a fine wallcovering by Louis W. Bowen, New York City.

Paints

Use of carefully coordinated shades for Victorian façades—rather than deadly white—has increased each year, and more major paint firms are addressing themselves to the needs of the majority of American buildings which date from the Victorian period. There are smaller paint companies that have put together period paint collections which are carefully conceived and

these are also listed following. The reader, however, is also advised to consider the use of custom-mixed colors. There is almost always at least one paint merchant in any area who enjoys the challenge of matching one shade to another. It costs more, of course, to have this done, but if you plan to live with the color for at least a few years, it should be done right.

Allentown Paint

Bright, cheerful, and durable, Allentown's Pennsylvania Dutch paints can keep old houses looking their best. The line includes an exterior paint with a linseed-oil base that is notable for its excellent hiding surface, high spreading rate, good color retention, and mildew resistance. Ten ready-mixed colors, including Parsley, Cherry Red, and Rich Straw, are available. For house trim, shutters, porches, arbors, boats, roofs, lawn furniture, tools, and masonite siding, Allentown makes an alkyd paint with a bit of linseed oil for easy spreading. Its eight colors include dark green, maroon, and bright red. The Pennsylvania Dutch collection also encompasses an indoor/outdoor enamel in eight colors for primed concrete or wood floors, green and red alkyd roofing paints, and latex interior and exterior paints in both pastels and bright colors.

For further information, write:

Allentown Paint Manufacturing Co.,
 Inc.
Box 597, E. Allen & N. Graham Sts.
Allentown, PA 18105
(215) 433-4273

Antique Color Supply

Cynthia Keefe, president of Antique Color Supply, calls milk paint "the purist's alternative to latex," and it certainly is the most authentic reproduction finish available for some walls, woodwork, and furniture. A rough texture, a flat finish, and superior

hardening qualities give this time-tested formula an antique look that will survive years or decades of use. Three sizes—1-ounce, 6-ounce, and 12-ounce—are available in eight colors: Barn Red, Pumpkin, Mustard, Bayberry, Lexington Green, Soldier Blue, Oyster White, and Pitch Black. The dry powder lasts forever if it is sealed tightly, and mixed paint can be sealed and refrigerated for as much as two days. There's no need to finish the painted surface, but you can if you like; it can be sanded for a distressed look and a lighter color or coated with linseed oil, polyurethane, or varnish to deepen the color.

Brochure available for a self-addressed, stamped envelope.

Antique Color Supply, Inc.
Box 711
Harvard, MA 01451
(617) 582-6426

Laura Ashley

Coordinating colors are the key to Laura Ashley's painted interiors. The firm markets a range of colors in satin gloss and vinyl flat emulsion paint to complement papers, fabrics, and tiles offered by the firm. The oil-based satin, available in one-liter cans, covers 15 square meters (160 feet) in rich hues like Kingfisher, Burgundy, Tropical Green, and Sapphire. Available in 2.5-liter cans (each covers 12 square meters, or 127 square feet), the flat latex colors are softer: Cream, Light Plum, Pale Moss, etc. Lighten this water-based paint

with white paint or water to reach the perfect shade.

Home furnishings catalogue, $4.

Laura Ashley
Dept. B117, Box 5308
Melville, NY 11747
(800) 367-2000

Chromatic

With as many colors as Baskin-Robbins has flavors, Chromatic offers its Japan line. These concentrated paste colors take to wood, paper, or metal, suiting them to furniture and floors, walls and metalwork. Use them decoratively, for lettering, staining, antiquing, glazing, and even for tinting flat paints. Chromatic's line outstrips all other Japan colors in popularity, enhancing historic restorations across the country with hues of American Vermilion, Van Dyke Brown, and Refined Lampblack.

Chromatic paints are available nationally. Write or call for further information.

Chromatic Paint Corp.
Box 105
Garnerville, NY 10923-0105
(800) 431-7001

Cook & Dunn

Cook & Dunn's Historic Colors recall the colonial and Victorian periods in living color. Subdued hues of Cobblestone, Classic Ivory, Beige, and Limestone deepen in other shades within the line to Cranberry, Concord Green, and Cape May Blue. Sandwiched between are hues of Heather, Ashford Blue, Amber Hall, and Jersey Clay. These gloss, semi-gloss, and flat enamels come in latex or oil base (alkyd).

Cook & Dunn's Rustic Stains have a special alkyd fortified oil recipe that thwarts blisters and cracks when used outdoors on siding, shingles, and fences, as well as indoors on ceilings, paneling, and beams. These solid colors, from pale Palomino to Olive Black, hide wood grain but show texture. Use semi-transparent stains to protect and enhance new outside wood structures while letting grain and texture through, or use on un-finished woodwork and paneling.

If you have any difficulty finding Cook & Dunn finishes, just contact:

Cook & Dunn Paint Corp.
Box 117
Newark, NJ 07101
(201) 589-5580

Dutch Boy

Dutch Boy's family of interior paints includes two groups of alkyd paints suitable for old houses. The company's Custom Deep and Custom Medium colors range from earthy pinks, beiges, golds, a medium olive called Edgecombe, and a dusty light blue called Cicely to a collection of oranges, a brick-red color called Ruby Port, and several deep, vivid blues. Most of the Custom Medium colors are available in both flat and semi-gloss enamel; Custom Deep paints are sold only in semi-gloss. Dutch Boy's flat alkyd wall paint is at its best when used on interior walls, ceilings, and woodwork. The semi-gloss enamel is applicable to a variety of surfaces, including masonry, concrete, wood or metal trim, furniture, and plaster ceilings and walls.

Dutch Boy paints are distributed nationally; if you have trouble locating a dealer in your area, contact:

Dutch Boy
1370 Ontario St.
Cleveland, OH 44101
(216) 566-3140

Finnaren & Haley

Whether you're intending to re-paint a colonial or a Victorian house, you're likely to find what you need at Finnaren & Haley. The company has two lines to suit the old-house lover's tastes. For one of these lines, Authentic Colors of Historic Philadelphia, Finnaren & Haley joined forces with the National Park Service to scientifically evaluate the original colors of several historic buildings. Their research resulted in the pro-

duction of thirty-one paint colors, ten of which have been certified by the National Park Service. Available in interior or exterior formulas with alkyd oil or acrylic water bases, the colors include Long Gallery Blue, Quaker Gray, and Congress Hall Tan. Two of the most interesting colors, Todd House Bronze and Yellow, were reproduced from the walls of the house in which James Madison met his future wife.

Finnaren & Haley makes a line of historic paints especially for Victorian homes as well. It features sixteen deep interior and exterior colors, including a cheerful yellow called Lombard, a light navy blue called Tudor, and Belle Meade, a medium green. The collection also includes trim colors and floor finishes.

If you have difficulty locating a Finnaren & Haley dealer or would like more information about the company's products, contact:

Finnaren & Haley, Inc.
2320 Haverford Rd.
Ardmore, PA 19003
(215) 649-5000

Fuller-O'Brien

Fuller-O'Brien classes its line of paints called the Victorian Palette as part of a multi-media national trend toward Victorian styles, affecting everything from makeup to ceramic tiling. After gleaning over 200 colors during a year-long research project, the firm whittled its offerings to 70 hues, with the help of architects, stylists, and the president of New Jersey's Cape May Historic District Commission, a group that rigidly enforces historical accuracy in that locale. Fuller-O'Brien's interior and exterior paints have brightened Cape May's 600 Victorian homes. The palette awaits your choices.

Local suppliers should be easy to find; contact the company for further information.

Fuller-O'Brien
2700 Glynn Ave.
Box 864
Brunswick, GA 31521
(912) 265-7650

Glidden

Glidden's "American Color Legacy" features heritage colors in flat and glossy finishes. To complement colonial structures of wood, granite, and fieldstone, shades of brown and gray—Tea-party, Cromwell, and Oregon Trail, among others—are suitable. Accents of deep blue, gold, green, and red set off the more muted tones to advantage. Soft washes of color over adobe and stucco suit coastal Pueblo, Mission, and Spanish Colonial styles and harmonize with desert surroundings. Deep Victorian colors like Thicket, Sleepy Hollow, Manor Brown, Weathervane, and Main Street round out the spectrum of traditional hues from Glidden.

Glidden paints should be available locally, but suppliers can be located by contacting:

Glidden Coatings & Resins
925 Euclid Ave.
Cleveland, OH 44115
(216) 344-8000

Martin-Senour

Authorized by the Colonial Williamsburg Foundation, Martin-Senour's line of Williamsburg paints faithfully reproduces colors used on the buildings in the historic town, Virginia's colonial capital. Combining modern quality with traditional beauty, the paints are available in three types: interior flat latex, interior satin gloss latex enamel, and exterior stain gloss latex. The interior flat latex colors are soft and muted. Each of the twelve colors, including King's Arms Rose Pink, Wythe House Gold, and Pelham Gray, is available in four shades so that you can make your walls and ceilings as dark or light as you choose. The thirty-four interior stain gloss paints range in intensity from the pale, grayish Palace Dining Room Pearl Blue to the vibrant Raleigh Tavern Chinese Red. Martin-Senour recommends these paints for kitchens, bathrooms, and woodwork. For the outside of the house, thirty-five colors are available, including Palace Arms

Red, Bracken House Biscuit, and Market Square Tavern Green. They can be applied to wood, metal, masonry, or asbestos siding.

Martin-Senour also makes a whitewash that adds texture to bare walls and blends perfectly with stone, brick, or woodwork.

If you cannot find a Martin-Senour dealer nearby, contact:

The Martin-Senour Co.
1370 Ontario Ave. NW
Cleveland, OH 44113
(216) 566-3178

Benjamin Moore

Both 18th- and 19th-century homes can benefit from Benjamin Moore's Historical Color Collection of interior and exterior paints. The interior paints, appropriate for plaster, wallboard, wood, metal, and (occasionally) masonry, come in three different latex finishes and one type of enamel. The eighty standard colors range from a clear, icy Woodlawn Blue to a soft, rich Buckland Blue and from the subdued Windham Cream and Hepplewhite Ivory to the strong, captivating Georgian Brick and Plymouth Brown. The selection of latex and enamel exterior paints contains fewer colors, but these retrieve in beauty what they lose in variety. Hadley Red, Philipsburg Blue, and Lafayette Green are particularly striking.

For further information or to locate a dealer near you, contact:

Benjamin Moore & Co.
51 Chestnut Ridge Rd.
Montvale, NJ 07645
(201) 573-9600

Muralo

Muralo's contribution to the cause of historic preservation is its collection of Restoration Colors, interior and exterior paints designed to give period homes the look of serenity and elegance they demand. The selection includes a number of grays and several browns ranging from the creamy beige of Hopewell to the rich

chocolate of Athenaeum Brown. Greens and blues make discreet appearances, as do white, black, a traditional red called Kendall Lodge, and a soft yellow called Exmoor Hall.

If you have trouble locating a distributor in your area, contact:

The Muralo Co., Inc.
148 E. 5th St.
Bayonne, NJ 07002
(201) 437-0770

Old-Fashioned Milk Paint

In Egypt, skim milk was a prime ingredient for paint. In fact, skim milk and buttermilk, in combination with lime, whiting, and other coloring, form a prized finish seen throughout Europe. Early Americans knew that milk paint's distinctive flat, grainy finish coats surfaces with color and protection; today even the strongest strippers don't faze this paint. Its powdered form facilitates shipment, discourages spoilage, and basically renders the paint as indestructible in storage as it is tenacious in application. Precise measurement, thorough mixing, and careful straining yield the inimitable milk paint, an authentic and durable finish that's held its popularity for centuries.

The Old-Fashioned Milk Paint Co. offers pint, quart, and gallon packages of powdered paint in several shades, including Barn Red, Pumpkin, Mustard, Bayberry, Lexington Green, Soldier Blue, Oyster White, and Pitch Black.

Brochure and color chart available.

Old-Fashioned Milk Paint Co.
R.R. 1
Box 65
Ashby, MA 01431
(617) 386-7550

Olympic

It's sad to watch beautiful wood age badly, succumbing to warping, cracking, rot, and mildew. Give your old house a fighting chance with Olympic's weather-screening stains. Brushing or

sanding and a thorough cleaning prepare new, already stained, or weathered wood to receive coats of the oil-enriched, water-repellent screen, in tints ranging from the semi-transparents to the dark solids that camouflage discolored wood.

Olympic dealers are eager to provide further information—or contact the company directly.

Olympic Stain
2233 112th Ave., NE.
Bellevue, WA 98004
(800) 426-6306

Pittsburgh Paints

Pittsburgh Paints' Historic Colors, well-suited to period homes, come in several formulations, for a variety of uses. You may select Satinhide alkyd enamel for indoor surfaces, Sun-Proof oil or acrylic house and trim paint for durable outdoor coats, or different enamels (Quick Dry Gloss, Water Base Gloss, or Floor, Deck and Patio) for interior/exterior use. The color names suggest their historic appropriateness: Bunker Hill, Amish Blue, Alamo Stone, Kentucky Blue Grass, and dozens of others add color authenticity to a colonial or Victorian home.

Pittsburgh Paints' brochures include helpful samples of color combinations suitable for colonial houses. These paints are available across the country—write or call for information on local suppliers.

Pittsburgh Paints
1 Gateway Center
Pittsburgh, PA 15222
(412) 434-3131

Pratt & Lambert

The Edison Institute's 12-acre Henry Ford Museum and Greenfield Village, a 210-acre, open-air demonstration of America's evolution from farm society to contemporary industry, provide hefty historical resources for Pratt & Lambert's Early Americana line. Colors drawn from a range of historical items, from fabrics to carriages, compose the wide span of interior and exterior paints.

Pratt & Lambert also offers 300 calibrated shades of solid rustic stains, in latex or alkyd. Varieties span Country Reds, Weathered Browns, Earthen Golds, Sandy Hues, Landscape Greens, and Coastal Blues.

The products of this nationally distributed brand should be easy to find; contact the company if you have any difficulty locating suppliers.

Pratt & Lambert
75 Tonawanda St.
Buffalo, NY 14207
(716) 873-6000

Cleaners and Finishes

How easy it would all be if you could just paint, and leave it at that. Unhappily, there are often layers of paint or other coatings which have to be removed first. And sometimes either before or after one has painted, surfaces require special treatments. Because it is tedious work, just about anything that makes the removal of old paint easier and less time-consuming is eagerly embraced by the homeowner. Much the same can be said for easy-to-apply coatings, preservatives, and stains. One has to exercise extreme caution, nevertheless, in the use of paint removers and other substances. Not only can they be extremely caustic, and require special handling, but they could inflict serious damage to surfaces. Each of the substances presented in the following listings has been tried and found true for its intended purpose.

Abatron

LiquidWood and WoodEpox, innovative compounds from Abatron, revitalize decorative and structural wood and furniture. Treated pieces are generally fully functional and stronger than before. LiquidWood and Wood-Epox are recommended for treating wood that must be retained for reasons of shape, size, or aesthetics. Mix together Liquid-Wood's transparent resin and hardener and spray, pour, or brush the formula onto wood to render it strong and water resistant. Reinforced areas can then be sawed, carved, planed, sanded, or painted. When cracks and holes exist, use LiquidWood as a primer for WoodEpox, a resin and

hardener paste that fills and builds on damaged wood. The non-shrinking adhesive putty can be stained or dyed at the time of mixing. The photographs here show the adhesive and shaping properties of WoodEpox. Use one or both versatile compounds to rescue the wood you thought was beyond saving.

Brochure available.

Abatron, Inc.
141 Center Dr.
Gilberts, IL 60136
(312) 426-2200

Cabot Stains

Cabot's Centennial Selection of oil-base solid color stains is perfect for a variety of applications. The stains are water-repellent, weather-resistant, and can be applied easily over previously stained, painted, or sealed surfaces. They can be used on shingles, siding, well-cured masonry, clapboards, rough-sawn wood, or primed metal, and the available colors are as appealing as the versatility. They include a rich, dark Mission Brown, a soft Old Virginia White, Driftwood Gray, and traditional Barn Red.

Cabot's stains are distributed throughout North America. If you have trouble locating a supplier near you, contact:

Samuel Cabot, Inc.
1 Union St.
Boston, MA 02108
(617) 723-7740

Daly's

When it comes to stains, sealers, fillers, finish removers, wood bleaches, cleaners, and finishes of almost every conceivable type for almost every conceivable woodworking job, you can't beat Daly's. More than fifty years ago, Walter J. Daly began creating a family of wood finishing products. Over the years, Daly's has developed and tested hundreds of new product ideas. The best of these (to date) are represented by the twenty-three standard products carried by the firm and listed in its catalogue. Despite (and perhaps because) of the excellence of its wood finishing products, Daly's is not a nationally recognizable brand. But Daly's word-of-mouth reputation among professional wood finishers, craftsmen, and serious do-it-yourselfers has helped spread Daly's products to every area of North America and to many foreign countries.

One of the unique things about Daly's is that the products work with each other to create wood finishing systems. And with the range of products available, users can undertake fairly complex wood finishing projects and know that each product will do exactly what it's supposed to do to produce results that are beautiful and

long lasting. To show how these systems work, Daly's has developed several work flow charts covering practically every type of wood finishing project from cleaning and finishing the teak decks on a boat, to stripping and finishing antique furniture in the home. These charts are available from Daly's and from dealers who carry Daly's products. They're also available as part of an excellent book, "Wood Finishing Class Notes," that can be pur-

chased from the company for $3.

For more information about Daly's products, send $1 for the firm's catalogue. With it you'll receive a complete set of work flow charts and a list of Daly's dealers in your area.

Daly's
3525 Stone Way N.
Seattle, WA 98103
(206) 633-4276 or
(206) 633-4200

19th Century

To keep your antiques looking their best, try some of the products listed in the catalogue of the 19th Century Hardware & Supply Co. This engaging catalogue, designed to simulate a Victorian advertising piece, includes all

sorts of hard-to-find goodies—from Briwax ("the furniture wax of kings") and Sheradale Antique Wax to old-fashioned hide glue and Never-Dull, the "magic wadding polish." Try the Tibet Almond Stick to wipe out scratches

in wooden furniture. Or choose a specialized protective compound for bread boards, salad bowls, wooden forks and spoons called Kitchen Wood Care. Non-toxic, it leaves no residual taste and easily preserves fine wood. Note that among the many polishes, adhesives, oils, and cleaners available from 19th Century is a complete line of Daly's wood finishing products.

Catalogue, $2.

19th Century Hardware & Supply
Co.
Box 599
Rough & Ready, CA 95975
(916) 432-1040

QRB

Ron Hack's father, a European cabinetmaker, taught him a great deal about wood. That knowledge, combined with his college work in chemistry, led Hack to create a particularly simple and effective refinishing system. The entire process takes minutes instead of hours.

The first step is the application of QRB paint remover, which contains no water, no caustic chemicals, and no acid activators to raise the grain. It requires no scraping or sanding and will not damage veneer, glue joints, or nylon brushes. The remover evaporates slowly to give you more working time, but once you're done, you can begin refinishing the piece immediately; there's no need to wait several hours for the remover to dry.

The refinishing compound is even easier to apply. Made of tung oil modified with tol oil, it penetrates the wood fiber, hardening the wood while creating a clear alkyd coating. Water-repellent, it can have a flat, satin, or gloss surface. Dust won't stick to it as it dries, so you don't have to sand between coats.

QRB also makes a stain-matching kit and a product that covers scratches. Send a self-addressed, stamped envelope for a helpful, free brochure with information on refinishing your furniture.

QRB Industries
3139 N. U.S. 31
Niles, MI 49120
(616) 683-7908

Decorative Painters

Painters who undertake special ornamental work, most of whom are also stencil artists, are becoming more common. Their talents are especially called for in the restoration of highly decorative Victorian-style buildings which employ a wide variety of ornamental devices and colorful effects. We are learning also that the colonial period of our history was not quite as sober and monochromatic an era as had once been thought. Careful research has uncovered evidence that various types of finishes were used on woodwork and walls, and that many of them were false or imitation treatments meant to suggest marble, a fine hardwood, or even plaster.

If you are considering stencil decoration, study the various alternatives carefully. Stenciling has become all the rage and, unfortunately, artists of little or no ability are on the loose. Stenciling, like any other artistic technique, should be executed only by those who have mastered its method. Its use should also be limited. Once begun, the temptation to apply designs nearly everywhere is hard to resist.

ARJ Associates

Ali Reza Jahedi has brought the best of Old World decorating techniques to America. A native of Iran, he was well trained in his home country as well as in England. He and his associates are superbly suited to undertake the most complicated restoration projects as well as original new commissions. While some decorative artists have talent only as trompe l'oeil painters or restorers of *faux* finishes, the ARJ group is accomplished in plaster and mosaic work as well. Gilding and stenciling are other talents whch have been exhibited in commercial and residential work in the Boston area, the group's home base, New York, and Pennsylvania.

Jahedi is shown at work applying the finishing touches to a ceiling medallion in the Old Court House in Cambridge, Massachusetts, a massive project completed in 1984.

ARJ Associates
310 Washington St.
Brighton, MA 02135
(617) 783-0467

Biltmore, Campbell, Smith Restorations

The American branch of a famed English restoration firm, Biltmore, Campbell, Smith has been in existence since 1982. In the past four years it has completed some of the most important painting restoration projects in North America, including the rotunda of the Pennsylvania State Capitol, the Damascus Church in Lumpkin, Georgia, Flagler College, St. Augustine, Florida, and the Atlanta-Biltmore Hotel in Atlanta, Georgia. In each project, the firm cleaned and expertly restored such valuable artwork as murals, ceiling paintings, and wall decorations.

Although the restoration of paintings is its forte, the group of artists and technicians is also skilled in more basic decorative techniques as graining, marbling, stenciling, and gilding. The group's work is always on display at the Biltmore Estate in Asheville, North Carolina, headquarters for the firm. It is here that an apprenticeship program for aspiring restoration craftsmen is also conducted.

Biltmore, Campbell, Smith
    Restorations, Inc.
One Biltmore Plaza
Asheville, NC 28803
(704) 274-1776

Larry Boyce & Associates

A view of what is described as a meditation room in a San Francisco town house best displays the work of Larry Boyce and his troupe of decorative artists. Imaginative and accomplished, they succeed in making the traditional visually exciting and aesthetically pleasing.

When San Francisco first became

known for its exuberantly decorated buildings in the 1970s, Larry Boyce was one of the pioneer painters. He could bring almost any decaying gray hulk of a building to life with the right combination of colors and textures. Since that time, his circle has expanded, and so have the projects undertaken throughout the United States by his associates. At present, the group is at work on the Vice-President's Office in Washington's Executive Office Building, restoring its late-Victorian ornamentation. Soon they will be moving on to other important rooms in the great Second Empire building.

While stenciling is the primary art practiced by Boyce and his associates, they are also skilled in freehand painting, gilding, and glazing.

Larry Boyce & Associates
Box 421507
San Francisco, CA 94142-1507
(415) 626-2122 or
(415) 923-1366

Bob Buckter

Bob Buckter has given almost every type of exterior new beauty by applying his considerable skill and a lot of paint. Italianate, Queen Anne, and Stick Style houses have been designated San Francisco landmarks after receiving his expert touch. The colors

are chosen to suit the client's taste and to enhance the structure's best features. This plain Oak Street façade has been brought back to life with the addition of a pale green paint, a bold forest green trim, and two cartouches.

Buckter also applied soft colors and delicate details to an eye-pleasing building at the corner of Vallejo and Laguna. Although Buckter usually works in the San Francisco area, he sometimes does color consulting by mail.

Brochure available.

Bob Buckter
3877 20th St.
San Francisco, CA 94114
(415) 922-7444

John Canning

A superior craftsman with a feel for the authentic, John Canning excels at characteristically Victorian decoration. Born and trained in Scotland, he has practiced his trade in America for a number of years and is well known for his work at Yale University's Battell Chapel, the Connecticut State Capitol in Hartford, and other Connecticut institutions. He is shown at work in the Capitol's Hall of Flags.

There is hardly a decorative technique—stenciling, stria, mottling, stippling, crosshatching, gilding, trompe l'oeil, graining—which is not within his grasp.

John Canning
132 Meeker Rd.
Southington, CT 06489
(203) 621-2188

David Cohn

David Cohn's principal love is stenciling and freehand painting on as large a scale as possible. His design inspirations come from a variety of sacred and profane sources such as an Old World cathedral tile floor, a 1930s linoleum design, and a late-Victorian floral wallpaper. His work is eclectic, mixing a bit of this and that, and therefore quite original. He'll tackle just about any surface—floor, wall, or ceiling—in any style desired by the customer, and in any setting, residential or commercial. The result is never anything short of wonderful.

David Cohn
240 Waverly Pl.
New York, NY 10014
(212) 741-3548

Craftsmen Decorators

The addition of decorative painting to certain elements of a house can turn ordinary materials into strikingly elegant details. Craftsmen Decorators can add touches of old-fashioned luxury by gilding, glazing, graining, or marbling a variety of surfaces.

The trompe l'oeil marbleized wainscoting illustrated here is an example of the company's fine work. No literature is available, but Craftsmen Decorators can supply numerous references.

Craftsmen Decorators
2611 Ocean Ave.
Brooklyn, NY 11229
(718) 332-2106

The Day Studio-Workshop

Founded by JoAnne Day in 1975 in San Francisco, the studio-workshop is among the best known in North America today. Working from coast to coast, the staff is able to undertake both restoration and new design projects.

Craftspeople at the Day Studio-Workshop know their art well enough to teach it to others. Two-day seminars for professionals and non-professionals are held each year at various locations on the East and West coasts. These cover glaze formulas, color mixing, tools and supplies, as well as

basic business techniques for the new decorative painter. Fully demonstrated are wall glazing and painted finishes, including graded shading, provincial distressing, trompe l'oeil, pickling, and silk and linen finishes. There are additional workshop sessions throughout the year in San Francisco.

For further information, contact:

Day Studio-Workshop, Inc.
1504 Bryant St.
San Francisco, CA 94103
(415) 626-9300

Designed Communications

Partners Suzanne Kittrell and Rebecca Rogers Witsell have fashioned a very successful business as restoration artists. So successful have they become that there is now a demand for them to create new work in addition to their restoration work, a request which both artists are happy to oblige.

Every restoration job that they undertake begins with thorough historical research and technical analysis of ornamented surfaces. Only when they are satisfied that they know the story behind the faded or altered surface do they begin their cleaning and re-painting. Stenciling is their specialty, and Kittrell and Witsell

have become experts on late-19th and early 20th-century ornamentation of this type. But they are also accomplished in graining, marbling, and other faux finishes.

Most of Designed Communications' work has been accomplished in the Little Rock area, but they are available to work farther afield. Illustrated is the restored dining room in the Cornish House, Little Rock.

Designed Communications
704 Boyle Bldg.
103 W. Capitol
Little Rock, AR 72201
(501) 372-2056

EverGreene Painting Studios

The rare material is unavailable. Or it's fragile. Or it won't last. These reasons, as well as economy, promote the use of skillfully painted *faux* finishes. Lapis lazuli and limestone, malachite and marble, tortoiseshell, precious wood, and more have been mirrored in paint for centuries. With clients like the Guerlain department of Bergdorf-Goodman and the U.S. Government, EverGreene has built a deservedly high reputation.

EverGreene champions decorative techniques such as stippling, polychroming, fresco secco, stria, color washing, gilding, scagliola, and antiquing.

Brochures available.

EverGreene Painting Studios
365 W. 36th St.
New York, NY 10018
(212) 239-1322

David Fisch

David Fisch is more than a decorative painter. He has been painting since childhood and specializes today in transforming walls and more with highly decorative borders, reliefs, and freehand oil painting of exceptional skill and imagination. His trompe l'oeil work—illustrated in these room-end landscape panels —is more than visual trickery. What is captured in a seeming

third dimension is a dream-like world, yet another dimension. Fisch's murals and trompe l'oeil paintings have received praise from *House & Garden, House Beautiful* and *The New York Times Magazine*. We gladly add our praise to theirs.

David Fisch
1014 S. Main St.
Spring Valley, NY 10977
(914) 352-7588

Gamut Art Interiors

Hellgah and Hellmuth Dieken are natives of West Germany who have become important ornamental artists on the American scene. Their unique wall paintings often resemble old oil frescoes and have clear historic roots in European design and decoration. The Diekens' mastery of the ancient arts of stenciling and trompe l'oeil is impeccable.

Clients of the talented couple have included European aristocrats as well as important American enterprises, including Trump Tower in New York City. Illustrated is the front hall of a model apartment which they painted in that towering Fifth Avenue building.

Gamut Art Interiors
12441 Nedra Dr.
Granada Hills, CA 91344
(818) 366-8862

George Studios

Richard George's work, usually commissioned for private homes, includes the standard repertoire of *faux* finishes and painting. His restoration of *objets d'art*, however, draws particular attention. Porcelain restoration is a specialty, and gold leafing is available, as well. His work is accomplished with an appropriate fine hand.

George Studios
45-04 97th Pl.
Corona, NY 11368
(718) 271-2506

Lynn Goodpasture

Magically transforming ten floors of sheetrock to marble, Lynn Goodpasture proved her competence at marbling with a mammoth project for Equitable Life in New York City. An independent contractor for homeowners, architects, and designers, Goodpasture includes among her considerable skills stenciling (illustrated here), gold leafing, and other painting techniques, executed on any interior surface.

The artist also custom paints furniture and floorcloths, and she has taught stenciling at New York City's Cooper-Hewitt Museum.

Goodpasture is ready to travel on the job. She has extensive restoration experience and enjoys working with architects to emphasize the merging of ornament and structure.

For more information, contact the artist.

Lynn Goodpasture
42 W. 17th St.
New York, NY 10011
(212) 989-5246

Grammar of Ornament

During its eight years of existence, Grammar of Ornament has achieved impressive restoration work at many sites in the Rocky Mountain region, including the U.S. Mint and the Museum of Western Art, both in Denver; the Wheeler Opera House in Aspen, Colorado; and the Grant-Kohrs Ranch in Montana. The partners in the firm—Ken Miller and Larry Jones—have an understanding of period ornamentation, how it was applied and how it can be properly restored.

Illustrated is a stenciled frieze design used for one room in the oldest remaining single-family dwelling in downtown Denver. The execution of this type of decorative finish is the primary focus of the firm's work, but also offered are site and finish analysis, documentation, research, drawings, full-scale color renderings, and samples.

Marbling, stenciling, gilding, glazing, and graining are offered for projects of almost any size and of any period design.

The Grammar of Ornament, Inc.
2626 Curtis St.
Denver, CO 80205
(303) 295-2431

Judith Hendershot

Judith Hendershot has made her reputation as a painter of ceilings in both residential and large commercial spaces. She is primarily a stencil artist, capable of restoring the work of such masters of ornament as Louis Sullivan and creating new designs for old spaces. Despite her deserved reputation, ceilings are only one of the areas in which she wields

her brushes and templates. Walls and floors also receive professional attention.

Hendershot works primarily in the Chicago area and has her studio in Evanston. On large projects, she calls upon the assistance of a talented crew of artists who welcome the opportunity to undertake such fulfilling work. Illustrated is one project of this kind—a stenciled ceiling for Daniel Burnham's Railway Exchange Building in Chicago, now the Santa Fe Center.

Judith Hendershot
1408 Main St.
Evanston, IL 60202
(312) 475-6411

Merilyn M. Markham

Years ago, theorem paintings—typically flowers and fruits in soft pastels on velvet or paper—were

the exercises of cultured young girls in female academies. Today, Merilyn Markham re-creates the effect of those special paintings in the unusual shaded look of her stenciling. She works her designs on floors, furniture, or walls. Here, Markham fills in one more detail on a painted fireboard. Markham uses oil paints and designs and cuts custom stencils for various decorative effects. She is willing to travel on assignments.

Merilyn M. Markham
22 Mammoth Rd.
Londonderry, NH 03053
(603) 889-2658

Megan Parry

Parry is one of America's best known stencil artists. Her work, however, goes well beyond the limits of traditional decoration. Trompe l'oeil, *faux* marble, and many more finishes and techniques fill out her repertoire. The projects for which she is best known today combine simple, classical stenciled motifs within very contemporary settings and involve freehand painting as well as a strong color palette. Il-lustrated is a frieze design for the upper lobby wall in the Blake Street Building, Denver, Colorado. The design combines hand-painted and stenciled Corinthian columns and Romanesque arches. Just below the ceiling is a stenciled egg-and-dart molding.

Megan Parry
1727 Spruce St.
Boulder, CO 80302
(303) 444-2724

Phyllis Parun Studios

Do you want to add to the beauty of a period house or to recapture the colors of fading stenciling, marbling, or graining? Phyllis Parun provides a variety of decorative painting services and will also restore damaged or faded decoration. Her specialty is gilding, so if you want to add or repair gold leaf on furniture, frames, or architectural elements, give her a call. The studio's address is:

Phyllis Parun Studios
2562 Verbena St.
New Orleans, LA 70122
(504) 944-2859

To leave a message or to make an appointment, call:

(504) 949-8876

Edward K. Perry Co.

Few decorating firms have more experience in restoration work than the Perry Co. Boston-based, the company is especially noted for its expertise in the field of colonial-period building restoration. One of the most recent projects involved the famous Paul Revere House in Boston's North End. The exterior of the building was restained and the interior woodwork refinished. Wallpaper was also repainted. The original restoration of the building was completed by the grandfather of the firm's current president in 1908.

The company researches and tests its materials continuously to insure that they are both appropriate and effective for the job. In addition to projects involving painting and refinishing, the firm is also noted for its trompe l'oeil work, oil and water glazing, graining, mural painting, marbling, and stenciling. Work on new structures is also undertaken by Perry. Illustrated is the lobby in the Boston Design Center in which the firm executed five different marbleized finishes.

Edward K. Perry Co.
322 Newbury St.
Boston, MA 02115
(617) 536-7873

Robson Worldwide Graining

Graining, marbling, and art decoration 'round the globe is the goal of Robson Worldwide Graining. A list of project sites serves as adequate recommendation for the firm headed by Malcolm Robson:

Kensington Palace, Grosvenor House, Woodlawn Plantation (Mount Vernon), the Jaffa Village (United Arab Emirates). Clients have included Margaret Thatcher, Ava Gardner, the Beatles, and the Duke and Duchess of Kent.

Contact fifth-generation craftsman Malcom Robson for further information.

Robson Worldwide Graining
4308 Argonne Dr.
Fairfax, VA 22032
(703) 978-5331

ing. It is, of course, a cleverly painted flat surface. In addition to *faux* plasterwork, the Tromploy craftsmen are also well versed in the *faux* painting of sandstone, marble, malachite, and even cobblestone.

Tromploy, Inc.
400 Lafayette St., 5th Floor
New York, NY 10003
(212) 420-1639

Tromploy

Today's interest in trompe l'oeil is superbly reflected in the many projects undertaken by this New York-based firm. Tromploy, headed by Gary Finkel and Clyde Wachsberger, serves as both a studio for the execution of intricate designs and a gallery for their display of furniture and other objects. The members of the firm also range far and wide in their decoration of interiors. Illustrated is what appears to be an elaborately modeled plaster ceil-

Valley Craftsmen

From a "marble" pillar in an elegant Baltimore hotel to a splendid piece of ornate gilding, the work of Valley Craftsmen shows great skill. Valley Craftsmen's *faux bois* treatment mimics marquetry, adds a natural look to painted wood, or lightens an old finish without actually harming the original. Specialty uses of the technique include over-graining, preferred in rehabilitation work as an alternative to replacing injured but interesting woodwork, and graining for elevator doors, satisfying fire codes without sacrificing an authentic look. Valley Craftsmen uses *faux* marble when structural problems or economy prohibit use of the actual material. *Faux* limestone, malachite, and granite finishes are also part of the firm's repertoire.

Glazing work include techniques such as stria, stippling (or spong-

ing, for a more pronounced effect), and frottage. Colored or metallic stenciling is routinely performed. Trompe l'oeil work is easily within the grasp of this firm's craftsmen, as is the more unusual art of oriental brush painting.

For more information, contact:

Valley Craftsmen, Ltd.
Box 11
Stevenson, MD 21153
(301) 484-3891

Waterman Works

Scott Waterman is still in his twenties, but he has managed in a short time to acquire the experience of a much older decorative painter. He began his work several years ago at Atlanta's famous Fox Theater. Since then Waterman has become known for fine restoration painting, gilding, graining, glazing, and stenciling as well as contemporary work in new homes and apartment buildings in the Atlanta area. Illustrated is a section of a marbleized fireplace executed in several different finishes.

Although he is known primarily for projects in his home territory, Scott Waterman is available for work in other areas as well.

Waterman Works
266B Oxford Pl., N.E.
Atlanta, GA 30307
(404) 373-9438

Wiggins Brothers

David and Gerard Wiggins carry on the tradition of itinerant New England stencil artists. They travel throughout the region decorating homes with traditional early 19th-century patterns that have become well known and appreciated once again—eagles of freedom, doves in flight, weeping willows. Their painting, however, goes beyond the merely symbolic and ornamental. Murals depicting various stages and scenes of everyday country life are also rendered on canvas and plastered walls. Folk art at its very best—spirited and inspired—is the special contribution of the Wiggins brothers.

Wiggins Brothers
Box 420
Hale Rd.
Tilton, NH 03276
(603) 286-3046

Papers

Ever since wallpaper could be inexpensively produced in continuous rolls by high-speed printing presses in the mid-19th century, papers have found numerous practical and decorative uses in the home. Today's homeowner will find papers similarly useful and ornamental. Available in various finishes and textures, modern papers are generally easier to hang and to keep clean than the old-fashioned variety. There are hundreds of well-documented reproduction designs from the 18th and 19th centuries to choose from, as well as thousands of adaptations and interpretations of traditional florals, stripes, and geometrics. Slowly but steadily, the old practice of using two or three papers in a room is once again gaining favor. Wallpaper borders can be effectively used to create cornice and frieze designs; other papers are appropriate for use on the ceilings or as wall panels. Special embossed and textured Victorian papers such as Lincrusta Walton and Supaglypta are being produced once again and are especially appropriate and attractive substitutes for wainscoting in hallways and dining rooms.

Laura Ashley

Each year the Laura Ashley wallpaper collection becomes more comprehensive. It has expanded far beyond the small-print sprigged country florals for which it was first famous. Ashley papers now include a good selection of stripes, moirés, and geometrics, several in bright, vivid colors. Many of the wallcoverings are suitable for formal rooms, and include 19th-century arborescent prints; Victorian designs in flowers, stripes, and swirls; and adaptations of period designs.

Of special interest are wallpaper borders in eighteen designs and many colorways. Featuring conveniently washable surfaces, the borders come in 4¼" widths and 11-yard lengths. Particularly appealing are numerous floral designs, a Greek key fret, and a richly detailed pattern of pointed arches.

Laura Ashley papers and fabrics are available through the firm's many retail outlets and through its home furnishings catalogue.

Home furnishings catalogue, $4.

Laura Ashley
Dept. B117, Box 5308
Melville, NY 11747
(800) 367-2000

Bentley Brothers

With Frederick Walton's invention of Lincrusta, a linoleum-like compound, in 1877, Victorian houses enjoyed the benefits of durable, relatively inexpensive embossed wallcoverings. The cost of such products was reduced and their versatility increased when a heavy, embossed paper called Anaglypta was introduced ten years later. Today, a British company called Crown Decorative Products Limited, whose wallcoverings are distributed in the United States by Bentley Brothers, makes five types of embossed materials that re-create the look of Anaglypta and Lincrusta. Two of them are almost identical to the originals. Crown's Supaglypta is a very heavy embossed paper made of cotton

fibers and pulp. Design 655, illustrated here, shows how Supaglypta can transform a wall.

Crown's version of Lincrusta is also comparable to the original. Beautifully shaped, it is waterproof and extremely durable, which makes it perfect for high-traffic areas. Such dados as design 1951 will survive quite a bit

of abuse. A wide range of available patterns includes a neoclassical frieze (design 1955) and a luxurious wall-covering (design 1589) and its companion frieze (design 1957).

Bentley Brothers also distributes Crown's Anaglypta, an embossed paper lighter and more fragile than its namesake. However, it is capable of accepting pattern rich in detail, like design 335, a delightful paper bursting with delicate leaves.

Anaglypta Vinyls come in two weights and are easy to clean and excellent for areas with high humidity. A series of heavy, embossed border papers called Pelmets features variety of design and strength derived from cotton fibers in the paper.

Anaglypta, Anaglypta Vinyls, Supaglypta, and Pelmets can be applied to walls or ceilings with heavy-duty vinyl wallpaper paste; Lincrusta requires a special glue. Bentley Brothers recommends that you allow a professional to install Anaglypta and Lincrusta for you.

All of these wallcoverings should be painted and can be repainted many times; a number of interesting effects can be achieved, including the appearance of pressed copper or tooled leather.

Brochure and samples, $2. For more information or to locate a dealer near you, contact:

Bentley Brothers
918 Baxter Ave.
Louisville, KY 40204
(800) 824-4777 or
(502) 589-2939

Louis W. Bowen

Pastel-colored flowers on fragile vines entangle the statues in Obelisk, a two-panel pattern from Louis W. Bowen. The pale columns against a lustrous gold or silver background will add a grand touch of the Oriental to your home. Bowen's extensive line

of wallcoverings includes scenics with over two dozen panels and small-scale repeating patterns, so there's something for the most formal or the coziest room in the house. The company has also released a line of fabrics intended to complement its papers.

Louis W. Bowen has showrooms in New York, Los Angeles, San Francisco, Chicago, and Boston; for more information, contact:

Louis W. Bowen
950 Third Ave.
New York, NY 10022
(212) 759-5410

Bradbury & Bradbury

Exquisite hand-printed papers in a number of popular styles have made Bradbury & Bradbury one of America's leading suppliers of late-Victorian reproduction papers. This frieze paper, circa 1884 and typical of the firm's exquisite offerings, was copied from a pattern found in a home in Oakland, California.

The company makes several room sets composed of fillers, borders, and special decorations. The Anglo-Japanese room set is typical of papers designed in the 1880s, when Britain and America were fervently interested in all things Japanese. This wall design for an 11'-high room is assembled from the 36"-high by 18"-wide Sunflower panel, the 26"-high Eastlake dado, Claire's Willow Wall Fill, and the Eastlake frieze trimmed to 18" high.

Ceiling patterns can also be created from Bradbury & Bradbury's pieces. This exotic ceiling is made by using a border of Ivy Block Enrichment, the 18" Sunflower rosette on the Japanese Lattice background, and lines of

Eastlake Combination Ornament with joints formed by Sunflower corner blocks. Five color schemes are available: Aesthetic Green, a pale yellow-olive with gold, red, and blue details; Eucalyptus, predominantly dark rose and blue; Apricot, a combination of light rose, blue, and yellow; Dove Blue, a grayish blue with gold, white, and rose details; and Ashes of Rose, a blend of several pinks.

Bradbury & Bradbury's circa 1887 Neo-Grec room set re-creates the

atmosphere of the neoclassical. The company's suggestion for decorating an 11'-high room includes a 27"-high dado, a frieze trimmed to 18", and the Anthemion Wall Fill.

A Neo-Grec ceiling design consists of a border called Star Trellis Enrichment, the 3" Wave Border with Laurel Border corner blocks, an 8½" fret border, and the 24"-long Corner Fan. It also comes in five color schemes: Terra Cotta, a combination of brownish-reds and black with gold and blue details; Cream & Gilt, featuring cream, pinks, gold, and reds; Jasper Green, a pale grayish olive complemented by rose, white, and

gold; Dove Blue; and Ashes of Roses. Bradbury & Bradbury also makes a line of papers reminiscent of the designs of William Morris. If you're having trouble deciding on the perfect paper, feel free to make use of the company's design service. The fee is deductible from your wallpaper order, and you will be provided with drawings, cost and quantity estimates, and pattern samples.

Samples of Neo-Grec or Anglo-Japanese papers, $5. Literature available.

Bradbury & Bradbury Wallpapers
Box 155
Benicia, CA 94510
(707) 746-1900

Brunschwig & Fils

Brunschwig & Fils papers are hard to find; they're sold only through interior designers and a few retail outlets. Once you locate them, though, you'll be hooked. The company's selection spans several historical periods and reflects a dedication to beauty and authenticity that has become Brunschwig & Fils' hallmark. You can make the search a little easier by contacting the company's main office for further information.

Brunschwig & Fils
979 Third Ave.
New York, NY 10022
(212) 838-7878

Greeff

Long known and respected for its fine period papers, Greeff offers two collections especially designed to please old-house lovers. The Fox Hollow Collection features, among others, a pattern called East Riding. Thickly spread with full-blown roses, it comes in five colorways: gold and green on cream, turquoise and sage on natural, rose and blue on parchment, coral and praline on sand, and oyster and spruce on brick.

Greeff's Shelburne Museum Collection presents several designs inspired by antique crafts and artwork. Dutton Swag, derived from hand-stenciling found in the museum's Dutton House, is particularly useful. It can be used as a vertical stripe or cut and used to frame a room. It is available in blue spruce and coral on cream, leaf and apricot on natural, blue and red on putty, or blue on sky blue.

Grape Ivy Stencil has a similar source. Calling to mind the work of early itinerant painters, it comes in olive and copper on sage, colonial blue and copper on café au lait, olive and persimmon on sand, and blue and cranberry on putty. Complementary fabrics are available for all four colorways.

The other two papers shown here, which Greeff suggests using together, were taken from quilt patterns. Samantha, with its small flowers, was inspired by an appliqué quilt at the Shelburne Museum. It comes in rose and green on blueberry, brick and olive on sand, maize and spruce on brick, rose and mint on bottle (a dark olive), and tan and navy on wedgwood. Anna, a floral stripe adapted from the central motif of an 18th-century quilt, is available in colorways which include pink and sky, gold and aqua, peach and hemlock, and pink and sapphire.

Greeff has showrooms in Atlanta, Boston, Chicago, Dallas, Los Angeles, New York, Port Chester, San Francisco, Toronto, London, and Paris. For more information, contact:

Greeff Fabrics, Inc.
150 Midland Ave.
Port Chester, NY 10573
(914) 939-6200

Katzenbach & Warren

Since 1940, Katzenbach & Warren has been licensed to reproduce patterns from Colonial Williamsburg. Old papers have been carefully copied, and fabric designs have been adapted for use as wallpapers. These photographs show two selections from the Williamsburg Museum Prints collection in use.

Two Katzenbach & Warren wallpapers adorn this room. The Williamsburg paper is Avalon, taken from an 18th-century fabric which may have been of French origin. It features delicate bouquets and grapevines. The pattern at the bottom of the wall and lining the curio cabinet is Brandon, a

paper with a tiny leaf and dot motif.

Diamond Floral's large and small floral vines are separated by narrow vertical stripes with a diamond lozenge design. It is an adaptation of an 18th-century linen and cotton fabric from Pro-

Capturing everything from the simplicity of late-18th-century America to the ornate complexity of Victorian England, Scalamandré re-creates the beauty of antique wallcoverings and ceiling papers. Skill and commitment to authenticity make this firm a leader in its field, as does its willingness to execute special projects. Scalamandré often reproduces designs for individual sites. For more information, contact the company.

Scalamandré, Inc.
950 Third Ave.
New York, NY 10022
(212) 361-8500

Schumacher

Specializing in papers from the 19th century, Schumacher produces a number of painstakingly accurate reproductions. The selection includes late-Victorian American and English wallcoverings and borders, Baroque papers, and French papers from 1840 to 1870.

The company also offers a collection of wallpaper adaptations inspired by architectural details found in classic American homes. These papers are part of Schumacher's National Trust for Historic Preservation Collection. Illustrated are two of these designs, Drayton Hall Crown Moulding and Drayton Hall Columns, each inspired by the carved paneling found in the Great Hall of the South Carolina mansion. The background paper is Manchu, an adaptation of a Chinese silk robe design, and is available in cream, peach, rose dust, and slate colorways.

A second collection of wallpaper designs has been adapted from objects in the Abby Aldrich Rockefeller Folk Art Center at Colonial Williamsburg. Details from 19th-century birth records, old quilts, paintings, and weather vanes have been translated into beautiful papers appropriate for many types of old houses.

vençe, France. The daybed alcove is decorated with a companion pattern called Milford, taken from the bands of small flowers in Diamond Floral.

Katzenbach & Warren has showrooms in New York, Los Angeles, San Francisco, Chicago, and Boston, and its papers can also be seen at dealers throughout the United States. For more information, call or write:

Katzenbach & Warren
950 Third Ave.
New York, NY 10022
(212) 759-5410

Sanderson

The papers of William Morris, whose striking flowers and foliage proved immensely popular in the late-Victorian era, are still in production today, thanks to Arthur Sanderson & Sons. Twenty designs, made with Morris's original blocks, are offered. Of course, not everyone in the late 19th century could afford these expensive papers, and the same is true now. With this in mind, Sanderson also manufactures silk-screened reproductions of the Morris designs which come a bit less dearly.

For more information, contact:

Arthur Sanderson & Sons
979 Third Ave.
New York, NY 10022
(212) 319-7220

Richard E. Thibaut

The classic porcelain still produced in Limousin, France, and commonly known as Royale Limoges china inspired Thibaut's Royale Limoges II collection of screen-printed wallcoverings and fabrics. Among 87 wallcoverings, 20 borders, and 35 fabrics are florals like the oversized Traviata, delicate Jardin, flamboyant Madras, and delicate, staid Kimono (shown here).

The fifth volume of Thibaut's Waterford collection includes fabrics and borders to accompany the 79 wallcoverings, which are strippable and washable and come already pasted and trimmed. The Bridgetown features gnarled vines and beautiful blossoms. Its companion paper is the scalloped Macon. Nassau shows abundant buds and vines. Nassau Tracery allows a pairing with a sparser version of the same.

Thibaut papers are produced with complete fidelity to designs of the past and with an authority that comes with continued contact with preservationists and museum creators throughout America.

Van Luit

Albert Van Luit's artistry and determination led him to found a business during the Depression to manufacture his own hand-printed scenic designs after the Chinese Revolution cut off the supply of such decorative papers, and in the 1980s to introduce two collections of wallcoverings in association with the Henry Francis du Pont Winterthur Museum.

Part of Van Luit's newest Winterthur collection, Simsbury was inspired by the museum's Simsbury Room, a setting based on a mid-18th-century Connecticut home. The drapes in this photograph are made of pure cotton sateen and are printed in the same pattern by Van Luit.

Covent Garden, with elaborate bands of birds, flowers, ribbon, and lace, reproduces the design of an English block-printed cotton chintz displayed at Winterthur. Also illustrated are Covent Garden Border and Coventry, two complementary accent designs with larger patterns than the model.

Altogether there are a dozen

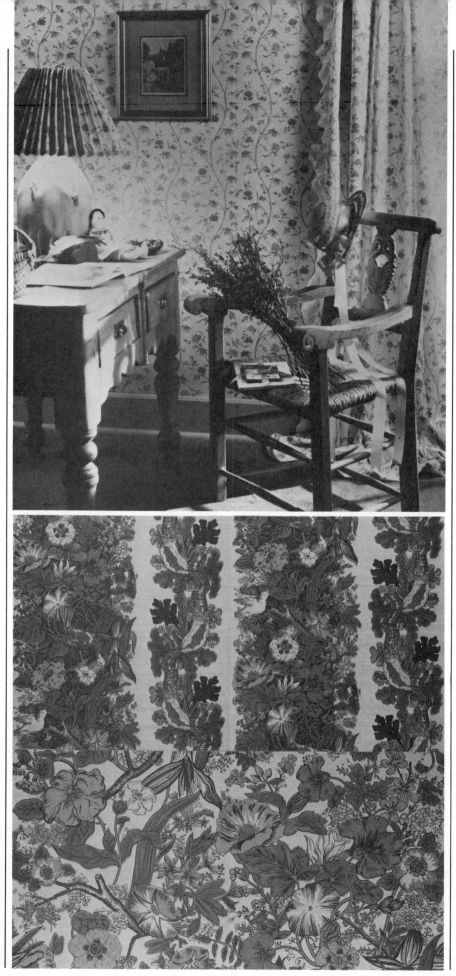

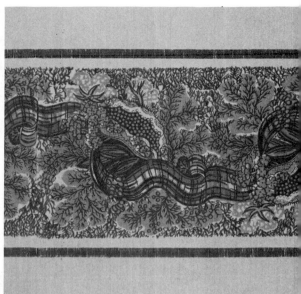

designs in this new Winterthur collection, each of which is coordinated with a matching fabric. And each design is offered in the color of the original piece as well as in a variety of suitable colors.

Van Luit showrooms are located in Boston, New York, San Francisco, Los Angeles, and Chicago. Contact the firm for further information regarding the availability of these papers.

Albert Van Luit & Co.
4000 Chevy Chase Dr.
Los Angeles, CA 90039
(818) 247-8840

Victorian Collectibles

It began with the purchase of 4,500 rolls of leftover wallpaper. To the surprise of the partners who bought them, they consisted of nearly 1,400 different sidewall, ceiling, border, and corner paper patterns dating from 1860 to 1910. Exposed to little or no light, they retained their original brilliant colors, and they were quickly reproduced by the newly formed Victorian Collectibles.

This photograph of a room from the General Crook House in Omaha, Nebraska, shows how striking and elegant the papers are. The sidewall and ceiling pattern is called Millard; it repeats every 10″, and its complementary 18″-high border repeats every 19½″. Millard appears again in the

medallion unless you specify otherwise. Documentary or contemporary colors may be selected. Canvas and paper may be combined. For an extra fee, Victorian Collectibles will provide design assistance and submit a pencil sketch and colors to you before beginning the painting.

The photographs show a corner design called Liberty Bird, which was first reproduced for the Grand Opera House in Oshkosh, Wisconsin, and a room in a house that survived the Chicago fire. The sidewall paper and 9" border are Dayle, and the hand-painted ceiling is in a pattern called Dayle Companion. The corners and joints are also hand-painted.

Brochure, $2.

Victorian Collectibles, Ltd.
845 E. Glenbrook Rd.
Milwaukee, WI 53217
(414) 352-6910

The Wallpaper Works

Museums, historical societies, restaurants, and television and motion picture art directors, as well as private individuals, have made use of the products sold by The Wallpaper Works. Not reproductions but original wallcoverings manufactured several decades ago, they feature vivid colors and large, sharp patterns. Number 16007 has a bold

next illustration, along with Fortino, an elaborate pattern with an 18" border, and Emperor, which has a 9" border. An elegant fleur-de-lis design called Dayle can be seen on the drawing table.

The company also remembers that it's practically a crime to leave a Victorian ceiling unadorned. Two basic types of ceiling treatments are available: paper and canvas. Victorian Collectibles has a number of non-directional ceiling papers and borders in stock. A painted background can be added to surround the ceiling paper. Hand-painted canvas is also available and includes four corners, four joiners, and a center

floral design on a dark background; number 15811 features rich bouquets of roses in a pattern reminiscent of late-Victorian papers.

Two sample books containing about 175 papers are available for examination, as are color photographs. Both require a deposit which is refunded when the material is returned. If you have a good idea of what you'd like, The Wallpaper Works can supply individual swatches at no charge.

The Wallpaper Works
Box 261, Station C
Toronto, Ontario, Canada M6J 2P4
(416) 366-1790

Waverly

Adaptations of traditional designs from Waverly are especially useful for the budget-conscious home decorator. Reasonably priced and

available in almost all fabric shops, Waverly's cottons cover a wide spectrum of period designs. Shown is American Beauty from the Liberty Legacy collection. The rose and ribbon motif is reminiscent of both papers and fabrics widely used in North America and England in the early decades of this century. American Beauty

is available in a 54″-wide cotton print as well as on washable, strippable, vinyl-coated paper.

For further information, write to:

Waverly
Dept. OH
79 Madison Ave.
New York, NY 10016

Other Suppliers of Paints and Papers

Consult List of Suppliers for addresses.

Cleaners and Finishes

The Canal Co.
Finnaren & Haley, Inc.
H & H Decors
Prospect Products
The Settlers

Decorative Painters

Koeppel/Freedman Studios
Marsh Stream Enterprises

Partridge Replications
Victorian Collectibles Ltd.

Papers

Ohmega Salvage
San Francisco Victoriana
Steptoe & Wife Antiques Ltd.

8.
Fabrics

Ever since the advent of machine-printed textiles in the early 1800s, it has been possible to drape and cover up almost any object or element in a room at a reasonable cost. Before that time, fabrics at the window were minimal and the primary use of expensive material was in bed hangings. Gradually, throughout the 19th century, more and more fabric was employed. No one is known as a draper today, but those who knew how to arrange fabric artfully around a chair or at a window were as important a century ago as painters and other decorators are in the 1980s. Historians are continually researching early uses of fabric. When we think we know it all, there is yet another new discovery—about the use of muslin, for example, or unbleached cotton. The manufacture of reproduction designs continues to grow each year. Many of these materials were prepared originally for a particular house restoration and may be available now only on a custom-order basis. Other reproductions, however, are part of the regular stock of the fabric manufacturers and merchants. Included in this category are many of the museum collections, such as those carrying the Sturbridge Village or Williamsburg designation. There are also "adaptations" of traditional designs which may be perfectly suitable for period decorating. To adapt a design is usually to make it somewhat less complex in coloration or detail so as to lower the cost of its production. In addition, many designs that were originally woven are now adapted as prints.

The following pages comprise a swatch book of reproduction fabrics and suitable adaptations. Unfortunately, it is not possible to present these designs in color. It is also impossible to represent all the different kinds of materials that are available. But, within the limits of reason and taste, a home renovator should have no problem selecting appropriate materials, given the wide range of price, style, and quality available but only hinted at in the present chapter.

Georgiana and Bolton Vine, companion fabrics in the Stately Home Collection of Stroheim & Romann, New York City.

Amazon Drygoods

Amazon Drygoods stocks a variety of fabrics and sewing notions; some are hard to find at ordinary fabric stores, and some are available at lower prices than you might pay locally. Pure cottons, synthetics, and cotton and synthetic blends are in stock or can be obtained. Several come in over twenty colors, and slipper satin comes in eighty-four. Amazon also features unusual trims and lace, and the store's proprietor, Janet Burgess, can locate and order museum-documented fabrics if you can't locate them near home.

Catalogue, $2.

Amazon Drygoods
2218 E. 11th St.
Davenport, IA 52803
(319) 322-6800

Laura Ashley

Coordinating with paints, with patterns often available in wallpaper as well, Laura Ashley's distinctive fabrics come in a variety of weights and twenty-one colorways for a range of attractive uses.

Country furnishing cottons, printed with miniature florals or bolder patterns, come in 48" widths of pure cotton, with a maximum length of 38 yards. Easy care is a plus: wash or dry clean this fabric.

For light upholstery and curtains, Ashley's cotton sateen drawing room fabric is appropriate. An innovation from the late-Victorian period, this material features abstract and floral patterns, including the flamboyant Emmeline, the ribbons and flower tufts in Garlands, and the exotic leaf motif of Venetia. Fade-resistant dyes on these 45" widths of cotton (continuous lengths of up to 35 yards) render drawing room fabric likewise washable or suitable for dry cleaning.

An Indian original, adopted in Europe during the 1800s, pure cotton chintz is still ideal for drapes, chair covers, and much

more. Patterns like the riotous English Garden and wide-blooming Joy typify the appealing designs that grace this fabric. Dry clean chintz to preserve its sheen. Widths of 48" are available in a maximum length of 35 yards.

Laura Ashley fabrics and papers

are available through the firm's many retail outlets and through its home furnishings catalogue.

Home furnishings catalogue, $4.

Laura Ashley
Dept. B117, Box 5308
Melville, NY 11747
(800) 367-2000

Brunschwig & Fils

Brunschwig & Fils's fine materials include cottons, silks, wools, linens, and even horsehair. Always a stickler for authenticity, this firm has gathered and reproduced period patterns from Delaware's Henry Francis DuPont Winterthur Museum, from the Musée des Arts Décoratifs in Paris, and from Richmond, Virginia's Valentine Museum.

To view Brunschwig & Fils fabrics, consult an interior designer or try the home decoration department of a selected retail outlet. Contact the firm for more information.

Brunschwig & Fils
979 Third Ave.
New York, NY 10022
(212) 838-7878

Carter Canopies

Calling these hand-tied fishnet canopies "the frosting on a cake," Carter Canopies adds a new dimension to an old-fashioned bed. Executed in pure cotton, the designs include this Double Diamond pattern, as well as Single Diamond, Large Scallop, Lover's Knot, Straight Edge, and Margaret Winston. All custom canopies are hand washable and available in white or natural tone. The firm also supplies custom-made dust ruffles of permanent-press muslin, fluffy and full, plain or bordered with lace or eyelet, in white or natural.

Brochure available.

Carter Canopies
Box 808
Rte. 2, Box 270-G
Troutman, NC 28166-0808
(704) 528-4071

Greeff

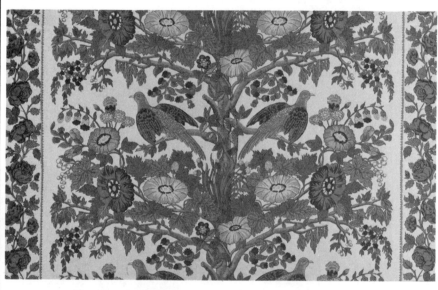

For over fifty years, Greeff has been producing high-quality prints and woven fabrics, many of which are historical reproductions or adaptations.

Easily at home in a period room, East Riding comes from the Fox Hollow Collection. A screen print on 100% cotton, it comes in a 36" width with a vertical repeat of 12⅝". The beautifully plumaged birds and flowering trees in this pattern find their complement in Greeff's East Riding wallpaper, festooned with roses.

Greeff products are available through the firm's showrooms in Atlanta, Boston, Chicago, Dallas, Los Angeles, New York, Port Chester, San Francisco, Toronto, London, and Paris, or through decorating departments in selected retail stores. Contact the firm for further information.

Greeff Fabrics, Inc.
155 E. 56th St.
New York, NY 10022
(212) 888-5060

Museum of American Textile History

Antique textiles need careful preservation to last for further generations. Their organic fibers fray from handling, environmental factors (light, pollution, soil-ing, temperature fluctuations), and vermin. To that end the Museum of American Textile History founded the Textile Conservation Center in 1977, establishing facilities for intensive laboratory analysis. The Textile Conservation Center cleans, fumigates, dries, and performs chemical analyses, photographic documentation, and light microscopy on historic textile works. Services include on-site inspections and work on textiles so large or so delicate as to prohibit transport. Appraisals, dating, and authenticating services are not available, but "first aid" and emergency work, as well as specific lectures and workshops, are offered.

Brochure available.

Museum of American Textile History
Textile Conservation Center
800 Massachusetts Ave.
North Andover, MA 01845
(617) 686-0191

Partridge Replications

Nancy Cook, handweaver and expert seamstress, brings her notable talents as a period interior designer to Partridge Replications. Skilled in selecting and making appropriate accessories for 18th- and 19th-century homes, she offers consultation, design, and sewing services. Cook can provide perfect bolsters, linens, blankets, table linens, floor coverings, or handwoven items for your house. She specializes in bed hangings made from museum-documented fabrics purchased from major fabric manufacturers. The photograph shows one of her bed

hangings and another of her specialities—custom-made window draperies.

Brochure available.

Partridge Replications
63 Penhallow St.
Portsmouth, NH 03801
(603) 431-8733

Raintree Designs

A cheerful bedroom emerges with a little help from fabrics by Raintree Designs. Assembled by British designer Victoria Morland, the fabrics are intended to evoke the atmosphere of an English country house. Roses and ribbons in wisteria, pale pink, and soft moss form a pattern called Bronte, which covers the walls and bed. Soft ruffles of Plain Jane, a simple, striped fabric, trim the bed hangings. Rose Swag serves as a complementary wall border. In the foreground, a side chair and ottoman are neatly upholstered with wisteria-and-white Clover Plaid; the lamp table is draped with a pretty design called Emily.

For information on these and other fabrics, contact:

Raintree Designs, Inc.
979 Third Ave., Suite 503N
New York, NY 10022
(212) 477-8594

Rue de France

Pamela Kelley, president of Rue de France, makes periodic voyages to France to choose the lace patterns offered by this firm. Crafted from a machine-washable synthetic to wear extremely well, the material successfully simulates more delicate cotton lace. Rue de France offers many different types of curtains and other decorative items. The firm also provides lace by the yard.

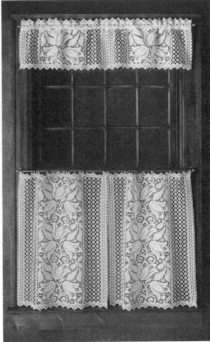

The Victorian Belle Fleur pattern, shown here as a valance, may also be ordered for door or café curtains, flat panels, and tiebacks. It comes in a natural tone.

When more of a screening effect is desired, choose a denser design like Chambord. Select anything,

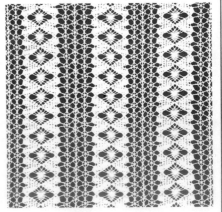

from door curtains to pillows, in natural or beige, all featuring this vertical design of hearts in a close lattice.

Rue de France also offers cheerfully colored screen-printed fabrics. Printed in France, the Provençal collection includes Campano and Campano Bande, either by the yard, or in ruffled tiebacks (standard and custom widths). Colors range from rose or raspberry to earth, teal, blue, and cream and blue. Coordinating wallpapers are a delightful plus.

In white on navy, navy on white, tangerine, and gray on blue, the closely-patterned Bonis adds a touch of country—tiebacks or by the yard. Cushions and tablecloths are also available.

Catalogue, $2. Sample book, $2. (Refundable upon first order.)

Rue de France
78 Thames St.
Newport, RI 02840
(401) 846-2084

Scalamandré

With no mention of Scalamandré, a listing of high quality, historically accurate fabrics would be sadly lacking. The firm's designers and Long Island mill craftsmen dedicate themselves to re-creating patterns they find preserved in hundreds of landmark North American and European homes and fine museums worldwide.

Scalamandré's admirable offerings are available only through interior designers or decorating departments of select stores. Contact the company for further information.

Scalamandré, Inc.
950 Third Ave.
New York, NY 10022
(212) 980-3888

Schumacher

Both precise reproductions of traditional fabric designs and adaptations of classic patterns have been specialities of Schumacher for many years. The firm is well known for its Winterthur and Colonial Williamsburg

collections, and was one of the first American companies to introduce accurate copies of Victorian papers and fabrics. Now Schumacher is introducing its National Trust for Historic Preservation collection.

The room setting was photographed at Chesterwood in Stockbridge, Massachusetts, the home of famed sculptor Daniel Chester French and now a National Trust property. All of the fabrics and papers used in the room are from the new collection. The cotton/linen blend used to cover the wing chairs is named, appropriately, Chesterwood. It is a hand-screened scenic design available in summer green, autumn, and spring blossom. Used as a table covering is Filoli Tapestry, a

tapestry weave from Europe inspired by the luxurious woven fabrics found at Filoli, another National Trust property in California.

For more information on Schumacher fabrics, contact designers, selected retail stores, or the firm itself.

F. Schumacher & Co.
939 Third Ave.
New York, NY 10022
(212) 213-7900

Kathleen B. Smith

Whether you're planning to make a reproduction of a 17th-century sampler or to furnish a whole house with fabrics appropriate to the 18th century, Kathleen B. Smith can supply the materials.

Two years as an assistant to the textiles curator of Colonial Williamsburg gave her a strong background in colonial weaving and needlework, and she selects her tools, fibers, and dyes on the basis of their authenticity. Her skills have been recognized by several museums, which have used her dyed textiles and hand-woven fabrics in their period rooms.

Smith dyes her own thread with vegetable colors. She sells worsted yarn in two weights and in fifty shades, including crimson, coral, black, walnut, blue, purple, and green. Perfect for canvaswork, crewelwork, or fine knitting, it comes in 120', 240', 480', and 960' skeins. Smith also dyes two-ply and seven-strand silk for embroidery or sewing in thirty-four colors. It's strong, smooth, and lustrous and won't catch on your hands as some silk threads will. Since dye lots vary, be sure to get as much as you'll need for the en-

tire project; also keep in mind the sensitivity of natural dyes to direct sunlight.

Smith's specialty is the reproduction of 18th-century fabrics. She has a number of types in stock, most of them hand-woven. They include plain and striped ticking, plain and patterned cottons, canvas, fustian, worsted and woolen twills, worsted tabby, linens in various weights and textures, linsey-woolsey, silk in three weights, and a wool and linen coverlet fabric. The wool fabrics get the benefit of her fifty vegetable dye colors. Linens are usually left natural or bleached in her shop, avoiding the bluish tinge created by commercial bleaching.

Linen, cotton, and wool trimming tapes and other hard-to-find items can be purchased from Smith; she is also expert at selecting bed and table linens appropriate for your house. Some, like the wool- or hair-stuffed mattresses and the imported Irish feather pillows and bolsters, are purchased from other makers; some, like her linen towels, pillowcases, tablecloths, bolster cases, and plain linen or cotton damask napkins and tea-cloths, she researches extensively and sews herself. On the latter items, the hidden seams are machine-sewn and the visible ones hand-sewn, but entirely hand-sewn items are also available.

Literature available. Samples of 50 worsted colors, $4; samples of 34 silk colors, $3; samples of various natural and white threads, 50¢; samples of reproduction fabrics, $2; samples of trimming tapes, $2; list of bed and table linens with swatches, $1. Single samples free with self-addressed stamped envelope.

Kathleen B. Smith
Box 48
W. Chesterfield, MA 01084
(413) 296-4437

Stroheim & Romann

From the archives and furnishings of five carefully selected British homes, Stroheim & Romann has chosen ten fabrics—five woven and five printed—that reflect a fine design history from British, French, Italian, Chinese, Indian, and Islamic sources. The "Stately Homes" prints—twenty-eight colorways for four designs in cotton, glazed chintz and one cotton sateen print (all 54" wide)—include the asters, peonies, and vines of

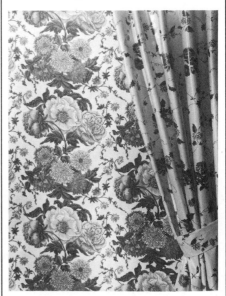

Georgiana, which shows well with the smaller pattern of Bolton Vine (used here in the drapery). Both come from the historic Chatsworth House.

Lennoxlove (named for a castle in Scotland) is a sateen print revealing an Oriental influence in its weaving of hybiscus and iris and exotic birds. The accompanying drapery, in the Italian Renais-

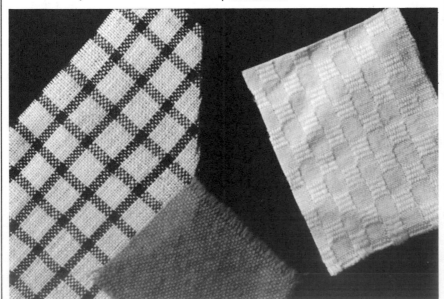

sance's Exeter pattern, hails from the baroque Burghley House. Exeter is a brocade—one of the five woven designs (thirty colorways) in the "Stately Homes" collection.

Exeter also pairs with Hardwick, another design from the Chatsworth House. Hardwick's silver filagree-like threads outline a French-inspired, woven floral pattern.

Stroheim & Romann has also introduced the JAB European Collection of lace panels from Scotland. Lacy Chantilly (51" by 102") is 95% cotton and 5% polyester. Of the same composition, Graziano (55" by 102") is a scattering of large bouquets with a simpler border of small, leafy fans.

Tosca (98" by 106"), 100% polyester blend, depicts a table set with a bountiful centerpiece of roses. A background of regular stripes and leaf patterns ranges above a wavy hem. Because of its unusual width, this panel could be used as a bedspread.

Contact Stroheim & Romann for information about its fifteen branch locations and for general information on its fabric collections.

Stroheim & Romann, Inc.
155 E. 56th St.
New York, NY 10022
(212) 691-0700

Vintage Valances

Made-to-order valances (with or without matching custom side drapes) are the specialty of Vintage Valances. Neo-classical choices include this 48" by 48"

toga-type drape. A Greek Revival design, 48" by 36", shows twin swags and tails. A lined valance with a decorative border, again fashioned after the toga's folds, spans 54" by 36".

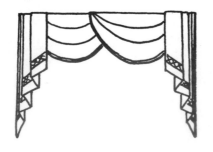

Victoriana enthusiasts will enjoy the multiple draping folds of this design (60" by 36"); with its swags, side tails, and fringe, it's ideal for the dining room or parlor.

This flat valance demonstrates another variation on the Victorian. Choose a suitable bottom contour to outline your window with an elaborate hemline.

Flannel interliners and other special features are readily available from Vintage Valances. Request matching mantel drapings, dressing tables, or other items, but order all fittings for one room at the same time to guarantee the same dye lot.

Under the heading "Helpful but Hard to Find Accessories," Vintage Valances offers adjustable flat curtain rods. Inside-mounting and lacking returns, they can suspend lace curtains beneath valances, showing off fancy woodwork. Wooden-roller window shades, in cotton or scrubbable vinyl, and cafe rods with the look of polished or antique brass round out the selection. Note that while the rods imitate period hardware, they do not have its distinctive weight.

Catalogue with sketches and photographs, $12.

Vintage Valances
Box 635
Whitmore Lake, MI 48189-0635
(313) 878-6670

Waverly Fabrics

With fabrics from Waverly, a designer look doesn't have to be prohibitively expensive. Most patterns coordinate with the company's washable vinyl wallcoverings and an array of decorative accessories. Designs from the Flower Show collection come in hues of alabaster, plum, colonial blue, china white, peach, blush, and forest. Illustrated is "Botanicals," featuring authentic

drawings of plants and trees. Four traditional floral and ribboned patterns are also available in the collection, and all are appropriate for draperies, tablecloths, valances, and bedspreads.

Waverly fabrics are available at retail stores throughout the country.

Contact the company for further information.

Waverly Fabrics
79 Madison Ave., Dept. OH
New York, NY 10016
(212) 644-5900

Other Suppliers of Fabrics

Consult List of Suppliers for addresses

Angel House Designs
Louis W. Bowen
The Canal Co.
Richard E. Thibaut
Victorian Collectibles

9.
Furniture

Good antique or reproduction furniture is hardly an essential for an old house, unless one is attempting to re-create a period mood. We always urge in *The Old House Catalogue* that you buy antique—whether from fine shops, flea markets, or the garage sale down the street. It usually costs less than the reproduction variety, and has a resale value many times greater. There are pieces, however, which one can't find easily or at all, and for these one must turn to a craftsman who has studied and mastered the techniques of the old furniture masters.

We have come to appreciate good reproduction chairs and beds. The stresses and strains of everyday life are too much for the majority of antique objects that are used for sitting at the table or for sleeping. There are many manufacturers of both kinds of furniture, and we strongly urge that one shop very carefully. Pieces that are joined rather than merely glued will last a great deal longer. Inquire also into the kinds of woods that are used. The material that now passes for wood in many reproduction pieces is little more than veneered composition, and if subject to stress, will sink like putty.

In assembling a set of period room furniture, there should be some attempt made to avoid sameness of look. Remember that the belongings of any family are usually acquired over a period of time—not bought all at once. Even the proud owner of a new Victorian parlor or bedroom suite in the late 1800s was likely to have left room for his or her grandmother's rocker or chest. Nothing looks quite so phony as an all-new matching set of furniture, particularly one—as is the practice today—which is finished in a high gloss. The curse of lamination has afflicted the furniture industry, although it is unlikely that any of the craftsmen included in the following listings would apply such a finish.

Enfield side table, a fine reproduction of an original Shaker piece by Shaker Workshops, Concord, Massachusetts.

Alexandria Wood Joinery

Alexandria Wood Joinery specializes in custom furniture design and manufacturing, as well as careful repair, stripping, and refinishing—always under your directions. Because work is done solely on a custom basis, no literature is available, but calls and letters are welcome.

Alexandria Wood Joinery
Plumer Hill Rd.
Alexandria, NH 03222
(802) 744-8243

Angel House

Angel House displays its hand-crafted, upholstered period furniture reproductions in the 1731 John Watson House, which serves as its showroom. Among the Angel House pieces featured there are the Martha Washington and the Concord Tavern chairs and graceful swan sofas. Country sofas come in lengths of 54", 66", 72", 76", or may be custom ordered. The Deerfield Parsonage

chair shown here is of Queen Ann design. It stands 45" tall and the seat measures 20" by 20". Inviting love settles include the Ipswich Homestead, inspired by Chippendale and Hepplewhite, and the Essex Grist Mill, taken from a 1790 Connecticut River Valley piece. Hard and semi-hard woods form sturdy frames supported by maple legs. Dacron and foam cushions are as comfortable

as down and feathers, but require little care. Angel House welcomes the opportunity to work to custom order.

Catalogue, $2.

Angel House Designs
RFD 1, Box 1
Rte. 148
Brookfield, MA 01506
(617) 867-2517

Robert Barrow

Although he specializes in Windsor chairs, making about twenty kinds, Robert Barrow also manufactures a lovely tavern table. The 23" by 29" oval top is made of pine, and the sturdy base, of maple. It stands 27" high and can be stained and varnished or painted with milk paint in black, barn red, blue, green, or mustard. Barrow also makes tall

post beds, tea tables, and New England maple-and-ash ladder-back chairs with woven rush seats.

Catalogue, $3.

Robert Barrow
412 Thames St.
Bristol, RI 02809
(401) 253-4434

Michael Camp

After thousands of hours of study and research, Michael Camp has developed what he calls an "18th-century attitude" that he deems crucial to completing exacting reproductions of that era's furniture. Hand joinery, careful planing and scraping, and painstaking attention to books, photographs, and sketches combine to render this furniture exceptional. Entire period interiors may include

pieces like the Boston blockfront chest (31¼" high by 34¾" wide by 22⅝" deep) in the background here, or the graceful Connecticut lowboy shown in the foreground, which measures 30½" high by 33½" wide by 19½" deep.

Camp generally executes his reproductions in maple or pine, but can substitute cherry, figured maple, mahogany, or walnut. Hand-finished light and dark

stains glow with a deep sheen; and various hues of milk paint are available.

Catalogue, $3.

Michael Camp
636 Starkweather
Plymouth, MI 48170
(313) 459-1190

Marion H. Campbell

After an early career spent planning and overseeing construction for steel bridges and large buildings, professional engineer Marion Campbell turned back to his first love—classic woodworking—with advantageous results for anyone who loves American period furniture. Treasured family heirlooms afforded Campbell the opportunity for careful study of historic pieces. Among the careful

reproductions he has crafted are this Queen Anne lowboy, an elegant piece in carved cherry.

One of Campbell's most challenging projects was the re-creation of a case to house an 18th-century David Rittenhouse clock movement (the original had burned). More than 100 hours of work resulted in an exquisite walnut case finished with hand-rubbed linseed oil and beeswax. The Queen Anne case shown here shows the same high-quality, meticulous work. Campbell works in walnut, cherry, mahogany, and other fine woods. He suggests that photos or designs accompany your requests for custom pieces.

Brochure, 50¢.

Marion H. Campbell
26 E. 3rd St.
Bethlehem, PA 18018
(215) 865-2522

Mailing address:

39 Wall St.
Bethlehem, PA 18018
(215) 865-3292

Caning Shop

For nearly twenty years, The Caning Shop has supplied first-quality caning materials for the craftsman and the do-it-yourselfer. Among the specific items imported from the jungles of Indonesia and Malaysia are cane, rush, splints, fiber, and wicker. Seagrass, rawhide, and Danish seat cord round out the wide selection. Pressed fiber seats combine cellulose, leather, and resin for durability. Tools you may need are available, including chisels, clamps, matt knives, clippers, and shears. A good selection of books is also offered.

Catalogue, $1.

The Caning Shop
926 Gilman St. at 8th
Berkeley, CA 94710
(415) 527-5010

Chestnut Hill

Readers of *The Fourth Old House Catalogue* will remember the work of Gerald LePage. He's moved his business and changed its name, but the quality of his work remains excellent. Some of his new products include New England-style carved chests and boxes made without the aid of power tools, New York and Pennsylvania-style spoon racks made with old wood whenever possible, a maple joint stool, a lattice-work carved document box patterned after a North-Shore Massachusetts original, and the fancy Rhode Island porringer top table shown here. Also new to LePage's chair line is a beautifully proportioned Connecticut comb-back Windsor chair with an intriguing angle to the arms. The original is in a private collection.

Catalogue, $2.

Chestnut Hill Furniture Manufactory
65 Chestnut Hill Rd.
East Hampton, CT 06424
(203) 267-8780

Country Bed Shop

While the Country Bed Shop's craftsmen have improved on the wobbly rope spring bedsteads that are a legitimate part of American tradition (the bolted frames are more solid and can be assembled by only one person, rather than the five needed for the original), they still use hand tools for all phases of construction and decoration. The exacting skill that characterizes their work shows in this intricately shaped post for a Goddard Chippendale bed, a style dating from the mid-18th century. Honduras mahogany and cast-brass bed bolt covers are the materials used.

An exact replica of a rare Queen Anne tester bed, a style dating from the early 1700s, is crafted of maple. Cherry, mahogany, or walnut would be equally suitable.

Catalogue, $4.

Country Bed Shop
R.R. 1, Box 65
Ashby, MA 01431
(617) 386-7550

Design for Sleep

Design for Sleep specializes in hard-to-find luxury bedding for odd-size antique and reproduction beds. The company can special order rabbet-frame box springs in custom sizes. Even its standard range encompasses a wide selection: twin, twin extra long, full, full extra long, queen, king, and California king. Mattresses from Design for Sleep's Magnus Collection, available in three firmnesses, are constructed of triple-tempered double-offset coils, three thicknesses of cotton upholstery felt, and a cover quilted from Belgian damask, polyester, and rayon over one thickness of foam and another of liner felt. The hand-tied box springs have an unusually thick frame and a dense support of twelve slats of Canadian spruce.

Design for Sleep
200 Lexington Ave.
Ste. 506
New York, NY 10016
(212) 685-6556

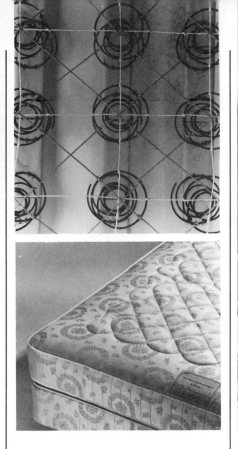

Henkel-Harris

Henkel-Harris crafts fine reproductions of 18th-century furniture using wild black cherry, mahogany, and walnut complemented by solid brass fittings. The architect's desk (in mahogany only) follows the lines of an original that Thomas Jefferson may well have used to draft plans for the University of Virginia at Charlottesville. Henkel-Harris's reproduction won the Thomas Jefferson Memorial Foundation's approval, as did this block-front bureau chest. The chest features

six dovetailed side drawers topped by a wide, locking drawer and comes in mahogany or cherry with brass fittings. The insides of the drawers are sealed, sanded and waxed; the exterior, hand-rubbed to a glowing finish. Other styles available from Henkel-Harris include Chippendale, Queen Anne, Satterfield, Mount Vernon, and Embassy.

Catalogue, $10.

For closest authorized dealer, contact:

Henkel-Harris
Box 2170
Winchester, VA 22601
(703) 667-4900

James Lea

Perpetuating a family tradition begun by his grandfather, James Lea crafts American period furniture from choice woods, using antique tools and finishing each piece by hand. Several different Windsor chairs are among Lea's specialities; the most widely known, a Bow Back Windsor whose original dates from 1770. Lea has used a variety of woods for this chair, including maple, oak, and cherry. Finishes can be light, dark, or antique green. Op-

tions for other styles of Windsors include brace backs, carved knuckle arms, comb rails, and hand-shaved spindles. Lea signs, dates, and numbers each piece. He welcomes requests for custom work.

Catalogue, $4.

James Lea
9 West St.
Rockport, ME 04856
(207) 236-3632

Lehman Hardware

Few pieces of furniture evoke a sense of the past more effectively than a roll-top desk. The tiny cub-

byholes and numerous drawers bring to mind images of dimly lit clerks' offices and letters with

century-old postmarks. Lehman Hardware sells desks designed to revive memories and extend the roll-top's romantic history. Amish-made with few power tools (none run by electricity), the desks are built of solid oak with raised panels on the sides and front. You can choose between a raised-panel and a plywood back. Seven drawers and eleven cubbyholes help you to keep things organized, and the 4′4″-wide, over 2-deep desk-top gives you plenty of room to work. The top is 30″ high for comfortable writing; the entire desk stands 3′10½″ high and measures 4′8″ wide by 2′6″ deep. The whole desk-top assembly lifts off for easy moving, and the desks are left unfinished to allow

you to match them to your other furniture.

Lehman carries other pieces of Amish-made furniture, most of which can only be seen at its stores in Kidron and Mt. Hope. J.E. Lehman encourages a visit to either store, but if you don't live in the area, the catalogue is worth examining.

Catalogue, $2.

Lehman Hardware & Appliances, Inc.
Box 41, 4779 Kidron Rd.
Kidron, OH 44636
(216) 857-5441

Edward Ludlow

The tapered legs, simple design, and solid construction of this mahogany Pembroke table bear witness to the superior craftsmanship of Edward Ludlow. Ludlow cuts dovetails by hand, uses mortise-and-tenon joints instead

of dowels exclusively, and hand finishes each piece. All his work is custom, much of it, restoration, so if you've got a damaged antique cabinet or an idea for a table, give him a call.

Edward Ludlow, Cabinetmaker
Box 646
Pluckemin, NJ 07978
(201) 658-9091

North Woods Chair Shop

Lenore Howe and Brian Braskie believe that hand-crafted products have a character that mass-produced furnishings cannot achieve, and their Canterbury rocker is a good example of that belief. Built of cherry (and

available in figured woods at an additional cost), each piece is signed, dated, and numbered. Four finishes make it easy to match the rocker with other colors in the room—ebony, a red-brown stain that blends well with mahogany or walnut, a honey-colored stain, and a natural oil finish that turns soft reddish-brown as it ages. The rocker's seat may be caned or tape-woven with fabric in one or two of ten colors, which include red-and-black striped, brown, green, beige, and red-and-green striped. Tape may be woven in a herringbone, checkerboard, basketweave, diamond, or radial pattern. The North Woods Chair Shop has a showroom which has regular hours, but it's best to call for an appointment.

Catalogue available. Color

catalogue with samples of finishes and seat tape, $3.

North Woods Chair Shop
RFD 1, Old Tilton Rd.
Canterbury, NH 03224
(603) 783-4595

Craig Nutt

Using considerable experience as a furniture restorer to augment his knowledge of historic designs, Craig Nutt has now turned his attention and his talent to creating original designs with a period flavor. The inspiration for this walnut and heart-pine table, inlaid with satinwood in a jonquil pattern, was an early 19th-century Georgia Piedmont piece. Nutt's

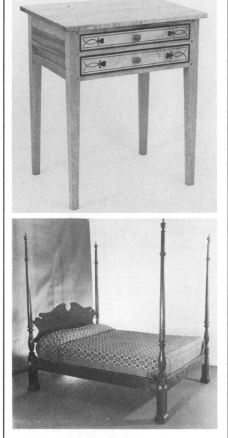

interpretation of a four-poster bed, executed in solid walnut, features traditional mortise-and-tenon joinery, bolted for extra strength. Nutt's work is often featured in exhibitions and he specializes in creating custom, one-of-a-kind pieces to special order.

Brochure, $1.

Craig Nutt Fine Wood Works
2014 5th St.
Northport, AL 35476
(205) 752-6635

Orleans Carpenters

Dick and Phoebe Soule take the Shaker tradition very seriously. Their furniture, like that of the Shakers, is made of fine woods with high-quality finishes. The simplicity and grace of their Shaker round table is characteristic of the religious sect whose work the Soules emulate. It is available in both solid walnut and solid cherry, either finished in Danish oil. Its 18" diameter and 24" height make it ideal for plants, lamps, or other medium-sized objects.

A two-step stool is one of Orleans Carpenters' new products. Crafted of cherry with walnut plugs, and finished with hand-rubbed Danish oil, it's a far cry from the ugly metal stools that are so commonly available.

Catalogue, 50¢. Brochures available.

Orelans Carpenters
70 Rock Harbor Rd.
Orleans, MA 02653
(617) 255-2646

Prospect Products

Prospect offers ready-made chair seats or, if you prefer, the supplies necessary to make them yourself. A hank of cane, available in widths of from $\frac{1}{16}$" to $\frac{5}{32}$", will cover three or four chairs. Various fibers are available, including seagrass and rush, sold by the pound. Binder cane finishes raw edges after weaving. Prospect stocks an array of idea books to give you inspiration and instructions, along with caning pegs, awls, and splints. Pressed fiberboard seats require less work; just trim the patterned seats with shears, a saw, or a craft knife, and paint, stain, or seal them. (Prospect has the finishes available to do the job).

Catalogue, $2 (refundable with order).

Prospect Products
8000 Rose Island Rd.
Box 70
Prospect, KY 40059
(502) 228-3493

Michael Reid

Fine woods and traditional methods combine in Michael Reid's Windsor chairs. Only one power tool, a lathe for turning the graceful legs, is to be found in Reid's shop; his hands and simple tools do the rest. The classic chairs he makes include a continuous arm, a sack back, a loop back, a child's chair, and the rod back shown. Seats are sculpted of pine with a U-shaped drawknife

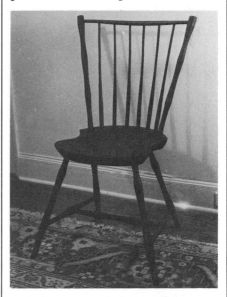

called a scoop. Oak spindles, maple legs, and oak backs are made from split logs instead of sawn boards; this ensures that the wood has a strength belied by the chair's delicate design. Reid will finish the chair with milk paint or leave it unfinished, if you prefer.

Michael M. Reid
132 Morey Rd.
Sharon, CT 06069
(203) 364-5444

Shaker Workshops

The beauty of simplicity characterizes Shaker life and furniture. A Shaker community in Enfield, New Hampshire first produced this side table, distinguished by its strong, slender legs and large (28¼" by 21") surface.

Crafted from the hard maple and pine often found at Shaker Workshops, it will arrive preassembled and finished, or can be ordered as a kit if you would rather do it yourself. From baskets to living-room furniture, Shaker Workshops' kits let you reproduce authentic Shaker designs for your own home, using only the common hand tools you probably have already. The kits lack no detail—glue, hardware, sandpaper, and stain accompany wood and instructions. Choice of stains includes light, medium, mahogany, and ebony. Or pick the natural sheen of Shaker Workshops' oil finish.

Seasonal catalogues, $1.

Shaker Workshops
Box 1028
Concord, MA 01742
(617) 646-8985

The Shop

For those who'd like to build their own reproduction hardwood furniture but aren't sure how to begin, The Shop offers a number of furniture kits, in addition to finished pieces. An icebox kit is available in various stages of completion. The finished oak icebox measures 40¼" high by 32½" wide by 16½" deep. The pieces necessary to make the box, in-

cluding the three panel Franklin doors, the panel sides, and the solid brass hinges and latches, can be ordered as a kit. If you're really ambitious, The Shop will mail the hardware and a set of plans. The Shop also restores, repairs, and custom-designs furniture.

Brochures available.

The Shop, Inc.
Box 3711, R.D. 3
Reading, PA 19606
(215) 689-5885

Smith Woodworks and Design

Todd Smith's inspiration is the Shaker aesthetic, and his work reflects the Shaker emphasis on simplicity, quality, and proportion. Each piece is finished according to its individual requirements and hand-rubbed to a satiny patina. Although Smith most frequently works in eastern white pine, black cherry, and maple, he is also willing to make furniture from red or white oak, black walnut, tulip poplar, Honduras mahogany, or any other available wood. Custom work is undertaken, and alterations may be made in most standard pieces. In addition to the cabinet and 6'-tall wardrobe shown here, Smith

also manufactures tables, cupboards, night stands, and a special line of Shaker chairs whose dimensions may not be altered, since they are exact reproductions. Made of solid maple with mortise-and-tenon construction, they are available in four traditional stains—ebony, mahogany, medium maple, and light maple. After staining, the wood is treated with an oil and wax coating. Seats are made of woven cotton tape, which comes in ten colors, including navy blue, maroon, olive green, black, light gray, and beige.

Brochure, $2.

Smith Woodworks and Design
Box 42, R.R. 1
Farmersville Rd.
Califon, NJ 07830
(201) 832-2723

Eldred Wheeler

Symmetry, graceful curves, elegant carving, and painstaking craftsmanship mark Eldred Wheeler's 18th-century reproductions. His cherry, maple, and tiger maple furniture has the feel of authenticity that only individual manufacture can create. Wheeler's pieces feature dovetail and mortise-and-tenon construction. All are hand finished. They make a durable, beautiful alternative to high-priced antiques.

Catalogue, $3. Brochure available.

Eldred Wheeler
c/o Partridge Replications
63 Penhallow St.
Portsmouth, NH 03801
(603) 431-8733

Robert Whitley

It's hard to imagine more impressive credentials than Robert Whitley's. He represents the third generation in his cabinetmaker family, and his list of commissions goes on and on. He's made duplicates of George Washington's leather covered trunks and compartmented document box, one of Benjamin Franklin's experimental machines, and a swivel-seat Windsor chair of the type used by Jefferson. His work has been displayed in Washington, D.C. and in the Hermitage in Leningrad. In addition to his contemporary walnut rocker, one of the finest we've seen, Whitley also repairs and refinishes furniture and does veneer and inlay work, gold leafing, and finish preservation, with the help of only two assistants. A wide selection of woods is kept in stock; each species is air-weathered, placed in heat-controlled storage rooms, and seasoned. In this picture, Whitley stands with copies of pieces that he made for the National Park Service's restoration of the Derby House in Salem, Massachusetts.

Literature available.

THE LEIGH PHOTOGRAPHIC GROUP

The Robert Whitley Furniture Studios
Laurel Rd.
Solebury, PA 18963
(215) 297-8452

Woodworkers' Store

If you are an inveterate do-it-yourselfer, or would like to become one, you'll find the catalogue issued by Woodworkers' to be an inspiration. It lists countless furniture projects in plan form, from an appealing high chair to a sturdy but portable platform bed and thirteen different styles of workbenches. Once you've chosen the plans for a project to suit you, check Woodworkers' supply of special tools—goggles, shields, and respirators—to make sure that the job is completed in safety.

Catalogue, $1.

The Woodworkers' Store
21801 Industrial Blvd.
Rogers, MN 55374
(612) 428-4101

Other Suppliers of Furniture

Consult List of Suppliers for addresses.

Aged Woods
Alfresco
Curvoflite
Dovetail Woodworking
The Joinery Co.
19th Century Hardware and Supply
 Co.

Nottingham Gallery
Second Impressions Antiques
Frederick Wilbur
Willsboro Wood Products
Wooden Nickel Antiques

10.

Outdoor and Garden Areas

Chances are that as you plan and sweat to restore your period home or to complete a new one in an early style, the last thing on your mind will be the grounds and gardens surrounding it. But eventually, when the last wall is painted and the last piece of furniture put in place, you'll be able to turn your attention to what is, after all, the setting for the house that has demanded and received so many hours of pleasurable toil.

There are a number of suppliers who can help you to achieve just the right effect, whether you want a pair of urns to flank your front entrance or a fountain to accent a formal garden. Some of them offer original pieces of statuary; others have antique molds from which to create fine reproductions. And there's no need to settle for an ugly prepackaged metal or wood shed in which to store garden equipment; a number of companies listed in this chapter can supply plans for period outbuildings to harmonize with the style of your home.

If you're fortunate enough to have purchased an old house with its original wrought-iron fencing still in place, you'll probably need some restoration work done. If the fence is long gone, you may want to replace it. A number of craftsmen listed in this chapter will duplicate an old pattern to your specifications, whether you need several hundred feet or just a few yards.

How a building is landscaped can prove as important an indication of its value as how the interior is decorated. The trees and shrubs found on the average residential property have much more than a decorative function; their imaginative arrangement provides environmental as well as aesthetic dividends. For the old-house owner blessed with mature plantings, the opportunities for improving on nature are many. A number of landscape architects specialize in old-house properties. Their knowledge of modern varieties of old-fashioned nursery stock and ways in which to simulate a period setting can be extremely helpful. Selected listings of these specialists in various areas of North America are featured in this chapter.

Pineapple hitching post with lion-headed column by Robinson Iron, Alexander City, Alabama.

Fencing, Gates, and Window Grilles

Fences don't always make good neighbors, especially when the material and design are downright ugly. Chain-link or cyclone fencing is not particularly recommended for enclosing the yard of an old house. Split-rail or stockade fencing may do just fine, and this type of fencing is available from lumber dealers everywhere. But if you have your heart set on a picket fence or an old-fashioned iron model, you will have to do some searching. Salvage yards (see chapter 1) often inventory materials of this type. If they can't be located, there are individual craftsmen and companies that still produce both wood and iron fencing and gates. Some of the best are included in the following listings.

Architectural Iron

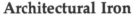

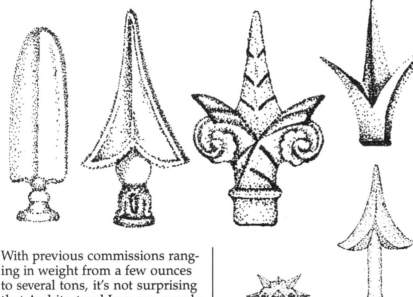

With previous commissions ranging in weight from a few ounces to several tons, it's not surprising that Architectural Iron can supply almost any iron fencing need. Much of the company's work is custom, and all of it is done with an attention to detail that justifies the staff's reputation as purists.

The variety, accuracy, and impressive detail of Architectural Iron's work is evident even in its smaller items, such as the finials shown here. They include a fluted spear whose original is from South Kensington, London, and whose curved top makes it an unusually graceful finishing touch; a classic pointed spear made distinctive by an interesting combination of shapes in the base; and an elaborate Gothic finial, appropriate for more ornate fences. The three-pointed finial was designed by Architectural Iron for a National Historic Landmark, the Jefferson Market Library in New York City. A Philadelphia commission occa-

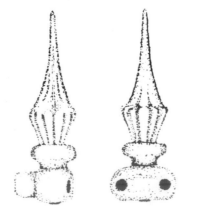

sioned the creation of two finials, a mace and a delicate spear. The finials range in size from 5½" high by 1¼" wide by 1¼"deep to 7½" high by 4½" wide by 2" deep. Some are flat-based; others are cored for pickets of various sizes and shapes. Architectural Iron also makes a set of end and line

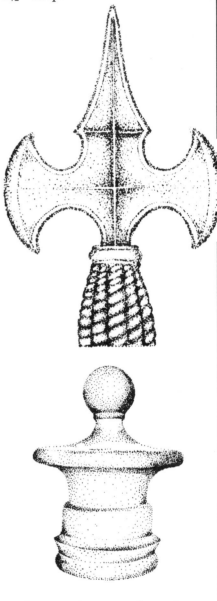

finials whose sloping, elongated silhouettes lend elegance to a fence. Both are 8½" high; the end finial is 2½" wide and 3" deep, and the line finial, 3" wide and 2½" deep.

Architectural Iron produces larger finials with equal excellence. The formidable fluted mace finial is a reproduction of a line post ornament from Christopher Park in Greenwich Village, New York. It has a flat base and measures 12" high by 8" wide by 2" deep. For a rounder, more solid look, the company makes a 9"-high post top for pipe with an outside diameter of 3½".

Among the company's specialties are rails and balusters. Model AIC 107, probably the only authentic

AIC 107

standard-size cast-iron railing made today, forms a graceful half-circle. It measures 2¼" in width and comes in 2' lengths, each weighing five pounds. Model AIC 110 is a considerably heavier top

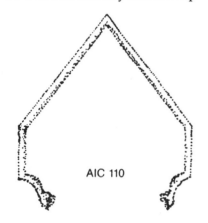

AIC 110

rail, measuring 4¼" high by 4" wide and weighing sixty pounds per 3' length. Its sharp slope and simple design make it impressive-looking; its solid, heavy construction adds strength to almost any fence.

Catalogue, $2.

*Architectural Iron Co.
Box 126, Rte. 6 W.
Milford, PA 18337
(717) 296-7722*

Cassidy Brothers

Cassidy Brothers specializes in wrought-iron fencing and offers both contemporary designs as well as historic styles such as the

richly accented one shown here. The firm welcomes restoration projects, and its craftsmen work to repair and augment broken fencing using the same forging and fastening techniques that produced the original. Old and new ironwork is protected with special finishes; latches and hinge parts are formed from stainless steel with sturdy bronze bushings.

Brochure available.

*Cassidy Brothers Forge, Inc.
U.S. Rte. 1
Rowley, MA 01969-1796
(617) 948-7611*

Custom Ironwork

It's hard to look at Custom Ironwork's selection of fences and gates without finding something that appeals to you. Almost any need can be met; fencing is available in 3', 4' or 5' heights and ranges from the very simple to the extremely ornate. One popular style (model 109) is actually relatively basic, with only two channels and widely spread spear-topped pickets, but curved pickets surrounding and surmounting the spears make the fence visually interesting. Model 110 is another simple fence that's useful as well as decorative. The tightly spaced ½" round pickets at the bottom help to keep animals out or in. Milled tops protect children from injury.

Victorian homes often demand more elaborate fencing, so Custom Ironwork makes several styles like model 114. The scroll inserts between the two bottom channels are hand made. Cast-

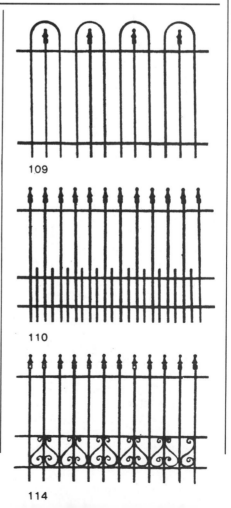

109

110

114

iron posts also come in a variety of styles. The standard post, whose 1" size is perfect for gates and corners, matches well with any of the company's fences. A ⅝" size is available for use as a line post. Scroll posts like model 830 are also sold to increase the Victorian splendor of fancy ironwork. They are manufactured in 3', 4', 5', and 6' heights.

Driveway gates come in four styles. Model 575 is made in 12', 14', and 16' widths. These gates are designed to swing open, but if that isn't possible, they can be set on a railway track. An electronic radio-controlled gate opener is an option. Spears are made in seven different styles to allow you to choose the best one for your needs. Custom Ironwork will send a representative anywhere in the United States to install its products on request.

Catalogue available.

Custom Ironwork, Inc.
Box 99
Union, KY 41091
(606) 384-4486

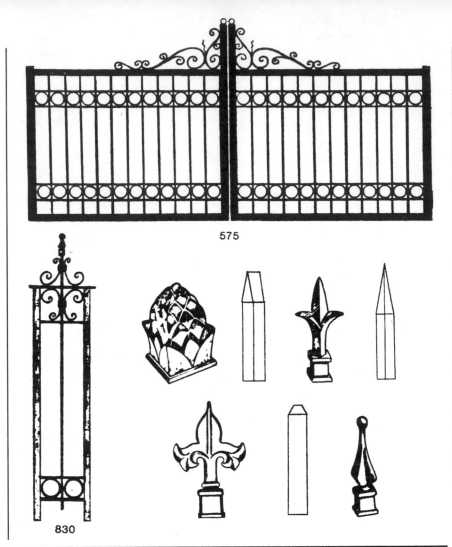

575

830

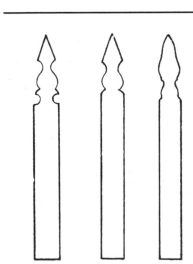

Mad River Woodworks

Simple fence pickets that would be perfect outside a colonial home often look too plain in front of more ornate houses. Mad River sells three styles of pickets with the more elaborate look required for such locations. All three measure 36" high by 3½" wide by ¾" deep. The company also sells a number of other wood products for old houses.

Catalogue, $2.

Mad River Woodworks
Box 163
Arcata, CA 95521
(707) 826-0629

Marmion Plantation

At Marmion, the 18th-century home of George Washington Lewis (nephew of George Washington), David Newhall III's company manufactures Diamond-head picket fencing. The design, which features a 4½"-high diamond with the lower sides slightly longer than the upper, is an accurate reproduction of a 300-year-old handcrafted original found at Marmion. It is perhaps the oldest early American wood fence to survive intact. The pickets are ¾" thick and 57" high; 2" gaps are recommended for yard fences. Marmion Plantation also makes 72"-high pickets which can be installed edge to edge for privacy. The pickets are sold unfinished, so that you can stain, varnish, or paint them as you please.

Brochure available.

Marmion Plantation Co.
R.D. 2, Box 458
Fredericksburg, VA 22405
(703) 775-3480

Nostalgia

Nostalgia is housed in the Savannah and Atlanta railroad building, on the site of the renowned Springfield Plantation, remembered for its importance during 1779's Battle for Savannah. Nostalgia upholds its historic legacy with custom work in iron fencing and gates. Many of Nostalgia's designs are faithful to specific historic styles from the

South. The heavily scrolled Habersham panel, (11¾" wide by 29¼" high), in cast iron or aluminum, is just one selection; others includes the Drayton Crest, the Gaston, and the York Street. Gates include the aluminum Kehoe (35" wide by 39" high), which duplicates a century-old Savannah relic.

Catalogue, $2.50.

Nostalgia, Inc.
307 Stiles Ave.
Savannah, GA 31401
(912) 232-2324

Nye's Foundry

In addition to a variety of cast-iron parts for home and industry, Nye's Foundry makes some products well suited to outdoor use. Decorative grates for trees and drains and tree guards to protect vulnerable roots and bark are only a few of the items available. Nye's also does quite a bit of custom casting, so the company may be able to help with special orders.

Nye's Foundry Ltd.
503 Powell St. E.
Vancouver, British Columbia, Canada
V6A 1G8
(604) 254-4121

The Old Wagon Factory

Perfect for creating an old-fashioned environment, The Old Wagon Factory's lattice-patterned garden gate accents period gardens, back yards, patios, pool areas, or front lawns. It's made of solid spruce and can be shipped primed and ready for painting or finished with gloss white enamel. Standard sizes measure up to 40" in height and 26" in width, although larger gates can be custom-made.

Catalogue, $2.

The Old Wagon Factory
103 Russell St.
Box 1427, Dept. OC86
Clarksville, VA 23927
(804) 374-5787

Rustic Home Hardware

It's possible to combine convenience with authenticity. You can have a self-closing gate outside your colonial home without sacrificing the period look. This colonial gate closer from Rustic Home Hardware saves effort and keeps your home's exterior looking as authentic as its interior. The gate closer comes complete with all the necessary hardware for installation.

Catalogue, $5.

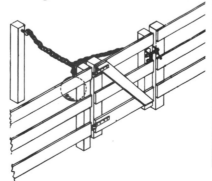

Rustic Home Hardware
R.D. 3
Hanover, PA 17331
(717) 632-0088

Schwartz's Forge

To Joel A. Schwartz, iron is not merely functional wrought metal, but an artistic medium that can be molded in imaginative ways. Schwartz's classic blacksmithing methods yield grilles, benches, and gratings—metalwork that in his words, "functions within, enhances, and complements its environment." Schwartz's Forge invites your questions, plans, sketches, and ideas for superb custom ironwork.

Brochure available.

Schwartz's Forge & Metalworks
Box 205
Forge Hollow Rd.
Deansboro, NY 13328
(315) 841-4477

If you're not fond of ordinary fencing, but would prefer something unusual, Silver Dollar has a style that's unique and complex. The Cornstalk fence, with its ripening ears and intertwined leaves, is made of cast aluminum, stands 4' high, and repeats every 1'. The fencing comes painted in one of four colors—white, black, medium dark green, or chocolate brown.

Catalogue, $2.

Silver Dollar Trading Co.
Box 394
1591 Main St.
San Elizario, TX 79849
(915) 851-3458

Stewart

Stewart Manufacturing offers a range of thick-walled steel tubing in both round and square models with measurements ranging from ⅜" to ⅞" across. Standard picket-top designs include the square apex, milled-point round, milled-point square, and forged-point square. Stewart also sells items difficult to find elsewhere, such as well heads in various styles and sizes and, for those blessed with substantial country estates,

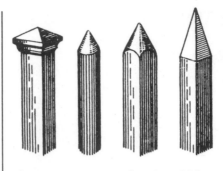

elegant gateway arches in widths ranging from 10' to 14'. The height of the archway is variable. A central motif, such as a coat of arms, may be added to any of Stewart's arch designs, whether plain or ornate. The company welcomes custom work and undertakes restorations of existing fencing; estimates, drawings, and specifications are provided at no charge.

Catalogue available.

Stewart Manufacturing Co.
511 Enterprise Dr.
Covington, KY 41017
(606) 331-9000

Outdoor Furniture

Until recently, about the only type of old-style outdoor furniture commercially available was the standard wood and iron park bench. While suitable in many locations where vandalism is a major problem, the look of this urban classic is rather forbidding. Now there are a number of suppliers of graceful lawn and terrace furniture with an old-fashioned appeal. Rustic wood chairs and tables are again being made of such materials as willow and ash, and there are craftsmen ready to supply carefully crafted iron benches, stands, chairs, tables, and settees.

Alfresco

It's hard to imagine a seat more relaxing and romantic than the old-fashioned porch swing. Alfresco's owner, Paul Wilbert, has been refining his porch-swing design for nine years, and the time seems to have been spent productively. His redwood swing

glides smoothly on 80' of sisal rope, hung by four points instead of only two. Measuring 24" high, 52" long, and 30" deep, it seats three comfortably, and Alfresco will be happy to make longer swings or to use other woods. The swing is oiled to provide protection against the elements, but if you'd like to paint it, the company will send you an unfinished version.

Literature available.

Alfresco
Box 1336
Durango, CO 81302
(303) 247-9739 or
(303) 259-5743

Gazebo & Porchworks

This porch swing from Gazebo & Porchworks features a tall, raked back made of split hemlock spindles. Bracketed arms and an intricately carved crest accent the swing, which is built primarily of clear vertical-grain fir. The seat is 16½" deep and the back, 27" high.

Gazebo & Porchworks ships the swing in four pieces and supplies the bolts for easy assembly. Finish the presanded swing in any way you like, and suspend it with the four hangers the company includes.

Catalogue, $2.

Gazebo & Porchworks
728 9th Ave. S.
Puyallup, WA 98371-6744
(206) 848-0502

Gravity-Randall

Outdoor areas can take on a period look with the addition of furniture from Gravity-Randall. Formerly known as Santa Cruz Foundry, this company makes two styles of sturdy iron benches. The delicately scrolled ends are painted in black or green. The simpler, lighter Estate bench has a seat and back of Douglas fir; oak is used for the heavier, more ornate Empire bench, which is available in 4', 5', 6', and 8' lengths.

The company also offers two types of table meant to lend Victorian elegance to your patio or yard. A pedestal table with a 24" marble or onyx top evokes images of European sidewalk cafes. If you prefer something more massive, you might take a look at Gravity-Randall's three-legged English Pub table. Equipped with heavy, highly decorated legs that curve gently inward, it was inspired by an 1842 design commemorating the abolition of slavery in the British colonies.

Gravity-Randall
208 N. Douty St.
Box 1378
Hanford, CA 93232-1378
(209) 584-2216

The Old Wagon Factory

Taking its inspiration from Thomas Chippendale's 18th-century pieces, The Old Wagon Factory makes an attractive line of garden furniture which includes a coffee table, an end table, an armchair, and two benches. The two-seater bench measures 35½" high by 38½" long by 18" deep; the

three-seater is 58½" long. Both are handcrafted from solid Douglas fir and finished with gloss white enamel. The company also makes a rustic solid pine bench which never requires staining or painting.

Catalogue, $2.

The Old Wagon Factory
103 Russell St.
Box 1427, Dept. OC86
Clarksville, VA 23927
(804) 374-5787

Robinson Iron

Robinson Iron makes just about everything that can be made in cast iron, and the results will be gratifying to those who appreciate that metal. The pieces are welded, not bolted, and are finished in one of four colors—white, black, verdigris, or terra cotta. Robinson's line of furniture is particularly striking. It includes a railroad bench; a patio set with a rose-and-lyre motif; a Janney table that incorporates dolphins, acanthus leaves, and rosettes; an exquisite, ornate French Renaissance settee; and a group of lawn furnishings based on an intricate fern design.

The curule stool originated in Egypt; its name is derived from the Roman magistrates who used it. Robinson interprets this old design in a delicate style that belies the solidity of the material used. The stool measures 16½" high by 15" wide by 14" deep and weighs thirty pounds.

Catalogue available.

Robinson Iron
Robinson Rd.
Alexander City, AL 35010
(205) 329-8484

Second Impression

Wicker is attractive, strong, and obviously versatile, as it is used to fashion everything from bird cages to beds, music stands, and sofas. Its properties have been well-known for many years; thus, today's antique shops, such as Second Impression, often have a variety of restored old wicker pieces on hand. Second Impression has furnished entire homes in wicker. Among the pieces the firm often has available are wing chairs with built-in magazine racks, heavy Art-Deco chaises, and ornate, square corner seats. Dan and Rosemarie Pokorski, proprietors of Second Impression, welcome the opportunity to help you design a room and can institute searches for special pieces you may have in mind. The company also stocks a variety of books chronicling the evolution of decorative, functional wicker furniture.

Catalogue available.

Second Impression Antiques
84½ Bay St.
Watch Hill, RI 02891
(401) 596-1296
Evenings: (401) 596-2661

Silver Dollar Trading

What's the point of having a beautiful period garden if there's nowhere to sit and enjoy it? Silver Dollar offers a variety of reproduction chairs and benches that includes a graceful aluminum chair with a fern pattern (model 1041). If you prefer benches, you might choose the Four Seasons bench (model 1010). The originals appeared in the late 1800s. Decorated with medallions illustrating the four phases of the agricultural year, the bench is 6' long and 3' high and made of aluminum and oak. The oak can be left natural and sealed with polyurethane finish or stained and then sealed.

If you'd like something a little more unusual, the cast-aluminum Circle bench (model 1090) may suit your taste. Its inside diameter of 31" allows it to surround fairly large trees for an interesting visual effect.

All aluminum pieces are painted in one of four colors: white, black, medium dark green, or chocolate brown.

Catalogue, $2.

Silver Dollar Trading Co.
Box 394
1591 Main St.
San Elizario, TX 79849
(915) 851-3458

Willsboro Wood Products

Adirondack cedar, a hardy wood that weathers to a beautiful gray sheen and doesn't rot even in the harshest climate, is the material of choice for the craftsmen of Willsboro. They cite the good condition of many century-old houses and barns constructed of Adirondack cedar as proof of the wood's durability. The furniture they offer is constructed using the finest methods (mortise-and-tenon joinery is standard). Among the company's most attractive offerings is the Tupper Lake settee, a rugged and comfortable two-seater. The Willsboro version of the classic Adirondack chair is crafted of oak. It may be left unfinished indoors, but the company suggests applying a preservative if you intend using it outdoors. The chair folds conveniently for storage; solid-oak planking and full-length oak peg construction insure strength and longevity.

Brochure available.

Willsboro Wood Products
Box 336
Willsboro, NY 12996
(800) 342-3373
(518) 963-8623 (NY)

Lawn and Garden Ornaments

Fountains and sculpture add a romantic and pleasing dimension to any outdoor scene. Sometimes we become so obsessed with the perfect lawn that we forget how commonly ornaments of various types were used in the past. The available amount of outdoor space will determine to some degree just how extensively durable objects of stone and iron such as urns, sculptural figures, birdbaths, sundials, and fountains may be employed. But even in the small outdoor area found around the typical town house, ornamental objects can be effectively used.

Cassidy Brothers

Having supplied hardware and handrails for projects as diverse as

Disney World's Epcot Center and the Ritz Carlton Hotel, Cassidy Brothers is obviously equal to any quality ironwork project you have in mind. Cassidy Brothers not only manufactures, but will draw up plans and oversee installation for, fences, grilles, gates, sundials, weather vanes, and much more. This 4' armillary sphere in Newburyport, Massachusetts is an example of the firm's superb ornamental ironwork. Cassidy uses construction methods and materials that may outlast the originals that spawn so many of its restoration projects.

Brochure available.

Cassidy Brothers Forge, Inc.
U.S. Rte. 1
Rowley, MA 01969-1796
(617) 948-7611

Good Directions

The racing sulky is a classic weather-vane figure, and Good Directions makes a fine version of it. The hollow, full-bodied figure is made of solid copper covered with an antique green finish. The directionals are brass, the rod, steel, and the ball-shaped spacers, copper. The top figure, like all Good Directions' weather-vane figures, may be purchased separately for use as a decoration. Some of the company's copper figures are available polished and

unlacquered instead of finished in antique green, but should be lacquered before outdoor use.

Catalogue available.

Good Directions, Inc.
24 Ardmore Rd.
Stamford, CT 06902
(800) 346-7678
(203) 348-1836

Marian Ives

More than ten years ago, Marian Ives made a codfish weather vane to sit atop her parents' Massachusetts boathouse. Since then, she has turned out grasshoppers and schooners, loons and butterflies, classical gods and ducks, employing her considerable skill in chasing and repoussé methods. Ives scorns soft soldering—she's restored too many antique vanes that corroded and fell apart as the seams disintegrated. The welded joints in her vanes won't come asunder. Ives works primarily in copper, but has used bronze or an alloy of the two on occasion. She also shapes and paints steel to make silhouette vanes and garden ornaments. Ives continues to build on her metalworking skills; some new vanes have heads of cast bronze, shaped through the

lost-wax technique. Ives will custom craft brass, copper, or steel weather vanes. A copper ball and a rod with lock groove for set screw accompany each vane.

Bronze cardinals (3¼″ tall) and gold leaf are decorative options.

Brochure available.

Marian Ives
Box 132
Norwell, MA 02061
(617) 659-4466

Robinson Iron

Whether you want a fountain that will make a perfect centerpiece for your lawn or a statue to guard the garden entrance, Robinson Iron can provide an ornament of beau-

ty and durability. The company keeps several cast-iron designs in stock which are firmly welded and painted white, black, verdigris, or terra cotta. Many of these designs are taken from exclusive pre-Civil War patterns. Robinson also does custom casting from drawings and restores partially destroyed metalwork. The company restored entrance posts at West Point Military Academy, using an old photograph and one corroded fragment. It also provided twenty-six tons of brackets, runners, column bases and capitals, lampposts, furniture, and fountains for The Courtyard, a Montgomery, Alabama, re-creation of part of the New Orleans Vieux Carré.

The pineapple hitching post, with its unusual top and lion-headed column, makes a handsome ornament for the driveway, next to the front door, or in the garden. It's 4′ high and 6¾″ wide at its base. Robinson also manufactures two different horsehead hitching posts and a unique post with a tree design. The base consists of a trunk with the branches sliced from it; at the top, the branches rise and twist to form the hitching loops. A pair of griffins would be handsome flanking an entrance way. Each lion's body and eagle's head stand 20″ high, 8″ wide, and 24″ long; the wings can also be welded to stand as high as the head, so that the statue can form a table base. The design for Robinson's whippet statue appeared at least as early as 1870. The cast-iron pieces used to make the 18″-high, 8″-wide, 35″-long statue vary in thickness from 1″ to 3″.

Robinson also casts urns and fountains that lend a classical look to almost any outdoor area. Twelve standard urn and vase styles are available; the Venetian fluted urn comes in five sizes, ranging from 16″ high and 13″ in diameter at the top to 34″ high and 29″ in diameter. Some sizes can be fitted with different bases. The Roman fluted fountain also comes in various sizes. As a three-

tiered fountain, it stands 65" high and measures 13½" wide at the base. The bottom bowl is 30", the middle, 24", and the top, 14" in diameter. The fountain can be purchased as a two-tiered version with either the top and middle or bottom and middle bowls. The former variation is 42" high; the second, 47" high.

Catalogue available.

Robinson Iron
Robinson Rd.
Alexander City, AL 35010
(205) 329-8484

Rustic Home Hardware

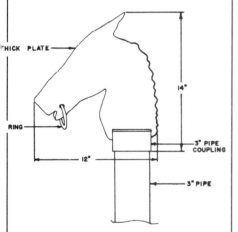

Rustic Home Hardware gives the classic horse-head hitching post a slightly different look by replacing the full head with a 1"-thick plate silhouette. A solid brass ring dangles from the horse's mouth. Measuring 14" high by 12" deep, the head mounts on a 54"-high, 3"-wide post.

Catalogue, $5.

Rustic Home Hardware
R.D. 3
Hanover, PA 17331
(717) 632-0088

Silver Dollar Trading

It's easy to give a garden a period flavor with outdoor ornaments like these from Silver Dollar. For a wall that needs adornment, there's a lion-headed lavabo available in cast aluminum or solid polished brass. It measures 20" high by 10½" wide.

Silver Dollar's Victorian urn is eye-catching enough to suit a

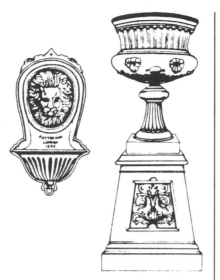

prominent location and would also look charming peeking through foliage. Made of aluminum and standing 4' high, it has a sloping base, ornate decoration, and graceful curves.

The aluminum pieces are painted in one of four colors: white, black, medium dark green, or chocolate brown. Silver Dollar carries a wide variety of other lawn and garden ornaments.

Catalogue, $2.

Silver Dollar Trading Co.
Box 394
1591 Main St.
San Elizario, TX 79849
(915) 851-3458

Travis Tuck

Travis Tuck is a metal sculptor who spends much of his workday fashioning pieces that will be seen on the rooftops of houses. His technique for crafting these fanciful weather vanes is not necessarily new, but he brings un-

common ability to his craft. Repoussé, the process of hammering and texturing a three-dimensional form from flat copper sheets, goes back as far as the art of metalsmithing itself and is a technique not too different from the one used to create historic vanes that have perched atop venerable structures for several hundred years. Pictured is one of Tuck's standard designs, the cod, which is a Massachusetts symbol. Other designs available are a sea eagle with prey, a ram, a weathercock, a Canada goose, and perhaps the most unusual, a humpback whale. Vanes are finished in any hue of paint, verdigris, gold leaf, or left natural to weather to a soft patina.

Brochure, $1.

Travis Tuck
Box 1832 C
Martha's Vineyard, MA 02568
(617) 693-3914

E.G. Washburne

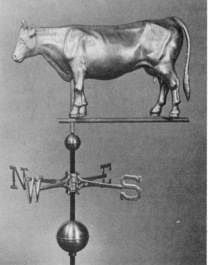

WILLIAM CHARLES STUDIO

E.G. Washburne was established in 1853, yet the art of making weather vanes that the firm perpetuates today is centuries older. Early designs in sheet metal or wood, usually silhouetting a fish, evolved to full-bodied, hammered copper horses, dogs, eagles, and even a docile, sturdy cow such as the one Washburne makes today. The company can custom make silhouette or three-dimensional vanes. Each complete vane has a steel spire, brass collar and cardinals, and two copper balls, and is shipped ready for mounting. The copper balls come in diameters ranging from 1½" to 12". Brass cardinals are available with letters standing from 2" to 12" tall. The vanes are finished with paint, verdigris, or gold leaf, or can be left natural, as you prefer.

Catalogue available.

E.G. Washburne & Co., Inc.
85 Andover St.
Danvers, MA 01923
(617) 774-3645

Frederick Wilbur

Frederick Wilbur specializes in architectural woodcarving and sign making. During the past decade he has carved a variety of traditional motifs for architects, as well as contemporary logos and reliefs for designers and other clients. His signs are hand-routed or carved or a combination of both; he can design them for you or use your own logo or artwork. Wilbur most frequently works with redwood, cedar, mahogany, and white pine. His redwood signs, generally 1½" thick, are given a natural finish, the letters painted, and a finish of exterior varnish applied to the whole. White pine or mahogany signs are completely painted, using three coats of primer and several of exterior grade color. Wilbur often uses gold leaf for lettering and decorative carving. His custom signs are well known throughout his native state, and his fame is spreading farther afield.

Brochure available.

Frederick Wilbur
Box 425
Lovingston, VA 22949
(804) 263-4827

Outdoor Structures

Outbuildings such as the gazebo, pavilion, carriage house, and barn have attracted more and more attention in the past few years. Back in the early 1900s, a prosperous country property might have contained a number of outbuildings, possibly including a summer kitchen, icehouse, carriage shed, privy, smokehouse, gazebo, springhouse, and a barn or two. There is very little practical need for many of these auxilliary structures today, but they do form a part of an historical record. Lack of utility notwithstanding, a gazebo or pavilion can provide a welcome shady nook on a hot summer day; the old-fashioned carriage shed is easily adapted for use as a garage and is a great deal more attractive than its usual modern counterpart. Barns, of course, are very fashionable today and are used for residential purposes as well as for animals and feed by country gentlemen and real farmers alike.

Amdega

One of the most prominent manufacturers of conservatories during the Victorian era was Richardson and Company, established in 1874. Richardson survived the first fifty years of the 1900s, when most makers of conservatories went out of business, and in 1969 Amdega took control of the company and revitalized it. Today, Amdega makes both custom and modular conservatories from fine red cedar. Based in the United Kingdom, the company ships its products worldwide, and its heritage of high standards and superior styling is apparent in every delightfully old-fashioned structure it produces.

Two standard designs with a number of variations make choosing the right conservatory easy. The octagonal version comes in lengths which range from 8'8" to 8'3½" and measures 12'1" wide by 10'9" high at the rooftop. The distance from the sash bottoms to the base is 18". Its double, 1¾"-thick doors can be hung on any side or front panel and come complete with brass hardware. Ventilation is provided by top-hung sashes held open by brass window stays. Optional plywood ridge cresting trims the roof in this picture.

The standard rectangular or lean-to model can range from 10'1" to 24'6¼" in length, with a depth of 9'11" or 7'6". Two heights are available—11'4½" and 10'9". The base shown here is made of brick; most of Amdega's conservatory bases are either brick or stone. Visible at the bottom edge of the roof is the standard gutter, which

discharges at ground level; below it is Amdega's optional timber dentil molding.

Several sash designs are available, including plain, divided vertically in half, rimmed at the top with a row of four small squares, and trimmed with arches formed by radial bars placed on both the exterior and interior surfaces of the glass. Toughened, laminated, tinted, or Georgian wired glass is optional, as is double glazing for more effective temperature control, reduced noise, and efficient energy use.

Custom designs, including combinations of the two standard shapes, are executed. Even grand

projects such as pool pavilions are undertaken. Amdega ships its conservatories in sections, but will erect and glaze its buildings if these services are required. A design consultant will offer suggestions and estimates at no charge.

Literature available.

Amdega Centre
160 Friendship Rd.
Cranbury, NJ 08512
(201) 329-0999

Gazebo & Porchworks

Lacy gingerbread designs for outdoor structures are a specialty at Gazebo & Porchworks, which offers a good selection of gazebo parts and kits. Rails, spindles, panels, and more are cut from red oak or hemlock. Parts can be arranged to form octagons or hexagons ranging in diameter from 6' to 12'. The gracefully arched arbor shown measures 70" wide by 89" high by 36" deep and is shipped sanded but unfinished so that you can choose your own paint or stain.

Catalogue, $2.

Gazebo & Porchworks
728 9th Ave. S.
Puyallup, WA 98371-6744
(206) 848-0502

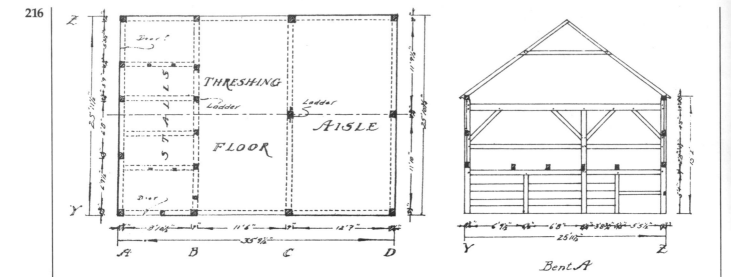

Bent A

New Jersey Barn

From carriage houses and corn cribs to a church, a mill, and a house built in 1740, New Jersey Barn can provide the parts for a variety of authentic old buildings. The company's name, however, indicates its specialty. Its staff scours the area for fine old barns, mostly made of oak, and disassembles them. The frames are photographed and blueprinted, then stored for later sale and reerection. The foundation, flooring, sheathing, and roofing are left to your contractor or architect.

Shown here are floor plans and cutaway views of two available barns. The 25'10¾" by 35'9½" Middleton-Waln is a circa 1790

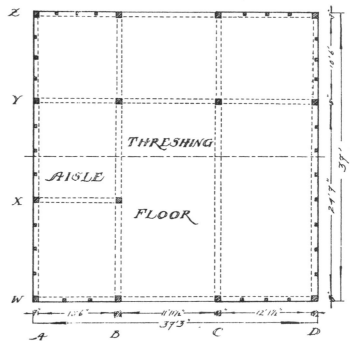

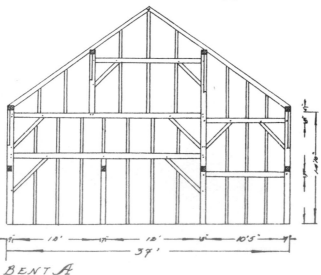

BENT A

English-style barn built in Cream Ridge, New Jersey. Dutch Pete's barn, 37' by 37'3", is a hybrid of the English and Dutch styles. It was built around 1800.

Brochure available.

The New Jersey Barn Co.
Box 702
Princeton, NJ 08542
(609) 942-8480

Landscape Architects

The site occupied by an historic house is almost as important as the structure itself, and so is its landscaping. Many old buildings enjoy a pleasant, attractive vantage point, their position having been chosen long before an area was fully developed. And old house owners usually appreciate the fact that they do not have to wait years for trees and shrubs to develop. Yet, the grounds of an older building are as subject to deterioration as the interior. Plantings have to be renewed, trees and shrubs kept properly trimmed and spaced, lawns reestablished. In many cases, the outlines of the original landscaping scheme— including gardens and lawn areas— have completely disappeared over the years. Whether it is a matter of renewing what is already in place or reestablishing the old, a landscape architect may be able to do wonders. Properly done, the work may save you maintenance time in the future; unquestionably, it will increase the value of your home.

Edsall & Associates

The scope of this firm's landscape architecture services should please even the most demanding. From feasibility studies, site evaluation and selection, master planning and site design, and quantity and cost estimates to drainage and grading specifications, irrigation, project management, and interior plantscaping, Edsall & Associates can handle practically any facet of your project. Over twenty awards from Ohio towns and cities testify to the company's excellence.

Edsall's reputation rests on projects like Concord Village, a community of twenty-six homes. Extensive research, especially at Colonial Williamsburg, resulted in an expert re-creation of 18th-century landscaping. All of the plants used were of the same genus as those at Williamsburg; species were selected on the basis of their suitability to the Ohio climate and their resistance to insects and disease. The project encompassed several aspects of landscape architecture beyond the selection of plants, including water sculpture, fencing, exterior lighting, designing private rear gardens for five of the homes, locating appropriate gazebos and trellises, and installing special pavements of handmade brick.

Edsall & Associates
754 Neil Ave.
Columbus, OH 43215
(614) 221-0580

Entourage, Inc.

You can get both the expertise of a superb design and construction firm and the benefits of a nonprofit organization's extensive research by calling one number. LaBarbara and Everett Fly head both Fly Associates and the nonprofit Entourage, Inc., which is committed to providing information, equipment, materials, and planning services for the general public. The two companies offer a vast range of historical preservation services, including archival and public records research, cartography, photography, master planning, design, assistance with historical landmark nominations,

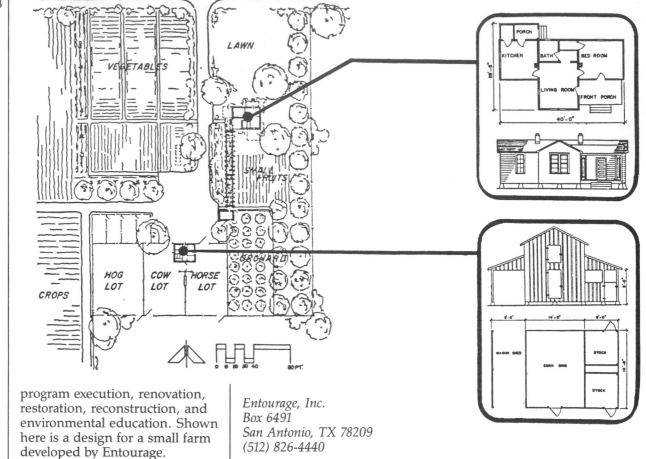

program execution, renovation, restoration, reconstruction, and environmental education. Shown here is a design for a small farm developed by Entourage.

Entourage, Inc.
Box 6491
San Antonio, TX 78209
(512) 826-4440

Jamie Gibbs and Associates

Jamie Gibbs's nine years of experience as a landscape architect and interior designer has taken him throughout the United States and to Europe and South America. Although he does some of his work with public and corporate spaces, ninety percent of his practice is residential, and seventy-five percent of his residential work is in older, suburban neighborhoods. One of his specialties is the restoration and re-creation of period gardens.

The author of three books, Gibbs has degrees in architecture, landscape architecture, horticulture, and historic preservation.

Jamie Gibbs and Associates
Landscape Architects and Interior
  Designers
340 E. 93rd St., Suite 14C
New York, NY 10128
(212) 722-7508

Kane, Liede and Ratyna

Historic landscape preservation is a specialty at Kane, Liede and Ratyna. Some of the firm's work has involved entire communities, although most of its sites are limited to one building and its surroundings. The company has executed a number of projects for the National Trust for Historic Preservation; one such endeavor is shown here. Lyndhurst, located

in Tarrytown, New York, is a Gothic-Revival mansion surrounded by a charming 19th-century park. Kane, Liede and Ratyna replanted key trees, removed foundation plantings introduced during this century, restored the stone walls, and rediscovered old walks. The firm is currently restoring a two-acre terraced garden for Oatlands, another National Trust property, in Leesburg, Virginia.

Brochure available.

Kane, Liede and Ratyna, P.C.
 Landscape Architects and Planners
70 Sarles Lane
Pleasantville, NY 10570
(914) 769-6600

Perennial Pleasures Nursery

Herb and flower gardens, ornamental shrubs, a sunken lawn, and grassy paths surround Rachel Kane's unusual nursery. Over three hundred varieties of plants indigenous to 17th-, 18th-, and 19th-century gardens include red and pink beebalm, Cupid's dart, dusty meadow rue, purple loosestrife, red campion, veronica, honesty, mignonette, and lady's mantle. The selection also includes a wide variety of herbs. Among them are sweet Cicely, elecampane, good King Henry, blue and pink hyssop, lime balm, perilla, horehound, and tansy. If you don't see what you need on Kane's plant list, ask; she's constantly acquiring new species.

Plant list available.

Perennial Pleasures Nursery
Box 147
East Hardwick, VT 05836
(802) 472-5512

Edward D. Stone, Jr. and Associates

A large, knowledgeable staff, versatility, and experience make EDSA capable of tackling almost any restoration project. The firm's practice is hardly limited to the Fort Lauderdale area; EDSA has offices in Orlando, Florida and Wilmington, North Carolina as well, and its planners and landscape architects have traveled as far from home as Taiwan, Yugoslavia, and Brazil. Currently, the company is providing site restoration, landscape consultation, master planning, and graphic design services for the Bonnet House, an early 1920s Florida estate.

Brochure available.

For more information, contact:

Edward D. Stone, Jr. and Associates
 Planners and Landscape Architects
1512 E. Broward Blvd., Suite. 110
Fort Lauderdale, FL 33301
(305) 524-3330

Other Suppliers for Outdoor and Garden Areas

Consult List of Suppliers for addresses.

Fencing, Gates, and Window Grilles

Architectural Antique Warehouse
Architectural Antiques Exchange
Bay Waveland Woodworks
Great American Salvage Co.
Robinson Iron
Schwartz's Forge & Metalworks

Outdoor Furniture

Architectural Antique Warehouse
Whit Hanks
Schwartz's Forge & Metalworks

Lawn and Garden Ornaments

Architectural Salvage Co.
Robert Bourdon, the Smithy
The Country Loft
Lehman Hardware and Appliances, Inc.
W.F. Norman Corp.
Period Furniture Hardware Co., Inc.
Remodelers' & Renovators' Supply
S. Chris Rheinschild
Schwartz's Forge & Metalworks

Outdoor Structures

Cape Cod Cupolas
Cumberland Woodcraft, Inc.
Historical Replications, Inc.
Silver Dollar Trading Co.
Vintage Wood Works

Landscape Architects

Office of Robert Perron
George E. Patton, Inc.

11.

Decorative Accessories

As any dictionary will tell you, an accessory is a supplement; an adjunct, rather than a primary object. Decorative accessories—mirrors, pillows, baskets, weather vanes, wall hangings, quilts, vases, etc.—can provide just the right finishing touch in a period decor. Unfortunately, they tend to be the last thing we think about when decorating a home, and we may have a tendency to buy such objects on impulse—from a flea market or garage sale, perhaps. Items bought in that way, however, frequently find their way back to the same type of sale a year or two later. But that doesn't have to be the case. There are many beautifully designed, well-made objects to enhance a period setting while serving a useful function as well. Some are illustrated in this chapter; many others are available from craftsmen and established firms listed in previous chapters.

Most of the objects recommended in the following pages are made by modern artisans. They are not antiques, although the methods and patterns followed are thoroughly based on tradition. Forms, too, resemble those from the past to a striking degree. The materials used are natural, not synthetic. The personal commitment to imaginative, well-wrought work is clearly evident in the objects themselves. There are far easier ways to make a good living than laboring at the forge, kiln, or workbench.

Antique accessories of the same quality and form may be priced several times more than reproductions or adaptations of old designs, and the profit therefrom keeps the dealer in business. We have no argument with those who make their livelihood by saving and selling such treasures, but there is a special kind of satisfaction that comes from helping to support present-day artistry. It is easy to decry most of the products of our materialistic society; the average gift shop is stuffed to the brim with absolutely worthless trash that cannot even be recycled. That is why it is such a pleasure to collect the work of living craftsmen whether they are employed by large companies or in workshops, or whether they labor in the luxury of solitude.

Eldred Wheeler's tiger-maple pipe box, available through Partridge Replications, Portsmouth, New Hampshire.

Amazon Drygoods

Amazon Drygoods is one of those tempting stores that sells a little bit of everything. Books, 19th-century clothing patterns, musical instruments, and walking sticks can be found here, as can fans of ebony, sandalwood, paper, and lace. A collection of tinware includes bowls, mugs, a coffee pot, a water pitcher, canteens, and a document box. Some of Amazon's merchandise is quite difficult to find elsewhere. For example, the "hot bricks" mentioned in 19th-century books were soapstone boot driers, which, when heated near a stove or oven and placed in a wet shoe, dry it slowly and evenly. These boot driers, which can also be used as pocket hand-warmers in the winter, are among the enormous variety of products sold at Amazon.

Catalogue available.

Amazon Drygoods
2218 E. 11th St.
Davenport, IA 52803
(319) 322-6800 or
(309) 786-3504

American Wood Column

For a display piece as impressive as the sculpture or pottery it supports, you might consider a wooden pedestal from American Wood Column. Fluted or plain columns, in diameters of from 6" to 10", can be cut to any height; Greek Ionic or Roman Corinthian capitals particularly suit these pedestals, and can be ordered in sizes ranging from 4" to 25" in diameter. The company suggests that one of its more ornate capitals, inverted, would make an unusual and arresting table base.

Brochure available.

American Wood Column Corp.
913 Grand St.
Brooklyn, NY 11211
(718) 782-3163

Baldwin Hardware

Inspired by an early 19th-century English Sheffield plate made circa 1810, this solid-brass Regency Shell bookend makes a handsome

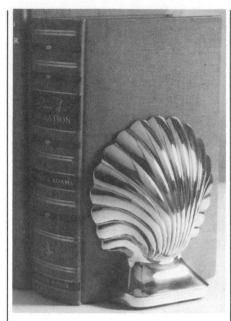

ornament on a desk or a bookcase. Its shape is reminiscent of the Classical Revival style. The lustrous finish of the polished brass is protected by a strong, clear baked-enamel coating.

Liberature, 75¢.

Baldwin Hardware Corp.
841 Wyomissing Blvd.
Box 82
Reading, PA 19603
(215) 777-7811

The Candle Cellar

The Candle Cellar's selection of hand-crafted country accessories includes these large and small herb drying racks. Model 1A, the large rack, consists of two 48"-high by 24"-wide native pine panels.

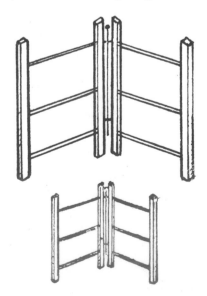

Dowels are provided, and assembly is simple. Model 1B, the smaller rack, has 14"-high, 12"-wide panels and is assembled prior to shipping. The Candle Cellar also makes wall boxes, plaques, doorstops, candles, ornaments, and trays.

Catalogue, $1.

The Candle Cellar and Emporium
Box 135
South Station
Fall River, MA 02724
(401) 624-9529

Coldstream Coverlets

Working in a converted garage on Canada's largest hand loom, which they built of timber from their own farm, Lorna and Walter McIntyre weave replicas of 18th- and 19th-century bedcoverings. The designs were extensively researched in museums and manuals of pattern drafts, and they are woven of white cotton thread and pure wool in one of seven colors: brick red, indigo, natural, ivory, beige, gray, or sable. Mothproofed, dye-fast, washed, and pre-shrunk, the coverlets, throws, and crib coverlets can be dry-cleaned or hand-washed. Each is initialed, dated, and numbered, and a matching certificate with information about the design's history is issued to the buyer.

Personalized lettering can be woven into the pattern, and custom work is sometimes undertaken, although the size of coverlets must always be 80" by 105". The pattern shown here, Monmouth, is based on an original which belongs to the Canadian Guild of Crafts in Montreal, and several like it have been found in Scottish communities.

Brochure available.

Coldstream Coverlets
R.R. 2
Ilderton, Ontario, Canada N0M 2A0
(519) 666-0393

Colonial Weavers

Weaving runs in Anda Bijhouwer's family. Her grandmother was a weaver, and many of her ancestors were weavers, so it seems natural that Bijhouwer should have tried her own hand at the craft. After restoring an antique loom, she copied an early 19th-century coverlet found in a neighbor's home. The result, the first of her "Phippsburg"

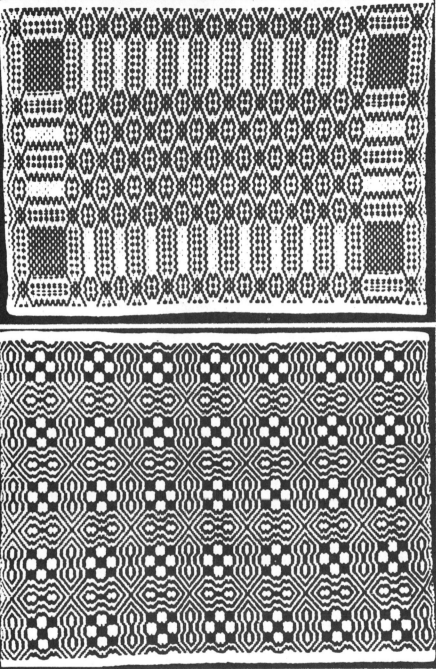

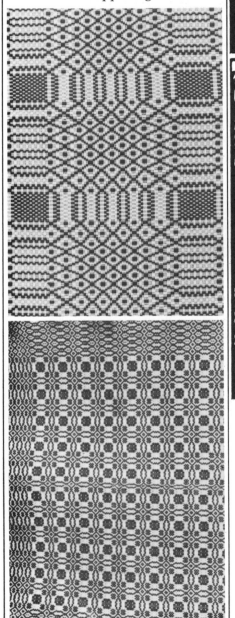

coverlets, was purchased by the Smithsonian Institution. Today, the Phippsburg pattern, with its complex blending of diamonds, rectangles, and other geometric figures, is one of Colonial Weavers' most popular designs.

A very common pattern for antique coverlets, the Whig Rose or Wedding Bands design, sports large flowers, interlocking circles, and an eye-catching border. It is also available in a summer and winter weave, which is reversible and more difficult to make than the more usual overshot weave. Bijhouwer's coverlets come in three sizes—66" by 110", 84" by 110", and 100" by 110". They consist of two or three panels sewn together, as old coverlets were. Fringe can be added to one end or three sides, and names, birthdates, or wedding dates can be woven into the design. Bijhouwer will analyze your heirloom coverlet and reproduce the pattern if you like; she weaves in about fifty colors and will dye thread to match your furnishings if you send samples of fabric, wallpaper, or carpeting.

In addition to coverlets, Colonial Weavers also makes tablecloths, table runners, pillows, and placemats. Two placemat designs, the delicate Martha Washington and the bolder, darker Anna Henrikkson's Fancy, are shown here. Woven in cotton and acrylic so that they can be machine-washed and dried, they measure 17" long and 12" to 13" wide, depending on the pattern.

Catalogue, $2.

Colonial Weavers
Box 16
Phippsburg Center, ME 04562
(207) 589-2033

Correia Art Glass

The Metropolitan Museum of Art and the Smithsonian Institution feature art glass from Correia in their permanent collections. The rare and time-consuming hand-blown technique used by Correia produces works suitable for door-knobs in an Abu Dhabi palace; one of the firm's commissions was the creation of two hundred sculptures to honor dignitaries and participants in the Los Angeles Olympic games. Cutting, engraving, and at least half a dozen polishing processes contribute to crafting each piece of Correia's art glass. Several lines of glass are available from the firm. The Etched Collection includes blue, black, and gold luster globes, vases, and paperweights, with butterflies, birds, and numerous sharp, abstract designs cut into their surfaces. The Silver Collection displays black and ruby glass apples, vases, and goblets swirled with glittering silver. The Iridescent collection features aqua, cobalt, and ruby tones, mixed with a changing sheen of other hues. Every piece is signed, dated, and registered, documenting it as the art that it is.

Brochures available.

Correia Art Glass
711 Colorado Ave.
Santa Monica, CA 90401
(213) 393-9794

The Fan Man

Kurt House, proprietor of The Fan Man, stocks and refurbishes early electric fans by Emerson, Robbins & Meyers, Adams-Bagnall, Westinghouse, and Century. The Luminaire, an Art Deco repro-duction featuring glass lotus-flower shades, was inspired by an artifact from the 4000-year-old tomb of King Tut. The Fan Man accepts trade-ins and supplies replacement fan parts in a strong cast-aluminum alloy or in solid brass. Vintage fans usually on hand in the shop include steam-driven, alcohol-burning, coin-operated, oscillating, ceiling, and gyro models. Reproductions come unfinished or in your choice of antique or bright brass, copper or antique copper, chrome, or pewter.

Catalogue, $2.

The Fan Man
4606 Travis St.
Dallas, TX 75205
(214) 559-4440

Ferguson's Cut Glass Works

Cary S. Ferguson, master glass cutter and beveler, offers a full line of brilliant-style tableware beautiful enough to please even the most demanding tastes. This piece, an example of his excellent work, is made of hand-cut lead crystal and features scalloped and serrated edges.

Brochure available.

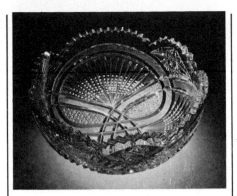

Ferguson's Cut Glass Works
4292 Pearl Rd.
Cleveland, OH 44109
(216) 459-2929

Import Specialists

The Museum of American Folk Art in New York City is the repository of a superb collection of decorative arts, and has given Import Specialists an exclusive license to reproduce certain designs from its collections of early Americana. Among Import Specialists' offerings are cotton-covered pillows stenciled with the Texas Star, Lincoln Log, and other classic quilting patterns in bright primary colors. Easy-to-clean vinyl placemats feature a checkered pattern reminiscent of oilcloth. Other designs are hand-printed on rag pillows, hand-printed cotton placemats, and kitchen towels.

For information on local distributors, contact

Import Specialists Inc.
82 Wall St.
New York, NY 10005
(212) 709-9633
(800) 334-4044

Lehman Hardware

Lehman Hardware was founded more than three decades ago to serve the largest Amish settlement in the United States. Its "Non-Electric Good Neighbor Catalog" lists a wide array of distinctive items useful even in today's high-tech society. An ornate cast-iron matchbox or simpler tin style in blue, green, or yellow can be wall mounted to keep an entire box of kitchen matches close at hand. Crafted from kiln-dried oak, a

watertight bucket holds 2½ gallons of liquid and is fitted with a handy rope bail. Tough, water-resistant white oak barrels and kegs serve many purposes: unlined kegs can hold homemade wine and come in sizes ranging from 1 to 15 gallons. Charred kegs (5 or 10 gallons) are famous for aging whiskey, but may be used for other liquids. Paraffin kegs will hold pickles, cider, or vinegar. Hinged railroad kegs like those found in old-fashioned general stores, treated with paraffin and varnish, come in 5-, 10-, 15-, and 20-gallon sizes. Furniture-grade kegs and larger, used charred kegs are also available. Older barrels

can be refurbished with Lehman's supply of hardwood faucets and bungs.

Catalogue, $2.

Lehman Hardware & Appliances Inc.
Box 41
4779 Kidron Rd.
Kidro, OH 44636
(216) 857-5441

M-H Lamp & Fan

M-H Lamp & Fan specializes in restoring antique ceiling fixtures, from the wiring to the wooden blades to the finishes. The company sells a number of such fixtures, including this Westinghouse ceiling fan, which dates from the first decades of the century. While its primary business is in restoring fans to individual request, M-H does maintain a limited stock of refurbished fixtures for sale, and also offers brass lighting fixtures that can be fitted to the fans.

Catalogue, $3.

M-H Lamp & Fan Co.
723½ N. Sheridan Rd.
Chicago, IL 60626
(312) 743-2225

Moravian Pottery & Tile Works

Located in a building that is a National Historic Landmark, the Moravian Pottery & Tile Works continues to produce tiles in the same way it has since the beginning of the century. Most are intended for walls and floors, but more creative uses include a set of stoveplates in Cross-and-Tulip, Lotus, and Trinity patterns. Each plate measures 7" by 6". Unusual inkwells in the Four Seasons and

Swan-and-Tower patterns display Moravian tiles on 4" cubes.

Catalogue, $4.

Moravian Pottery & Tile Works
Swamp Road
Doylestown, PA 18901
(215) 345-6722

The Old Wagon Factory

If you are looking for an alternative to the usual sisal or rubber doormat, The Old Wagon Factory may have the answer. Diagonals of pressure-treated Virginia pine surrounded by an 18" by 32" pine frame make a durable, unusual addition to an entryway. Other accessories offered by the firm include wooden planters, made of solid spruce coated in gloss white. Removeable inserts of galvanized metal protect flooring and prevent the planters from rotting. The three styles—raised panel, cross, and Chippendale—are each available in two sizes: 16" wide and long by 18" high, or 14" wide and long by 16" high. The raised-panel planter can be matched to a window box, which The Old Wagon Factory will cut to any size window up to 70". Made of solid spruce with pressure-treated bottoms, the boxes are painted either matte or gloss white at your option.

Catalogue, $2.

The Old Wagon Factory
103 Russell St.
Box 1427, Dept. OC86
Clarksville, VA 23927
(804) 374-5787

R. Wayne Reynolds

If you own a lovely old picture frame that's lost much of its gilding, or if you're looking for a reproduction mirror frame, R. Wayne Reynolds can help. His specialty is the regilding of antique frames and decorative art objects, but he also carries a line of picture and mirror frames in many styles. His list of previous commissions is impressive and includes restoring a 19th-century gilded picture frame for the White House and creating a coat-of-arms ornament for a reproduction of a 17th-century Dutch overmantle in the collection of the National Gallery of Art. Reynolds has also accepted commissions from the United States House of Representatives, the Department of the Interior, and the Smithsonian Institution's Museum of American History.

R. Wayne Reynolds, Ltd.
Box 28
Stevenson, MD 21153
(301) 323-1180

Shaker Workshops

Baskets have been among the most useful and decorative of accessories since Biblical times. Shaker Workshops, specializing in exquisitely simple and utilitarian reproductions of old Shaker furnishings, has replicated some of the most versatile baskets, from heavy, rugged oak to delicate reed splint. A sturdy herb-gathering basket is made of ingenious techniques that use neither wire

nor nails. Cheese baskets in a distinctive hexagonal weave range from 8″ to 19″ in diameter. Sets of square and round baskets serve myriad uses, from gathering berries to holding a dried flower arrangement. Do-it-yourselfers will appreciate Shaker Workshops' kits. Materials for a 7″ by 7½″ berry basket, a 14″ by 4¾″ cheese basket, or a 5″ by 8″ melon basket come with complete instructions.

Seasonal catalogues, $1.

Shaker Workshops
Box 1028
Concord, MA 01742
(617) 646-8985

Westmoore Pottery

An old, wood-fueled kiln still fires Westmoore's pottery, which is made using traditional methods that are centuries old, yet with modern touches that will be appreciated by 20th-century homemakers. Westmoore's pottery is made with leadless glazes and is dishwasher-safe; its redware can be used in either conventional or microwave ovens. Both contemporary and historic designs are made at the company kiln, and each piece attains a particular individuality because of the patterns of wood ash that inpregnate it.

Brochure available.

Westmoore Pottery
Rte. 2, Box 476
Seagrove, NC 27341
(919) 464-3700

Martha Wetherbee

Martha Wetherbee and her associate, Nathan Taylor, are preeminent basketmakers who have studied traditional American basketry for more than a decade. Their interests lie not only in the making of baskets but also in uncovering and documenting the lost history of the basketmaker's art in the Northeast; their knowledge of how a basket is made allows them to "read" basket history from a unique perspective. Recognized as authorities in their field, Wetherbee and Taylor are best known for the Shaker and Bushwacker baskets which they have researched and now reproduce at the shop adjoining their home. Among the styles they offer are a kitten-head basket edged with colorful printed triangles and a meticulously woven tatting basket.

Brochure available.

Martha Wetherbee Basket Shop
Star Rte., Box 35
Sanbornton, NH 03269
(603) 286-8927

Eldred Wheeler

Once ubiquitous features of New England public buildings, boxes such as this one held long clay pipes for the benefit of visitors. A flint was contained in the drawer for use in lighting the pipes, and after smoking, a visitor would break off the pipe tip and replace the pipe in the box for the next person. Although most such boxes were rarely designed for anything but function, the original of Eldred Wheeler's tiger maple version is a delightful exception to the rule. Its fan-carved drawer and painstaking scrollwork make it an excellent accessory for almost any colonial home. It measures 16¼″ high by 4″ wide by 4¼″ deep. The pipe box, as well as Eldred Wheeler's fine reproduction furniture, is

sold through Partridge Replications.

Catalogue, $3.

Eldred Wheeler
c/o Partridge Replications
63 Penhallow St.
Box 4104
Portsmouth, NH 03801
(603) 431-8733

Other Suppliers of Decorative Accessories

Consult List of Suppliers for addresses.

Angel House Designs
Architectural Antiques Exchange
Architectural Salvage Co.
Laura Ashley
The Country Loft
Curran Glass and Mirror
Granville Manufacturing Co., Inc.

Henkel-Harris
The Old Wagon Factory
Orleans Carpenters
Rue de France
Sunflower Glass Studio
Vintage Valances
Woodstock Soapstone Co., Inc.

LIST OF SUPPLIERS

List of Suppliers

AA-Abbingdon Affiliates, Inc.
2149-51 Utica Ave.
Brooklyn, NY 11234
(718) 258-8333

A-Ball Plumbing Supply
1703 W. Burnside
Portland, OR 97209
(503) 228-0026

Abatron, Inc.
141 Center Dr.
Gilberts, IL 60136
(312) 426-2200

Accurate Metal Weather Strip Co., Inc.
725 S. Fulton Ave.
Mount Vernon, NY 10550-5086
(914) 668-6042

Acorn Manufacturing Co., Inc.
Mansfield, MA 02048
(617) 339-4500

Aetna Stove Co., Inc.
S.E. Corner 2nd & Arch Sts.
Philadelphia, PA 19106
(215) 627-2008 or
(215) 627-2009

Aged Woods
Division of First Capital
Wood Products
147 W. Philadelphia St.
York, PA 17401
(800) 233-9307

A.J.P., Coppersmith & Co.
34 Broadway
Wakefield, MA 01880
(617) 245-1223

Alexandria Wood Joinery
Plumer Hill Rd.
Alexandria, NH 03222
(802) 744-8243

Alfresco
Box 1336
Durango, CO 81302
(303) 247-9739 or
(303) 259-5743

Allentown Paint Manufacturing Co., Inc.
Box 597, E. Allen &
N. Graham Sts.
Allentown, PA 18105

Amazon Drygoods
2218 E. 11th St.
Davenport, IA 52803
(319) 322-6800

Amdega Centre
160 Friendship Rd.
Cranbury, NJ 08512
(201) 329-0999

American Architectural Art Co.
1910 N. Marshall St., Dept.
OHC
Philadelphia, PA 19122
(215) 236-6492

American Olean Tile Co.
1000 Cannon Ave., Box 271
Lansdale, PA 19446-0271
(215) 855-1111

American Ornamental Metal Corp.
5013 Kelley St., Box 21548
Houston, TX 77026
(800) 231-3693

American Wood Column Corp.
913 Grand St.
Brooklyn, NY 11211
(718) 782-3163

Anderson Building Restoration
923 Marion Ave.
Cincinnati, OH 45229
(513) 281-5258

Anderson Pulley Seal
Box 19101
Minneapolis, MN 55419
(612) 827-1117

Angel House Designs
RFD 1, Box 1
Rte. 148
Brookfield, MA 01506
(617) 867-2517

Antique Color Supply, Inc.
Box 711
Harvard, MA 01451
(617) 582-6426

The Antique Hardware Store
43 Bridge St.
Frenchtown, NJ 08825
(201) 996-4040

Architectural Antique Warehouse
1583 Bank St.
Ottawa, Ontario, Canada
K1H 7Z3
(613) 526-1818

Architectural Antiques
121 E. Sheridan Ave.
Oklahoma City, OK
73104-2419
(405) 232-0759

Architectural Antiques Exchange
709-15 N. 2nd St.
Philadelphia, PA 19123
(215) 922-3669

Architectural Antiques West
3117 S. La Cienega Blvd.
Los Angeles, CA 90016
(213) 559-3019

Architectural Components
Box 249
Leverett, MA 01054
(413) 367-9441

Architectural Iron Co.
Box 126, Rte. 6W.
Milford, PA 18337
(717) 296-7722

Architectural Reclamation
312 S. River St.
Franklin, OH 45005
(513) 746-8964

Architectural Resources Group
Pier 9
The Embarcadero
San Franscisco, CA 94111
(415) 421-1680

Architectural Salvage Co.
103 W. Michigan Ave.
Box 401
Grass Lake, MI 49240
(517) 522-8516

Architectural Salvage Cooperative
909 W. 3rd St.
Davenport, IA 52803
(319) 324-1556

The Arden Forge
301 Brinton's Bridge Rd.
West Chester, PA 19382
(215) 399-1350

ARJ, Inc.
310 Washington St.
Brighton, MA 02135
(617) 783-0467

Art Directions
6120 Delmar Blvd.
St. Louis, MO 63112
(314) 863-1895

Artistry in Veneers, Inc.
450 Oak Tree Ave.
South Plainfield, NJ 07080
(201) 668-1430

Laura Ashley
Dept. B117, Box 5308
Melville, NY 11747
(800) 367-2000

Authentic Designs
The Mill Rd.
West Rupert, VT 05776-0011
(802) 394-7713

Authentic Lighting
558 Grand Ave.
Englewood, NJ 07631
(201) 568-7429

Baldwin Hardware Corp.
841 Wyomissing Blvd.
Box 82
Reading, PA 19603
(215) 777-7811

Ball & Ball
463 W. Lincoln Hwy.
Exton, PA 19341
(215) 363-7330

Barclay Products Ltd.
424 N. Oakley Blvd.
Chicago, IL 60612
(312) 243-1444

Barnstable Stove Shop
Box 472, Rte. 149
West Barnstable, MA 02668
(617) 362-9913

Robert Barrow
412 Thames Rd.
Bristol, RI 02809
(401) 253-4434

Bay Waveland Woodworks
1330 Hwy. 90 W.
Waveland, MS 39576
(601) 467-2628
Mailing Address:
Rte. 4, Box 548
Bay St. Louis, MS 39520

Beech River Mill Co.
Old Route 16
Centre Ossipee, NH 03814
(603) 539-2636

Bendix Mouldings, Inc.
235 Pegasus Ave.
Northvale, NJ 07647
(800) 526-0240
(201) 767-8888 (NJ)

Bentley Brothers
918 Baxter Ave.
Louisville, KY 40204
(800) 824-4777 or
(502) 589-2939

Besco Plumbing
729 Atlantic Ave.
Boston, MA 02111
(617) 423-4535

Biltmore, Campbell, Smith Restorations, Inc.
One Biltmore Plaza
Asheville, NC 28803
(704) 274-1776

Blaine Window Hardware
1919 Blaine Dr.
Hagerstown, MD 21740
(301) 797-6500

Blue Ridge Shingle Co.
Montebello, VA 24464
Virginia: (703) 377-6635
North Carolina:
(919) 395-5333

Bona Decorative Hardware
3073 Madison Rd.
Cincinnati, OH 45209
(513) 321-7877

Robert Bourdon, the Smithy
Box 2180
Wolcott, VT 05680
(802) 472-6508

Louis W. Bowen
950 3rd Ave.
New York, NY 10022
(212) 759-5410

Larry Boyce & Associates
Box 421507
San Francisco, CA
94142-1507
(415) 626-2122 or
(415) 923-1366

Bradbury & Bradbury Wallpapers
Box 155
Benicia, CA 94510
(707) 746-1900

The Brass Finial
2408 Riverton Rd.
Cinnaminson, NJ 08077
(609) 786-9337

The Brass Knob
2309 18th St. N.W.
Washington, DC 20009
(202) 332-3370

Brass Light Gallery
719 S. 5th St.
Dept. 5
Milwaukee, WI 53204
(414) 383-0675

Brasslight, Inc.
90 Main St.
Nyack, NY 10960
(914) 353-0567

The Broadway Collection
250 N. Troost
Olathe, KS 66061
(800) 255-6365
(913) 782-6244 (KS)
(800) 468-1219 (Canada)

Brunschwig & Fils
979 3rd Ave.
New York, NY 10022
(212) 838-7878

Bryant Stove Works, Inc.
Box 2048 Rich Rd.
Thorndike, ME 04986
(207) 568-3665

Bob Buckter
3877 20th St.
San Francisco, CA 94114
(415) 922-7444

Burdoch Silk Lampshade Co.
11120 Roselle St.
San Diego, CA 92121
(619) 458-1005

Busy Bridge Antiques
Rte. 1, Box 165A
Charlevoix, MI 49720
(616) 547-2740 or
(616) 536-3511

C & H Roofing, Inc.
1713 S. Cliff Ave.
Sioux Falls, SD 57105
(605) 332-5060

Samuel Cabot, Inc.
1 Union St.
Boston, MA 02108
(617) 723-7740

Michael Camp
636 Starkweather
Plymouth, MI 48170
(313) 459-1190

Campbell Center
Box 66
Mt. Carroll, IL 61053
(815) 244-1173

Marion H. Campbell
26 E. 3rd St.
Bethlehem, PA 18018
(215) 865-2522
Mailing Address:
39 Wall St.
Bethlehem, PA 18018
(215) 865-3292

The Canal Co.
1612 14th St. N.W.
Washington, DC 20009
(202) 234-6637

The Candle Cellar and Emporium
Box 135
South Station
Fall River, MA 02724
(401) 624-9529

The Caning Shop
926 Gilman St. at 8th
Berkeley, CA 94710
(415) 527-5010

John Canning
132 Meeker Rd.
Southington, CT 06489
(203) 621-2188

Canvas Carpets
Box 26
South Egremont, MA 01258
(413) 528-4267

Cape Cod Cupola Co., Inc.
78 State Rd.
North Dartmouth, MA 02747
(617) 994-2119

Carlisle Restoration Lumber
Rte. 123
Stoddard, NH 03464
(603) 446-3937

Carolina Craftsmen
975 S. Avocado St.
Anaheim, CA 92805
(714) 533-0894

Carson, Dunlop, & Associates
597 Parliament St.
Ste. 85
Toronto, Ontario, Canada
M4X 1W3
(416) 964-9415

Carter Canopies
Box 808
Rte. 2 Box 270-G
Troutman, NC 28116-0808

Cassidy Brothers Forge, Inc.
U.S. Rte. 1
Rowley, MA 01969-1796
(617) 948-7611

Cedar Valley Shingle Systems
985 S. 6th St.
San Jose, CA 95112
(408) 998-8550

Ceilings, Walls & More, Inc.
124 Walnut St.
Box 494
Jefferson, TX 75657
(214) 665-2221

Central Kentucky Millwork Inc.
2623 Regency Rd.
Lexington, KY 40503
(606) 277-1755

Chelsea Decorative Metal Co.
6115 Cheena Dr.
Houston, TX 77096
(713) 721-9200

Chestnut Hill Furniture Manufactory
65 Chestnut Hill Rd.
East Hampton, CT 06424
(203) 267-8780

Chromatic Paint Corp.
Box 105
Garnerville, NY 10923-0105
(800) 431-7001

Cirecast
380 7th St.
San Francisco, CA 94103
(415) 863-8319

City Lights
2226 Massachusetts Ave.
Cambridge, MA 02140
(617) 547-1490

Jamie C. Clark
685 Jackson Pike
Harrodsburg, KY 40330
(606) 734-9587

Classic Accents Inc.
Box 1181
Southgate, MI 48195
(313) 282-5525

Classic Architectural Specialties
5302 Junius
Dallas, TX 75214
(214) 827-5111

Classic Illumination, Inc.
2743 9th St.
Berkeley, CA 94710
(415) 849-1842

Clio Group, Inc.
3961 Baltimore Ave.
Philadelphia, PA 19104
(215) 386-6276

The Cobweb Shop
N 3956 N. U.S. 2
Iron Mountain, MI 49801
(906) 774-6560

David Cohn
240 Waverly Rd.
New York, NY 10014
(212) 741-3548

Monroe Coldren and Son's
723 E. Virginia Ave.
West Chester, PA 19380
(215) 692-5651

Coldstream Coverlets
R.R. 2
Ilderton, Ontario, Canada
N0M 2A0
(519) 666-0393

Colonial Furniture Refinishing and Stripping
Broad and Charles Sts.
Medford, NJ 08055
(609) 654-0660

Colonial Weavers
Box 16
Phippsburg Center, ME
04562
(207) 589-2033

The Color People
1672 Madison St.
Denver, CO 80206
(303) 388-8686

Combination Door Co.
Box 1076
Dept. OH
Fond du Lac, WI 54935
(414) 922-2050

Community Services Collaborative
1315 Broadway
Boulder, CO 80302
(303) 442-3601

Conant Custom Brass
270 Pine St.
Burlington, VT 05401
(802) 658-4482

Cook & Dunn Paint Corp.
Box 117
Newark, NJ 07101
(201) 589-5580

Correia Art Glass
711 Colorado Ave.
Santa Monica, CA 90401
(213) 393-9794

Country Bed Shop
R.R. 1, Box 65
Ashby, MA 01431
(617) 386-7550

The Country Loft
South Shore Park
Hingham, MA 02043
(800) 225-5408

Craftsman Lumber
R.R. 1, Box 65
Ashby, MA 01431
(617) 386-7550

Craftsmen Decorators
2611 Ocean Ave.
Brooklyn, NY 11229
(718) 332-2106

Creative Openings
Box 4204
Bellingham, WA 98227
(206) 671-6420

Cumberland Woodcraft Co., Inc.
Drawer 609
Carlisle, PA 17013
(717) 243-0063

Curran Glass & Mirror Co.
30 N. Maple St.
Florence, MA 01060
(413) 584-5761

Curvoflite
205 Spencer Ave.
Chelsea, MA 02150
(617) 889-0007

Custom Ironwork
Box 99
Union, KY 41091
(606) 384-4486

Dahlke Studios
Box 1128
Glastonbury, CT 06033
(203) 659-1887

Dalton-Gorman
1508 Sherman Ave.
Evanston, IL 60201
(312) 869-5575

Daly's
3525 Stone Way N.
Seattle, WA 98103
(206) 633-4276

Day Studio-Workshop, Inc.
1504 Bryant St.
San Francisco, CA 94103
(415) 626-9300

D.E.A. Bathroom Machineries
495 Main St.
Box 1020
Murphys, CA 95247
(209) 728-3860

Design for Sleep
200 Lexington Ave.
Ste. 506
New York, NY 10016
(212) 685-6556

Designed Communications
704 Boyle Bldg.
103 W. Capitol
Little Rock, AR 72201
(501) 372-2056

Designs in Tile
Box 4983
Foster City, CA 94404
(415) 571-7122

DeWeese Woodworking Co.
Box 576
Philadelphia, MS 39350
(601) 656-4951

Diamond K. Co., Inc.
130 Buckland Rd.
South Windsor, CT 06074
(203) 644-8486

Diedrich Chemicals Restorations Technologies, Inc.
300A E. Oak St.
Milwaukee, WI 53154
(800) 323-3565

Dovetail, Inc.
Box 1569
Lowell, MA 01853-2769
(617) 454-2944

Dovetail Woodworking
550 Elizabeth St.
Waukesha, WI 53186
(414) 544-5859

Dutch Boy
1370 Ontario St.
Cleveland, OH 44101
(216) 566-3140

Eagle Plywood & Door Manufacturers, Inc.
450 Oak Tree Ave.
S. Plainfield, NJ 07080
(201) 668-1460

Edison Chemical Systems, Inc.
25 Grant St.
Waterbury, CT 06704
(203) 597-9727

Edsall & Associates
754 Neil Ave.
Columbus, OH 43215
(614) 221-0580

Eighteenth Century Hardware Co., Inc.
131 E. 3rd St.
Derry, PA 15627
(412) 694-2708

Elcanco
60 Chelmsford St.
Chelmsford, MA 01824
(617) 256-9972 or
(617) 256-8809

Electric Glass Co.
One E. Mellen St.
Hampton, VA 23663
(804) 722-6200

Elephant Hill Ironworks
R.R. 1, Box 168
Tunbridge, VT 05077
(802) 889-9444

Entourage, Inc.
Box 6491
San Antonio, TX 78209
(512) 826-4440

EverGreene
365 W. 36th St.
New York, NY 10018
(212) 239-1322

The Fan Man
4606 Travis St.
Dallas, TX 75205
(214) 559-4440

Federal Street Lighthouse
38 Market Sq.
Newburyport, MA 01950
(617) 462-6333

Ferguson's Cut Glass Works
4292 Pearl Rd.
Cleveland, OH 44109
(216) 459-2929

Buddy Fife's Wood Products
9 Main St.
Northwood, NH 03261
(603) 942-8777

Finnaren & Haley, Inc.
2320 Haverford Rd.
Ardmore, PA 19003
(215) 649-5000

The Fireplace Mantel Shop
4217 Howard Ave.
Kensington, MD 20895
(301) 564-1550

David Fisch
1014 S. Main St.
Spring Valley, NY 10977
(914) 352-7588

Folkheart Rag Rugs
18 Main St.
Bristol, VT 05443
(802) 453-4101

F.P. Architectural
379 Eglinton Ave.
Toronto, Ontario, Canada
M5N 1A3
(416) 483-4085

Fuller O'Brien
2700 Glynn Ave.
Box 864
Brunswick, GA 31521
(912) 265-7650

Fypon, Inc.
22 W. Pennsylvania Ave.
Stewartson, PA 17363
(717) 993-2593

Gamut Art Interiors
12441 Nedra Dr.
Granada Hills, CA 91344
(818) 366-8862

Garrett Wade
161 Avenue of the Americas
New York, NY 10013
(212) 807-1155

Gaslight Time
823 President St.
Brooklyn, NY 11215
(718) 789-7185

Gazebo & Porchworks
728 9th Ave. S.W.
Puyallup, WA 98371-6744
(206) 848-0502

George Studios
45-04 97 Pl.
Corona, NY 11368
(718) 271-2506

Jamie Gibbs and Associates
Landscape Architects and Interior Designers
340 E. 93rd St., Ste. 14C
New York, NY 10128
(212) 722-7508

Glass Arts
30 Penniman Rd.
Boston (Allston), MA 02134
(617) 782-7760

Glen-Gery Corp.
6th and Court Sts.
Box 1542
Reading, PA 19603
(215) 374-4011
For information on Glen-Gery's flooring brick, contact:

Glen-Gery Corp.
Drawer S
Shoemakersville, PA 19555
(215) 562-3076

Glidden Coatings & Resins
925 Euclid Ave.
Cleveland, OH 44115
(216) 344-8000

Golden Age Glassworks
339 Bellvale Rd.
Warwick, NY 10990
(914) 986-1487

Good & Co.
Salzburg Sq.
Rte. 101
Amherst, NH 03031
(603) 672-0490

Good Directions, Inc.
24 Ardmore St.
Stamford, CT 06902
(800) 346-7678 or
(203) 348-1836 (CT)

Good Time Stove Co.
Rte. 112, Box 306
Goshen, MA 01032-0306
(413) 268-3677

Lynn Goodpasture
42 W. 17th St.
New York, NY 10011
(212) 989-5246

The Grammar of Ornament, Inc.
2626 Curtis St.
Denver, CO 80205
(303) 295-2431

Granville Manufacturing Co., Inc.
Rte. 100
Granville, VT 05747
(802) 767-4747

Gravity Randall
208 N. Douty St.
Box 1378
Hanford, CA 93232-1378
(209) 584-2216

Great American Salvage Co.
34 Cooper Sq.
New York, NY 10003
(212) 505-0070

Great Panes Glassworks, Inc.
2861 Walnut St.
Denver, CO 80205
(303) 294-0927

Greeff Fabrics, Inc.
155 E. 56th St.
New York, NY 10022
(212) 888-5060

Greg's Antique Lighting
12005 Wilshire Blvd., W.
Los Angeles, CA 90025
(213) 478-5475

Pat Guthman Antiques
342 Pequot Rd.
Southport, CT 06490
(203) 259-5743

H & H Decors
7958 Broadview Rd.
Cleveland (Broadview Heights), OH 44147
(216) 526-3788

Half-Moon Antiques
c/o Monmouth Antique Shoppes
217 Front St.
Red Bank, NJ 07701
(201) 842-7377

Hammerworks
75 Webster St.
Worcester, MA 01603
(617) 755-3434

Whit Hanks
1009 W. 6th St.
Austin, TX 78703
(512) 478-2101

Brian G. Hart
4375 W. River Rd.
Delta, British Columbia,
Canada V4K 1R9
(604) 946-8302

Hartco, Inc.
300 Main St.
Oneida, TN 37841
(615) 569-8526

Heart-Wood, Inc.
Rte. 1, Box 97-A
Jasper, FL 32052
(904) 792-1688

Hearth Realities
Box 38093
Atlanta, GA 30334
(404) 377-6852

Heartwood School
Johnson Rd.
Washington, MA 01235
(413) 623-6677

Judith Hendershot
1408 Main St.
Evanston, IL 60202
(312) 475-6411

Henkel-Harris
Box 2170
Winchester, VA 22601
(703) 667-4900

Heritage Lanterns
70A Main St.
Yarmouth, ME 04096
(207) 846-3911

Hickey/Hess Architecture and Design
230 Harrisburg Ave.
Lancaster, PA 19603
(717) 394-6053

Hippo Hardware and Trading Co.
201 S.E. 12th
Portland, OR 97214
(503) 235-4635

Historic Windows
Box 1172
Harrisonburg, VA 22801
(703) 434-5855

Historical Replications, Inc.
Box 13529
Jackson, MS 39236
(601) 981-8743

Marjory & Peter Holly
3111 2nd Ave. S.
Minneapolis, MN 55408
(612) 824-2333

Hurley Patentee
R.D. 7, Box 98A
Kingston, NY 12401
(914) 331-5414

Iberia Millwork
500 Jane St.
New Iberia, LA 70560
(318) 365-5644

Ideal Co., Inc.
Box 2540
Waco, TX 76702-2540
(817) 752-2494

Illustrious Lighting
1925 Fillmore St.
San Francisco, CA 94115
(415) 922-3133

Import Specialists, Inc.
82 Wall St.
New York, NY 10005
(800) 334-4044
(212) 709-9633 (NY)

Insul-Crete
4056 Bailey N.W.
Massillon, OH 44646
Canton: (216) 478-5751
Akron: (216) 376-1899

The Iron Shop
Dept. OHCF
Box 128, 400 Reed Rd.
Broomall, PA 19008
(215) 544-7100

Marian Ives
Box 132
Norwell, MA 02061
(617) 659-4466

The Joinery Co.
Dept. OHC
Box 518
Tarboro, NC 27886
(919) 823-3306

Jerard Paul Jordan Gallery
Box 71, Slade Acres
Ashford, CT 06278
(203) 429-7954

Kane, Liede and Ratyna, P.C.
Landscape Architects and Planners
70 Sarles Lane
Pleasantville, NY 10570
(914) 769-6600

Katzenbach & Warren
950 3rd Ave.
New York, NY 10022
(212) 319-7220

Kayne & Son
76 Daniel Ridge Rd.
Candler, NC 28715
(704) 667-8868

Kenmore Industries
Box 34, One Thompson Sq.
Boston, MA 02129
(617) 242-1711

Phyllis Kennedy
9256 Holyoke Ct.
Indianapolis, IN 46268
(317) 872-6366

Kentucky WoodFloors
4200 Reservoir Ave.
Louisville, KY 40213
(502) 451-6024

King's Chandelier Co.
Dept. OHC-1
Eden, NC 27288
(919) 623-6188

Mark A. Knudsen
1100 E. County Line Rd.
Des Moines, IA 50320
(515) 285-6112

Koeppel/Freedman Studios
368 Congress St.
Boston, MA 02210
(617) 426-8887

Kohler Co.
Kohler, WI 53044
(910) 264-3877

Kraatz Russell Glass
Grist Mill Hill
RFD 1, Box 320C
Canaan, NH 03741
(603) 523-4289

James Lea
9 West St.
Rockport, ME 04856
(207) 236-3632

Lehman Hardware & Appliances, Inc.
Box 41, 4779 Kidron Rd.
Kidron, OH 44636
(216) 857-5441

Linoleum City
5657 Santa Monica Blvd.
Hollywood, CA 90038
(213) 469-0063

London Venturers
2 Dock Sq.
Rockport, MA 01966
(617) 546-7161

Edward Ludlow, Cabinetmaker
Box 646
Pluckemin, NJ 07978
(201) 658-9091

Steven P. Mack Associates
Chase Hill Farm
Ashaway, RI 02804
(401) 377-8041

Mackall & Dickinson Architects
50 Maple St.
Branford, CT 06405-3590
(203) 488-8364

Mad River Woodworks
Box 163
Arcata, CA 95521
(707) 826-0629

Merilyn M. Markham
22 Mammoth Rd.
Londonderry, NH 03053
(603) 889-2658

Marmion Plantation Co.
R.D. 2, Box 458
Fredericksburg, VA 22405
(703) 775-3480

Marsh Stream Enterprises
RFD 2, Box 490
Brooks, ME 04921
(207) 722-3575

The Martin-Senour Co.
1370 Ontario Ave. N.W.
Cleveland, OH 44113
(216) 566-3178

Maurer and Shepherd Joyners Inc.
122 Naubuc Ave.
Glastonbury, CT 06033
(203) 633-2383

M.J. May Antique Building Restoration
505 Storle Ave.
Burlington, WI 53105
(414) 763-8822

The Mechanick's Workbench
Front St.
Box 544
Marion, MA 02738
(617) 748-1680

M-H Lamp & Fan Co.
7231 ½ N. Sheridan Rd.
Chicago, IL 60626
(312) 743-2225

Midwest Wood Products
1051 S. Rolff St.
Davenport, IA 52802
(319) 323-4757

Newton Millham
Star Forge
672 Drift Rd.
Westport, MA 02790
(617) 636-5437

Mister Slate
Smid Inc.
Sudbury, VT 05733
(802) 247-8809

Benjamin Moore & Co.
51 Chestnut Ridge Rd.
Montvale, NJ 07645
(201) 573-9600

Tom Moore's Steeple People
21 Janine St.
Chicopee, MA 01013
(413) 533-9515

Moravian Pottery & Tile Works
Swamp Rd.
Doylestown, PA 18901
(215) 345-6722

Mountain Lumber Co.
Rte. 2, Box 43-1
Ruckersville, VA 22968
(804) 985-3646 or
(804) 295-1922

The Muralo Co., Inc.
148 E. 5th St.
Bayonne, NJ 07002
(201) 437-0770

Museum of American Textile History
Textile Conservation Center
800 Massachusetts Ave.
North Andover, MA 01845
(617) 686-0191

The New Jersey Barn Co.
Box 702
Princeton, NJ 08542
(609) 924-8480

New York Marble Works, Inc.
1399 Park Ave.
New York, NY 10029
(212) 534-2242

19th Century Hardware & Supply Co.
Box 599
Rough & Ready, CA 95975
(916) 432-1040

Nixon Design Studio
835 15th St.
Wilmette, IL 60091
(312) 256-3531

Noral
c/o F.P. Architectural
379 Eglinton Ave. W.
Toronto, Ontario, Canada
M5N 1A3
(416) 483-4085

W.F. Norman Corp.
Box 323
214-32 N. Cedar St.
Nevada, MO 64772-0323
(800) 641-4038
Missouri customers, call collect:
(417) 667-5552

North Woods Chair Shop
RFD 1, Old Tilton Rd.
Canterbury, NH 03224
(603) 783-4595

Nostalgia, Inc.
307 Stiles Ave.
Savannah, GA 31401
(912) 232-2324

Nottingham Gallery
339 Bellvale Rd.
Warwick, NY 10990
(914) 986-1487

Nowell's, Inc.
490 Gate 5 Rd.
Sausalito, CA 94965
(415) 332-4933

Craig Nutt Fine Wood Works
2014 5th St.
Northport, AL 35476
(205) 752-6635

Nye's Foundry Ltd.
503 Powells St. E.
Vancouver, British Columbia, Canada V6A 1G8
(604) 254-4121

Office of Robert Perron
2326 S.W. Park Place
Portland, OR 97205
(503) 223-2266

Ohmega Salvage
Box 2125
2407 San Pablo Ave.
Berkeley, CA 94702
(415) 843-7368

Old Fashioned Milk Paint Co.
R.R. 1, Box 65
Ashby, MA 01431
(617) 386-7550

The Old Wagon Factory
103 Russell St.
Box 1427, Dept. OC86
Clarksville, VA 23927
(804) 374-5787

Old World Restorations, Inc.
Columbia/Stanley Bldg.
347 Stanley Ave.
Cincinnati, OH 45226
(513) 321-1911

Olympic Stain
2233 112th Ave., N.E.
Bellevue, WA 98004
(800) 426-6306

Omnia Industries
49 Park St.
Box 263
Montclair, NJ 07042
(201) 746-4300

Orleans Carpenters
70 Rock Harbor Rd.
Orleans, MA 02653
(617) 255-2646

Pagliacco Turning and Milling
Box 225
Woodacre, CA 94973
(415) 488-4333

Megan Parry
1727 Spruce St.
Boulder, CO 80302
(303) 444-2724

William H. Parsons &
Associates
420 Salmon Brook
Granby, CT 06035
(203) 653-2281

Partridge Replications
63 Penhallow St.
Portsmouth, NH 03801
(603) 431-8733

Phyllis Parun Studios
2562 Verbena St.
New Orleans, LA 70122
(504) 944-2859

Saxe Patterson
Box 15
Salazar Rd.
Taos, NM 87571
(505) 758-9513

George E. Patton, Inc.
1725 Spruce St.
Philadelphia, PA 19103
(215) 545-4643

Paxton Hardware, Ltd.
Dept. OHC
7818 Bradshaw Rd.
Upper Falls, MD 21156
(301) 592-8505

Pelnik Wrecking Co., Inc.
1749 Erie Blvd. E.
Syracuse, NY 13210
(315) 472-1031

Pennsylvania Firebacks Inc.
1011 E. Washington Lane
Philadelphia, PA 19138
(215) 843-6162

Perennial Pleasures Nursery
Box 147
East Hardwick, VT 05836
(802) 472-5512

Period Furniture Hardware
Co., Inc.
123 Charles St.
Box 314, Charles St. Sta.
Boston, MA 02114
(617) 227-0758

Period Lighting Fixtures
1 Main St.
Chester, CT 06412
(203) 526-3690

Edward K. Perry Co.
322 Newbury St.
Boston, MA 02115
(617) 536-7873

Pittsburgh Paints
1 Gateway Center
Pittsburgh, PA 15222
(412) 434-3131

Pocahontas Hardware & Glass
Box 127
Pocahontas, IL 62275
(618) 669-2880

Portland Stove Co.
Box 377
Fickett Rd.
N. Pownal, ME 04069
(207) 688-2254 or
(207) 775-6424

Pratt & Lambert
75 Tonawanda St.
Buffalo, NY 14207
(716) 873-6000

Preservation Associates
207 S. Potomac St.
Hagerstown, MD 21740
(301) 791-7880

The Preservation Partnership
345 Union St.
New Bedford, MA 02740
(617) 996-3383

Preservation Services, Inc.
1445 Hampshire
Quincy, IL 62301
(217) 224-2300

PRG
5619 Southampton Dr.
Springfield, VA 22151
(703) 323-1407

Price Glover Inc.
817½ Madison Ave.
New York, NY 10021
(212) 772-1740

Prospect Products
8000 Rose Island Rd.
Box 70
Prospect, KY 40059
(502) 228-3493

QRB Industries
3139 N. U.S. 31
Niles, MI 49120
(616) 683-7908

Raintree Designs, Inc.
979 3rd Ave., Ste. 503N
New York, NY 10022
(212) 477-8594

Michael M. Reid
132 Morey Rd.
Sharon, CT 06069
(203) 364-5444

Rejuvenation House Parts
901 N. Skidmore
Portland, OR 97217
(503) 249-0774

REM Associates
Box 504
Northborough, MA 01532
(617) 393-8424

Remodelers' & Renovators'
Supply
512 W. Idaho
Boise, ID 83702
(208) 344-8612

Renaissance Marketing, Inc.
Box 360
Lake Orion, MI 48035
(313) 693-1109

The Renovation Source, Inc.
3512-14 N. Southport Ave.
Chicago, IL 60657
(312) 327-1250

Restoration Supply
Box 253
Hawesville, KY 42348
(502) 927-8494

Restorations Unlimited
124 W. Main St.
Elizabethville, PA 17023
(717) 362-3477

R. Wayne Reynolds, Ltd.
Box 28
Stevenson, MD 21153
(301) 323-1180

S. Chris Rheinschild
2220 Carlton Way
Santa Barbara, CA 93109
(805) 962-8598

J. Ring Glass Studio
2724 University Ave. S.E.
Minneapolis, MN 55414
(612) 379-0920

Rising and Nelson Slate Co.,
Inc.
West Pawlet, VT 05775
(802) 645-0150

River City Restorations
623 Collier
Box 1065
Hannibal, MO 63401
(314) 248-0733

Riverbend Timber Framing, Inc.
Box 26
Blissfield, MI 49228
(517) 486-4566

Robinson Iron
Robinson Rd.
Alexander City, AL 35010
(205) 329-8484

Robinson Lumber Co., Inc.
Ste. 202
512 S. Peters St.
New Orleans, LA 70130
(504) 523-6377 or
(504) 523-6370

Robson Worldwide Graining
4308 Argonne Dr.
Fairfax, VA 22032
(703) 978-5331

McKie Wing Roth, Jr.
1001 Bridgeway, #234
Sausalito, CA 94965
(800) 232-7684

Roy Electric Co., Inc.
1054 Coney Island Ave.
Brooklyn, NY 11230
(718) 339-6311 or
(718) 761-7905

Rue de France
78 Thames St.
Newport, RI 02840
(401) 846-2084

Russell Restoration of Suffolk
5550 Bergen Ave.
Mattituck, NY 11952
(516) 765-2481

Rustic Home Hardware
R.D. 3
Hanover, PA 17331
(717) 632-0088

Saint Louis Antique Lighting
Co.
25 N. Sarah St.
St. Louis, MO 63108
(314) 535-2770

San Francisco Victoriana
2245 Palou Ave.
San Francisco, CA 94124
(415) 648-0313

Arthur Sanderson & Sons
979 3rd Ave.
New York, NY 10022
(212) 319-7220

Scalamandré, Inc.
950 3rd Ave.
New York, NY 10022
(212) 361-8500

F. Schumacher & Co.
939 3rd Ave.
New York, NY 10022
(212) 644-5900

Schwartz's Forge &
Metalworks
Forge Hollow Rd.
Box 205
Deansboro, NY 13328
(315) 841-4477

Scott's Antiques
Rte. 9, Box 536
Springfield, MO 65804
(417) 866-6303

Second Impressions Antiques
84½ Bay St.
Watch Hill, RI 02891
Watch Hill: (401) 596-1296
Evenings: (401) 596-2661

The Settlers
1437 W. Alabama
Houston, TX 77006
(713) 524-2417

Shaker Workshops
Box 1028
Concord, MA 01742
(617) 646-8985

Sheppard Millwork, Inc.
21020 70th Ave. W.
Edmonds, WA 98020
(206) 771-4645 or
(206) 283-7549

The Shop, Inc.
Box 3711, R.D. 3
Reading, PA 19606
(215) 689-5885

Shuttercraft
282 Stepstone Hill Rd.
Guilford, CT 06437
(203) 453-1973

Silver Dollar Trading Co.
Box 394
San Elizario, TX 78949
(915) 851-3458

Silverton Victorian Mill Works
Box 850-OHC
Silverton, CO 81433
(303) 387-5716

The Sink Factory
2140 San Pablo Ave.
Berkeley, CA 94702
(415) 548-3697

Smid Inc.
Sudbury, VT 05733
(802) 247-8809

Kathleen B. Smith
Box 48
W. Chesterfield, MA 01084
(413) 296-4437

Smith Woodworks and Design
Box 42, R.R. 1
Farmersville Rd.
Califon, NJ 07830
(201) 832-2723

Somerset Door & Column Co.
Box 328
Somerset, PA 15501
(800) 242-7916
(800) 242-7915 (PA)

Spiess Antique Building
Materials
228-230 E. Washington St.
Joliet, IL 60433
(815) 722-5639

Steptoe & Wife Antiques Ltd.
322 Geary Ave.
Toronto, Ontario, Canada
M6H 2C7
(416) 530-4200

Stewart Manufacturing Co.
511 Enterprise Ave.
Covington, KY 41017
(606) 331-9000

Edward D. Stone, Jr. and Associates
1512 E. Broward Blvd., Ste. 110
Fort Lauderdale, FL 33301
(305) 524-3330

Stroheim & Romann, Inc.
155 E. 56th St.
New York, NY 10022
(212) 691-0700

Sunflower Glass Studio
Box 99, Rte. 523
Sergeantsville, NJ 08557
(609) 397-1535

Sunset Antiques, Inc.
22 N. Washington (M-24)
Oxford, MI 48051
(313) 628-1111

Sunshine Architectural Woodworks
Rte. 2, Box 434
Fayetteville, AR 72701
(501) 521-4329

Superior Clay Corp.
Box 352
Urichsville, OH 44683
(800) 848-6166
(800) 282-6103 (OH)

David Swearingen, Bonded Locksmith
220 E. 6th St.
Jacksonville, FL 32206
(904) 356-5396

Tennessee Tub, Inc. & Tubliner Co.
6682 Charlotte Park
Nashville, TN 37209
(615) 352-1939

Terra Cotta Productions, Inc.
Box 99781
Pittsburgh, PA 15233
(412) 321-2109

Thermocrete Chimney Systems
7111 Ohms Lane
Minneapolis, MN 55435
(800) 328-6347
(612) 835-1338 (MN)

Richard E. Thibaut
706 21st St.
Irvington, NJ 07111
(201) 399-7888

Tremont Nail Co.
Dept. OHC, 8 Elm St.
Box 111
Wareham, MA 02571
(617) 221-5540

Tromploy, Inc.
400 Lafayette St., 5th Floor
New York, NY 10003
(212) 420-1639

Travis Tuck
Box 1832C
Martha's Vineyard, MA 02568
(617) 693-3914

Turncraft
Box 2429
White City, OR 97503
(503) 826-2911

Urban Archaeology
137 Spring St.
New York, NY 10012
(212) 431-6969

Valley Craftsmen, Ltd.
Box 11
Stevenson, MD 21153
(301) 484-3891

Albert Van Luit & Co.
4000 Chevy Chase Dr.
Los Angeles, CA 90039
(818) 247-8840

Venturella Studios
32 Union Sq. E., Rm. 1110
New York, NY 10003
(212) 228-4252

Vermont Cobble Slate
Smid Inc.
Sudbury, VT 05733
(802) 247-8809

Victorian Collectibles Ltd.
845 E. Glenbrook Rd.
Milwaukee, WI 53217
(414) 352-6910

Victorian Glassworks
904 Westminster St. N.W.
Washington, DC 20001
(202) 462-4433

Victorian Lightcrafters Ltd.
Box 350
Slate Hill, NY 10973
(914) 355-1300

Victorian Reproduction Lighting Co.
1601 Park Ave. S.
Minneapolis, MN 55404
(612) 338-3636

Vintage Lumber & Construction Co., Inc.
9507 Woodsboro Rd.
Frederick, MD 21701
(301) 898-7859

Vintage Plumbing and Sanitary Specialties
17800 Minnehaha St.
Granada Hills, CA 91344
(818) 424-3327

Vintage Valances
Box 635
Whitmore Lake, MI 48189-0635
(313) 878-6670

Vintage Wood Works
Dept. D691
Box 1157
513 S. Adams
Fredericksburg, TX 78624
(512) 997-9513

The Wallpaper Works
Box 261, Station C
Toronto, Ontario, Canada
M6J 2P4
(416) 366-1790

The Washington Copper Works
South St.
Washington, CT 06793
(203) 868-7527

E.G. Washburne & Co., Inc.
85 Andover St.
Danvers, MA 01923
(617) 774-3645

Watercolors
Garrison on Hudson, NY 10524
(914) 424-3327

Waterman Works
266B Oxford Pl. N.E.
Atlanta, GA 30307
(404) 373-9438

Watertower Pines
Box 1067
Kennebunk, ME 04043
(207) 985-6868

Waverly Fabrics
79 Madison Ave. Dept. OH
New York, NY 10016
(212) 644-5900

J.P. Weaver Co.
2301 W. Victory Blvd.
Burbank, CA 91506
(818) 841-5700

Westmoore Pottery
Rte. 2, Box 476
Seagrove, NC 27341
(919) 464-3700

Martha Wetherbee Basket Shop
Star Rte. Box 35
Sanbornton, NH 03269
(603) 286-8927

Eldred Wheeler
c/o Partridge Replications
63 Penhallow St.
Portsmouth, NH 03801
(603) 431-8733

The Robert Whitley Furniture Studios
Laurel Rd.
Solebury, PA 18963
(215) 297-8452

Wiggins Brothers
Box 420
Hale Rd.
Tilton, NH 03276
(603) 286-3046

Frederick Wilbur
Box 425
Lovingston, VA 22949
(804) 263-4827

Lt. Moses Willard, Inc.
1156 U.S. 50
Milford, OH 45150
(513) 831-8956

Williams Art Glass Studios Inc.
22 N. Washington (M-24)
Oxford, MI 48051
(313) 628-1111

Helen Williams/Rare Tiles
12643 Hortense St.
Studio City, CA 91604
(818) 761-2756

Williamsburg Blacksmiths
Rte. 9
Williamsburg, MA 01096
(413) 268-7341

Willsboro Wood Products
Box 336
Willsboro, NY 12996
(800) 342-3373
(518) 963-8623 (NY)

D.W. Windsor
c/o F.P. Architectural
379 Eglinton Ave.
Toronto, Ontario, Canada
M5N 1A3
(416) 483-4085

Windy Hill Forge
3824 Schroeder Ave.
Perry Hall, MD 21128-9783
(301) 256-5890

Woodbury Blacksmith & Forge Co.
Box 268
Woodbury, CT 06798
(203) 263-5737

Wooden Nickel Antiques
1408 Central Pkwy.
Box 991531
Cincinnati, OH 45202
(513) 241-2985

Woodstock Soapstone Co., Inc.
Airpark Rd.
Box 37H
West Lebanon, NH 03784
(603) 298-5955

The Woodworkers' Store
21801 Industrial Blvd.
Rogers, MN 55374
(612) 428-4101

Yankee Craftsman
357 Commonwealth Rd.
(Rte. 30)
Wayland, MA 01778
(617) 653-0031

Index